"Blown away by [this] eloquent memoir of Métis life and surviving the streets."

—EMMA DONOGHUE, *New York Times* bestselling author of *Room* (via Twitter)

"From the Ashes is an illuminating, inside account of homelessness, a study of survival and freedom. Jesse Thistle delivers a painfully lyrical book, a journey through the torrents of addiction and trauma, masterfully sliding in humor and moments of heart-expanding human connection. I found myself gasping out loud at parts, unable to put the book down. Jesse's story shows us that there is nothing that cannot be transformed."

—AMANDA LINDHOUT, *New York Times* bestselling coauthor of *A House in the Sky*

"The best stories are the ones that stay with you. *From the Ashes* will stay with me for a long time. Maarsii to Jesse for coming through to tell this story. It is an important one. The revolutionary kind. The kind of story that changes how you look at the world, that shows us how amazing human beings can be, so capable, strong, resilient, powerful."

—KATHERENA VERMETTE, internationally bestselling author of *The Break*

"A memoir of resilience, spirit, and dignity from a gifted storyteller. It is, at heart, also about the many shapes that love can inhabit. When you plan to read this book, clear your schedule. It will hold you in its grasp and won't let you go, like a great novel. It's all the more remarkable that this is not fiction. This book will stand out in my reading experience for a long time to come."

—SHELAGH ROGERS, OC, host and producer of CBC Radio One's *The Next Chapter*

"This is a work that should not be mistaken for a redemption story—it is a love story. About family. Community. A partner. Most of all: this is a love story about Jesse Thistle. How he came to love himself. Why he is worthy of love. And, importantly, how you will love him when you are done reading. This book signals change: in our understanding of worth, our compassion in the face of harm and self-harm, and the power and possibility that can exist in spaces we try to forget about. Jesse Thistle is amazing. His story is stunning. We will talk about colonial and other violence differently on Turtle Island because Jesse lived them and shared them with us. With an openness, candor, and generosity that is inspiring. Its uglybeautiful/hurtlove will resonate with you long after you finish turning the pages. I am proud to call him nisîmis (my little brother)."

—TRACEY LINDBERG, internationally bestselling
author of *Birdie*

"A courageously heartfelt journey from profound self-destruction to redemption."

—*Kirkus Review*

"Thistle makes an especially valuable contribution in today's growing national conversation about the historic and systemic racism of Black, Brown and Native American peoples, the driving force behind the out-of-proportion rates of homelessness, police brutality, deficient health care, incarceration rates, uneven administration of justice, and inadequate education in our nation—all these issues are covered in glaring honesty and brutal truth. A must-read for all Americans, but especially for educators, policy makers, and frontline workers.

—Dr. Sam Tsemberis, creator of Housing First,
CEO of the Pathways Housing First Institute,
and clinical associate professor at UCLA
Department of Psychiatry and Biobehavioral Sciences

"In this page-turner of a memoir—raw, honest, gripping, wrenching, and inspiring—Jesse Thistle gifts us with an intimate and bracing look into the realities, traumas, and triumphs of indigenous life in today's North America."

— Gabor Maté, MD, bestselling author of
In the Realm of Hungry Ghosts: Close Encounters with Addiction

FROM
THE
ASHES

MY STORY OF BEING INDIGENOUS, HOMELESS, AND FINDING MY WAY

JESSE THISTLE

ATRIA PAPERBACK

NEW YORK LONDON TORONTO SYDNEY NEW DELHI

ATRIA
PAPERBACK

An Imprint of Simon & Schuster, Inc.
1230 Avenue of the Americas
New York, NY 10020

First Atria Paperback edition June 2021

ATRIA PAPERBACK and colophon are trademarks of Simon & Schuster, Inc.

For information about special discounts for bulk purchases, please contact Simon & Schuster Special Sales at 1-866-506-1949 or business@simonandschuster.com.

The Simon & Schuster Speakers Bureau can bring authors to your live event. For more information or to book an event, contact the Simon & Schuster Speakers Bureau at 1-866-248-3049 or visit our website at www.simonspeakers.com.

Interior design by Carly Loman

Manufactured in the United States of America

1 3 5 7 9 10 8 6 4 2

Library of Congress Control Number: 2021933989

ISBN 978-1-9821-8294-6
ISBN 978-1-9821-8295-3 (ebook)

This book is dedicated to the families whose loved ones are taken, or disappeared, or lost to them. Those forever watching for their loved one to return home. I watch and wait with you.

It is also dedicated to Indigenous children who grew up with no sense of themselves through projects like the Sixties Scoop, residential schools, adoption, or other such separation from their nuclear family during which they were robbed of their Indigenous identity through no fault of their own.

The pages of this book speak to the damage colonialism can do to Indigenous families, and how, when one's Indigeneity is stripped away, people can make poor choices informed by pain, loneliness, and heartbreak, choices that see them eventually cast upon the streets, in jail, or wandering with no place to be. I dedicate this book to you. I walk with you. I love you. I know the loneliness and frustration you endure.

Lastly, I dedicate this book to my wife, Lucie, who loved me back into the circle. This also goes out to my brothers, Josh, Jerry, and Daniel; my mom and dad; and to my grandparents, who gave me a fighting chance. Our circle is strong; our fire burns; this book is but a torch from the hearth of our clans, and is hopefully enough to light the way for others to follow.

CONTENTS

CONTENTS

CONTENTS

CONTENTS

RECONCILIATION
2008–2017

INDIGENOUS AFFAIRS

at night
alone
when the dope sickness set in
and the begging became too humiliating
I'd wander from the ByWard Market to the Centennial Flame fountain
    on Parliament Hill
looking for respite from my addictions.

ashamed
i sat with my back to the Peace Tower
thrust my hand in the cool fountain water
fishing out the hoard of coins thrown by tourists and passersby.

the RCMP who guarded the fountain
always saw me coming
from way down at the bottom of the Rideau Hill
near the Milestones and Château Laurier
but he never stopped me.

instead he'd sit and wait for me
watch as I shovelled wet change into my pockets.
then, before I got too greedy,
rush out and chase me away.

he always let me escape.

we both understood what was going on

why I was there
stealing from the Centennial Flame.

PROLOGUE

*The kingdom of heaven suffers violence, and violent men take
it by force.*

Matthew 11:12

THE DEAD SILENCE SCREAMED DANGER.

Frenzied squeaks of jail-issued blue deck shoes on sealed cement followed by wet smacks, fast pops, loud cracks, and finally a dull thud confirmed it. A guy lay crumpled on the range floor, our range quartermaster told us. He wasn't conscious. His legs were seized straight, quivering uncontrollably. He had pissed and shit himself.

We didn't need to see it with our own eyes. The unseen, the unknown, in jail is often worse than the seen, the known.

The next day, after cell search, I heard that he had died en route to hospital.

Someone said he'd stolen a bag of chips from another inmate's canteen, but who knew?

Who cared?

It was jail justice. The thief got what he deserved. According to us, according to society. At least that's what I told myself. All I knew for sure was that I didn't know anything and I hadn't seen anything. I'd only heard it, but I wouldn't even tell the guards that much. I had to survive, and the only way you did that was by keeping your mouth shut, turning your head away.

What was I doing here in jail anyway? Why had I put myself in the midst of this filth, this horrible violence?

The answer was simple.

I did it to save my leg—and my life.

LOST AND ALONE

1979–1987

A LITTLE BOY'S DREAM

I had this tiny bag
Had it since my family fell apart
It was red and blue with an Adidas logo on the side
And a golden zipper—the zipper of all zippers!

I had this tiny bag
I took it everywhere with me
When we moved with Dad
Hopped out windows at night
When we ran and ran
On to our next place.

I had this tiny bag
Grandma asked me to unpack it
But I wouldn't do it.
She asked many times after that
But I kept it filled with all my things
Tucked away
Under my bed
Just in case.

I had this tiny bag
It had my old life inside
When I finally got the courage to get rid of it

I left it on my bed
Then jumped out my window
Down two stories
But the grass broke my fall.

"Why did you do that, Baby Boy?" Grandma asked.

"Because I always dream of dying," I said. "And I can't take it to heaven
   with me."

ROAD ALLOWANCE

MY KOKUM NANCY'S PALM FELT leathery in mine as we walked along-side of the train tracks. Stands of poplar swayed and bent in the wind, and she stood still for a second to catch her bearings and watch the flat-bottomed, late-spring clouds slouch by. She mumbled, then began thrusting her gnarled walking stick into the tall brush ahead, spreading it open, looking for flashes of purple or blue. Purple was a clear sign that the pregnant Saskatoon berry bushes were ready to give birth and ease the winter suffering of bears, birds, and humans.

Berries, Kokum said, knew well their role as life-givers, and we had to honour and respect that. We did that by knowing our role as responsi-ble harvesters, picking only what we needed and leaving the rest for our animal kin so they could feed themselves and their young. That was our pact, she said, and if we followed it, they'd never let us down.

My kokum wore brownish-yellow eyeglasses the size of teacup saucers, but her eyes could still see things my three-year-old eyes couldn't. I always tried to search out berry patches before she did, but she always got there first. Always.

As we waded deeper through the rail-side grass and reeds, a vast fleet of mosquitoes and gnats lifted from the ditch floor and enveloped our heads. A few flew into my mouth, choking me. I coughed and batted at the air.

"No, Jesse." Kokum grabbed my arms and held them. "They are our relatives. Never do that!" I'd never seen her angry before, but she was now.

As the black cloud intensified around us, she drew in a deep breath, closed her eyes, and spoke softly in Michif. She pointed to me and our half-full pail of berries, and then to the rat-root plant that protruded out of her dress pocket. Her voice sounded like warm summer air swooshing over the open prairie right before rain comes, and reminded me of when I'd accidentally disturbed the hornet's nest behind the smoke shed. There was no anger in her voice then. The plume of insects hovered mid-air for a second, then flew skyward and dispersed. Just like the hornets had done.

I looked at her in amazement, and my mouth opened but no sound came out. I strained to hear any buzzing, but there was only the call of a loon far in the distance followed by the shuffle of Kokum's moccasins.

"Oh, my silent one," Kokum said. "I just told them we have a job to do." Her brown face cracked into a smile. "I asked them to visit us later, if they must, but for now we need to concentrate." She brushed a few strands of hair from my face and hoisted me over a puddle. "Or maybe they're right, maybe it's quitting time. Let's get back, *chi garçon*; we have enough to make a good bannock."

I loved Kokum's bannock more than anything—even harvesting with her, listening to her stories, or hearing her sing. She made it whenever we visited. We lived in Prince Albert, Saskatchewan, about an hour's drive away from my grandparents'. Their cabin was in Erin Ferry, near Debden, just south of Big River, between the old Highway 1 on one side and the new Highway 55 on the other. The CN Railway cut right up the centre of the road allowance, connecting Debden to Big River and on to the rest of Saskatchewan.

My grandparents' log cabin wasn't like any other place I knew. Mom told us that her dad, Mushoom Jeremie Morrissette, had made it by hand from the surrounding aspen hardwood after our family lost our homestead in Park Valley, a few kilometres away. It took him one season to fell the trees, strip them of bark, and build it, and another half season to chink in the cracks with mud and moss, waterproof the roof, and make it ready for winter living. Nobody else had a neat house like my kokum and Mushoom, way out in the country in the middle of nowhere, with no water or electricity.

Mushoom said there weren't many people like us anymore, rebels who fended for themselves—maybe a few Arcand relatives down the road, but that was about it. The rest had sold out and got farms or went to the city to find work. He didn't own his land; it belonged to the Queen of England.

"She doesn't mind us being here," Mushoom said. "And it lets me hunt and trap freely and be my own boss, which I like."

He told us stories about how our people once had lived in large communities in handmade houses just like his all over Saskatchewan, living off the land, but that was before the government attacked us and stole our land during the resistance, before our clans fell apart.

I couldn't understand what he was talking about. I tried imagining villages of our people living like he and my kokum did, in their little log house, all squished onto little pieces of land owned by the Queen, and I couldn't. But there were beaver, muskrat, deer, bears, elk, and fish everywhere; forest, streams, and rivers all around to play in; and no neighbours for miles and miles.

"If someone tries to push us around, we just pick up and move somewhere else," Mushoom said. "We live like this to be free, like our ancestors."

I understood that.

When Kokum and I came back from berry picking, Mushoom was standing at the front door of the cabin. The elk-horn buttons that fastened his beige leather vest strained to hold it together over his rounded stomach. Kokum made all of Mushoom's clothes from animals he trapped and materials she traded for in Debden on her monthly visit to town.

"Where are Blanche and Sonny?" Kokum called to him, her brow wrinkling. My parents' car had been in the dirt driveway when we left to go picking, but now there was just my mushoom's plump horse drinking from the trough at the side of the house.

"They went into town. Should be back soon. Fire's ready, though."

Kokum nodded, picked up a pail of rainwater for the washing, and nudged Mushoom aside as she carried it inside. The smell of burnt hardwood licked all around my grandfather's bald head as he bent down to hug me. The press of his fancy vest against my exposed belly felt like thousands of soft pebbles. Blazes of prairie roses, windflowers, big bluestems, hyssops, leadplants, and asters decorated his clothing in beaded patterns that Kokum said were passed down to her from her Michif-Nehiyaw ancestors—mothers to daughters—for over two centuries.

When Mushoom played the fiddle at night, I loved watching moonbeams flickering over his beads—it looked like he was wearing rubies and diamonds all over. And when he tapped his feet to the rhythm of reels he told us were passed down from his grandfather's grandfather, the light lulled me to sleep.

Josh and Jerry were inside the cabin playing on the floor with the wooden toys Mushoom had carved for them while we were out. Jerry's was a captain's sword, and Josh's was a little marionette man that jigged when

Mushoom Jeremie and Kokum Nancy (née Arcand) Morrissette, in their road-allowance home in Erin Ferry, Saskatchewan.

you held the stick that protruded out its back. Mushoom could carve things in five minutes flat. Jerry always got the best toys because Jerry was his favourite grandson, being his namesake and all.

Sometimes Josh and I would get jealous of Jerry. He crawled all over Mushoom's stomach and they both bellowed until tears came out of their eyes. Or Mushoom would take Jerry into the woods to show him his traps and a thing or two about snaring rabbits. He never did that with us. He'd hug us, but it wasn't the same. Jerry even kind of looked like him: stout, thick-legged, and broad across the shoulders. He was like Mushoom, too: powerful, strong-willed, and stubborn.

Josh was tall and thin. Out of all of us, he looked the most "Indian," or at least that's what Mom would say when she brushed his long black hair in the morning. She always took her time with Josh, and I could see that he was her favourite. His skin was much darker than Jerry's and mine, and he looked more like Mom than Dad. Korean or Japanese almost. Everyone was proud of Josh. He was the oldest and smartest and talked the most, and whatever new clothes we got from our aunts and uncles went to him. I'd eventually get them, but not until after Josh and Jerry.

I was much smaller and skinnier than both my brothers and had blond shoulder-length hair. My skin looked like my father's—pinkish cream. People were always saying, "He looks like a little white boy" or "You sure he wasn't switched at the hospital?" Mom said it didn't matter, because I was special. She said that I was the largest of all her babies, a little over ten pounds when I was born in 1976—as long as a carnival hot dog with a huge oblong head—and the doctors were shocked when I came out.

"You didn't make a sound," Mom said. "No screams or whimpers or nothing, just a wet *plop* sound."

I stayed quiet my first three years. The most noise I'd make was a cry or an incomprehensible squeal of excitement.

"Look here," Mushoom said, as he placed me on the floor with my brothers. He pulled a small wooden knife out of his back pocket. It was just little enough for me to grasp. I waved it in front of him, and he jumped back. Jerry charged at me, coming to Mushoom's rescue. Mushoom scooped him up before he could impale me with his wooden sabre.

Heat and the smell of lard radiated from the wood stove. Kokum opened its door to chuck in a few logs, and the muscles on her arms rippled. She was strong. One time a dog almost bit Josh near the road and Kokum threw a cast-iron skillet at it with one flick of her wrist, like a ninja star. The skillet whistled thirty feet in the air and the dog ran into the forest whining and never bugged any of us again.

I watched her as she wiped the dirt off her hands and put rolled-up bannock balls in the skillet. As they hissed and spit into the air, I could hear my parents' car screeching to a stop outside. They were fighting, like always. Mushoom said something to Kokum in Cree. I thought she was going to toss the frying pan, oil and all, out the door at my dad. She just wagged her head, though.

Mom leaned in the front door and announced, "We're going home, boys. Pull your stuff together."

Dad didn't come in. I peeked out the door. Music was blasting from the car, the windows were rolled up, and the inside was flooded with smoke.

"But, Blanche," Kokum said, "we've picked berries for the bannock."

"Can't," Mom said. "Sonny needs to get back. Damn idiot's gotta meet someone. Come, boys, hurry it up."

My mother was just fifteen when she met my father in 1973 at her sister Bernadette's house in Debden, Saskatchewan. According to my aunties, my mother was just about the prettiest Native girl in all northern Saskatchewan—a Michif Audrey Hepburn crossed with Grace Kelly and Hedy Lamarr. Silken black hair down to her waist, jet-black eyes, and a smile like a midnight flame. They said men hovered around her like moths, and that when Dad first laid eyes on her, he tripped all over himself to catch her. He chatted her up, bought her stuff, and fawned over her. He looked like a bumbling fool, my aunties said, all the men did.

But Dad was different. He was an Algonquin-Scot, although my uncles tell me he knew himself as a white man. He wasn't much to look at—chubby around the middle, with a pockmarked face and broken fighter's teeth, and his usual jean outfit was slick with traveller's patina. But there was something charming about him, an ability to talk and a boldness. That apparently came from his rough blue-collar upbringing north of Toronto, where he learned to hustle or perish. He also loved rock music. Deep Purple, Foghat, Jethro Tull, Black Sabbath, Johnny and Edgar Winter—he knew all their songs and more, how they were written and the stories behind their creation.

Mom was stuck in the 1950s, listening to old country music—the Carter Family, Patsy Cline, Hank Williams, Bill Monroe, Don Messer, anyone of the sort. She did know some modern music—Bob Dylan, the Doors, the Guess Who, Joni Mitchell—but she couldn't match my father. My aunties said Mom told them Dad was like a jukebox, with info on all the hottest bands. That made him like a god in northern Saskatchewan,

My mother, Blanche Morrissette, and father, Cyril "Sonny" Thistle, in 1977 in Debden, Saskatchewan.

where no one knew anything about rock, or Led Zeppelin, or Jimi Hendrix, or anything.

It made him irresistible, Mom said.

The side of my mom's face was blue. It wasn't that way before she left. And her voice sounded the way I didn't like. Mushoom examined her, and I knew he could see her broken glasses sticking out of her pocket when she went into the back room. He pushed himself up from the table, swore, and reached for his axe.

I thought he was going to kill my dad. Josh, Jerry, and I all started crying.

"Stop, Jeremie," Kokum yelled. She pulled the axe out of his hand and threw it beside the stove. "This is between them," she said, her voice sounding the way it had when she spoke with the mosquitoes.

Mushoom sneered, then stared out the window. Dad didn't notice. I could see him drumming his hands against the steering wheel.

Mom came back with some things. "Sorry, Mom, Dad. Next time we'll stay for bannock." She picked up our toys, then piled us into the car. She was like a whirlwind—we didn't even have a chance to say goodbye. As soon as we were in the car, Dad floored it. The wheels kicked up a cloud of dirt, and I could just see my kokum and mushoom waving to us through it.

HORNET

DAD BURST THROUGH THE APARTMENT door, his dirty-blond mullet in full flight. He was grinning so widely his greasy handlebar moustache splayed out at both ends. In his hands were a coffee tin and a white plastic bag.

"Daddy got paid, boys!" He placed his bounty on the cardboard box that served as our coffee table, then fell backward onto the sofa. A plume of sour dust erupted from the cushions. The tin rattled, and a nickel spilled out over the edge and rolled a foot or two toward us.

When Dad opened his arms for a hug, Josh ran from his usual spot in front of the TV and grabbed his legs. Jerry and I were still watching television—a shark attacking an octopus on *The Undersea World of Jacques Cousteau*. A red cloud of ink filled the ocean water. As the octopus scurried to safety, we joined Josh and hugged Dad.

"I did what you said," Josh said. He still clung to Dad's jeans. "I kept an eye out and made sure no one came in the apartment while you were gone."

Josh was in charge of Jerry and me whenever Dad left us alone to go on a mission. He was five.

"Make sure to feed your brothers," Dad would say. "Don't let no one in. Hide in the vent behind your bed if anyone gets in. And don't turn the light on at night because they'll know you're inside. Got it?" Josh always nodded.

Even four-year-old Jerry was my boss. We were like a little tribe with Josh as our chief, Jerry as second-in-command, and me as the expendable warrior. I had to do the bidding of both. They made me stand on the chair to check the peephole when someone was at the door. They made me fish poo out of the toilet to smear on walls to get even with Dad for leaving us alone. And they always made me climb onto the counter to reach where Dad hid all the best food away in the top cupboard. It was dangerous to climb so high, but I was good, and I was never afraid of heights like Jerry and Josh were. Climbing came naturally, and the distance between me and the floor excited me and made me feel powerful—it was something my brothers couldn't do.

Dad would freak out when he found that we'd eaten his secret food—cans of Spam, peanut butter, loaves of bread, chips, and the odd jar of Cheez Whiz—which he never shared, and I always got the blame because I never talked, even when I played alone with my brothers, and even when I got a licking. Mom used to think I was mute, but I could speak fine, I just chose not to. My words belonged to me, they were the only thing I had that were mine, and I didn't trust anyone enough to share them.

Dad was only gone for a night this time, but in the kitchen, the cupboards only had a few unopened cans of beans and beets he'd gotten from the local food bank a few days before. Empty boxes of crackers and cans piled one on top of another, covering the countertops and cascading out over the stovetop. The fridge had a few half-drunk beer bottles, an old light bulb, and a hardened turnip. Sometimes he'd go away for two or three days and leave us nothing.

"Good boy." Dad rubbed Josh's head, then pushed the three of us off of him. Josh, Jerry, and I fell to the beer-stained carpet, like puppies bucked off their mom's teat, as Dad cradled his bag.

My mother had abandoned my father, my brothers, and me—that was the version of the story we were made to believe by my father's family. But it wasn't the whole picture.

Mom married Dad when she was just seventeen, and my father was twenty-two.

She gave him an ultimatum the day of their wedding: "Quit drinking and running around, or I'll leave you."

He promised her a life of sobriety.

Dad lasted three days before he drank himself into a stupor.

One day he took his anger out on everyone. Josh endured a beating and Mom received it even worse.

Mom had had enough of moving from apartment to apartment, room to room, of my dad wasting all the money and opportunity that came their way. She'd had enough of all the bullshit. She packed our bags while Dad was passed out on the couch, and the four of us moved to Moose Jaw.

Mom went to night school and began working at a local restaurant

YVONNE RICHER

My brothers, Jerry (*on the left*) and Josh (*in the middle*), and me (*on the right*) in 1979 in Moose Jaw, Saskatchewan. Our aunt Yvonne, my mother's sister, took this picture.

during the day. Life was steady—we stayed in one apartment, slept in beds instead of on piles of laundry, and ate frequent meals, and Mom didn't cry herself to sleep with bruises like before.

One day Dad showed up.

He was healthy, coherent, and his clothes were clean. He charmed his way through the front door, telling Mom he'd found a great job back east with his father, that he wasn't drinking and drugging, and that he'd found an apartment and could afford to keep us boys if she allowed us to go with him. He wasn't trying to get back with her—he knew not to go there.

"I'll return them after a few months. You have my word, Blanche."

I think Mom decided to let us go with Dad because she wasn't thinking straight—she was exhausted—and Dad knew how to sound convincing when he wanted something and could exploit Mom's weaknesses. He had skills from years and years of hustling.

Mom let us go. I could smell the pine scent in her hair as we hugged goodbye on the veranda.

I didn't blame her. Dad could sell the Brooklyn Bridge to New York City officials if he really wanted to, or so people said. He was just that good at lying.

"Look here," Dad said as he broke open the bag and an avalanche of cigarette butts spilled onto the floor. He grabbed my brother's arm and placed him in front of the butts beside the TV. "Jerry, you roll the best. Take my Zig-Zags and do like last time."

Jerry peeled out a rolling paper and set to work ripping open the largest butts onto a sheet of paper. The smell of mouldy smokes filled the apartment. Dad then poured the contents of the tin onto the carpet. The coins were like falling treasure and Dad looked like a pirate, like Captain Hook in the Peter Pan book Mom used to read us before bed.

"Josh, count 'em up," he said. "Jesse knows what pennies are. Just let him pick them out before you get started."

Josh nodded and got my attention. "Like last time, Jesse. Remember?" He held up a penny and told me to dig. I shoved my hand in the pile and began picking out what looked to me like nuggets of gold.

"Dad," Josh said before we got too far. "We haven't eaten since yesterday morning and it's nighttime now. We're hungry. Did you bring anything?"

"Shit. I forgot. Count it up. We'll go to the store and get something after. Promise."

I watched as he pulled a small Baggie filled with white powder out of his jean jacket pocket. He held it up to the light and flicked it, then made his way to the washroom and slammed the door.

Josh sighed and began helping me. My stomach gurgled. He looked over at me. It was Josh's job to feed us. Sometimes he'd leave Jerry and me alone for a while and walk to the convenience store to beg for money to buy food. We'd seen Dad do it and knew how to do it, too. It usually took Josh a couple of hours, but he always came back with chips and pop and other goodies. He was my hero, my chief!

Sometimes, when we got really hungry, Josh even took Jerry and me over to ask for change in front of the hockey arena around the block. It was the best spot because we could buy gigantic hot dogs there. We shared bites. The hot meat burst with such flavour that my jaw would ache up around my ears, and my tongue swam in pools of saliva. Drool would sometimes spill out of my mouth onto my shirt before I even took a bite.

Dad's treasure shimmered in front of the TV. The wildlife program was still playing, and a whale drifted through blue water, calmly scooping mouthfuls of food, as Josh and I rifled through the silver and gold pile, and images of those hot dogs piled high with ketchup and mustard and relish and everything else floated through my head.

I noticed light peeping out of the washroom. Dad must've slammed the door so hard it bounced open a crack. I dropped the gold pennies I had in my hand and crawled over quietly to see what he was doing. Josh trailed behind.

Dad was on the toilet, hunched over with a spoon in one hand, a blue lighter in the other. Red flame licked the bottom of the spoon and bubbles spit droplets into the air. Dad's forehead was wet, sweat dripped onto the tile floor, and that see-through thingy I'd found one day underneath the sofa was by his side.

Dad had told me it was a man-made hornet, and that kids shouldn't play with it because they'd end up getting stung by accident, and the medicine it carried could make young boys so sick they could die. The black stripes on its see-through body looked scary, like the blue-and-black hornets I saw flying in the prairie roses, the kind that stung me when I went to see Kokum Nancy.

Dad picked up the hornet, put it near the spoon, and it sucked the medicine into its belly. Then he wrapped his leather belt around his arm and held one end in his teeth, pulling back with his head like my uncle Paul's dog did whenever we played tug of war. I could see green veins on his arm and hand. He jabbed himself with the hornet and red shot into the hornet's body. I pushed my face right up against the crack trying to get a better look, as bad butterflies swam all through my guts.

It looks just like the red ink that the octopus shot into the ocean right before it escaped the shark, I thought. I wondered if my dad could run away, or if a shark would get him. The softness of Kokum's voice whispered in my ears, as the smell of sweet Saskatoon berries filled my nose. The butterflies flew up my body and out the top of my head.

Dad let go of the belt, moaned, and toppled off the edge of the toilet. I pushed the door open and ran to him. He didn't move, and his eyes were closed. I looked back at Josh. He stood in the arch of the doorway, a dark river spreading down the front of his brown corduroys.

TRASH PANDAS

THE PINK NEON SIGN ON the corner store drooped down to one side and flickered off and on. The light strobed against the window I was standing in front of, staring at the huge ice-cream cone on the advertisement taped against the inside of the glass.

"Jesse, pay attention," Dad said and pushed my shoulder. Blankets of dead leaves swirled alongside the building when the wind picked up, and Dad tucked his head into the collar of his jean jacket. I saw an old man wearing a hat approach from the path over near the grass. Dad headed him off by the corner. I tried to focus.

"Excuse me, sir," Dad said. "I was wondering if you had some spare change? I got three kids, and they haven't eaten today." Dad sounded polite as he motioned over at us, and we stood, hands out, with big eyes, just like Dad taught us. "We'd really appreciate anything."

The man peeled his trench coat open, searched his pockets, and shrugged. "Sorry, fella. Don't have change to spare." He moved past us and entered the store. The entrance bell rang—it was a sound that meant defeat and more begging. I watched through the window as he bought milk and bread. He got some change back. When he came out, I ran over and tugged his leg, trying to make his quarters and dimes jingle in his pocket, to let him know I knew he had change. He kicked me away. "You should be ashamed," he said to my dad.

"Fuck you," Dad fired back and flicked his cigarette in the man's direction. Dad was shivering. Josh sighed, and Jerry wrapped his arms around Josh in a bear hug and squeezed until Josh laughed and begged him to stop. Dad was busy searching the sidewalk and found a half-smoked butt near a trash bin.

"I'm not eating out of there again," Josh said, his eyes focused on my father and the bin. He kicked the wall. "We're not supposed to."

Dad put the butt in his mouth and lifted the lid off the garbage container. "You never know what you'll find."

He was right. A couple of days ago, when Dad had taken off, Josh took Jerry, leaving me in the apartment. I'd watched out of our window and could see Jerry as he made a beeline toward the bin, climbed up, and dove into the pool of black trash bags. He looked like a raccoon. After a few minutes, he emerged clutching some old bread, a couple of packs of cold cuts, and a few dented cans. He tossed them to Josh, but Josh fumbled and dropped them like an outfielder having a bad day. The bread and meat were still good, just a little green around the edges. When we picked that off though, it was as good as new.

"Nothing in here, boys. Pickup was last night." Dad shut the bin lid and pulled his collar up. His cigarette went out. The November wind bit through our clothing, and we huddled together. We'd been out for a few hours and hadn't come up with any change. Everyone seemed to be in a rush or didn't have enough to spare. We always shared what we had, and I didn't understand why people were so mean and wouldn't share with us.

"Listen," Dad said, "I have a plan." He knelt down in front of Jerry and Josh, placing his hands upon their shoulders. "I've done it with Josh before, but we're all here today, so I think it'll work better."

Josh perked up, but Dad didn't even glance at me. I stuck my tongue out.

"Now, now. You're only three, but you can help, too, Jesse." Dad patted my bum. "Josh knows the drill. Just follow behind him and do what he says."

Josh put his arms around Jerry and me and pulled us close. "Just stay beside me and run when I tell you," he whispered. "Go straight back to the apartment and don't follow Dad!"

Dad winked at Josh. "That's right, son."

I was so jealous of Josh.

I held on to Josh's sleeve when we entered the store. Jerry was right beside me ogling the rows of chips and candy. The storekeeper looked down at us but then fixed his eyes on Dad, who walked ahead, leaving us behind. Before I knew it, he was by the milk and pop near the back of the store. His head darted around—down at the floor, over to the chocolate bars, up to the lights—like he didn't know what he was looking for. Inch by inch, Josh nudged us closer and closer to the first aisle near the front door.

I'd never seen Dad move around like that, like a freaked-out squirrel. He looked scared and funny all at once, opening and closing doors. Suddenly, he disappeared. I stood on my tippy toes to see what he was up to.

Smash! A river of milk flowed out from the dairy section. It was followed by the noise of another broken bottle.

"What's going on over there?" the storekeeper shouted as he came out from behind the till and went to investigate.

I was looking in the direction of the milk aisle, trying to catch a glimpse of Dad, but Josh pulled me close, yanked open my drawers, and stuffed in a few bags of chips, a handful of pepperettes, and a loaf of bread. I was shocked, food sticking halfway out of my waistband. Jerry was already at the door ten feet away, holding it open, his pants, too, bulging to the brim with goodies. Josh pulled my shirt and nudged me toward Jerry. I stumbled a few steps before Jerry grabbed my arm and walked me out the front door.

When our shoes touched the sidewalk outside, he pivoted toward the trash bin and dragged me until I almost fell flat on my face. The bell on the door rang as it closed behind us. Josh hurried by with a bunch of gum in one hand, and licorice and more pepperettes in the other. He directed us to a cedar bush a couple of feet behind the bin. We nestled under the cover of the branches and waited for Dad.

When he emerged from the store, he was flailing his arms and arguing with the storekeeper. The storekeeper screamed back, waving around a mop, pointing back into the store. Dad skipped backward a few steps then took off toward the park.

No one noticed us watching through the bush's boughs.

I thought, *This was fun.* I was happy to be working together with everyone. And we now had tons of food.

A FATHER'S LOVE

I dreamed of my birth, all wet from the womb
Blinding light overhead, emergency room

Behind newborn cries, my little hands grasped
"A son!" called the doc, while my tiny lungs gasped

"Oh, happy day," my mother did cry.
"Come, let me hold him," a tear in my dad's eye.

The strength of Father's arms tight around me
He swayed back and forth; his love did surround me

Then, out of nowhere, Dad yanked with a dash
Swung by my legs, he chucked me right in the trash!

"Don't need that." He laughed and slammed down the lid.
He dusted his hands. "Who the fuck needs a kid!?"

THE RED BARON

"DAD DIDN'T COME HOME AGAIN last night," Josh said as he jumped off the top bunk, thudding down on the wooden floor. He began rocking the lower bunk. Its rusty springs squeaked with each push. Jerry groaned and pulled the covers over his body, exposing my legs. The chill of the morning air through the holes in my Mighty Mouse PJ bottoms jolted me wide awake. Jerry took up three-quarters of the bottom bunk, which I shared with him, but that was okay, even if I only got the outside sliver of the mattress to sleep on, because his body was warm and soft and reminded me of a teddy bear. I yawned and rubbed my stomach.

"I know," Josh said. "That's why I'm trying to get you up. Dad took off with all the change when he woke up. He said he'd come back with food but hasn't." He shoved the bunk again, this time hard enough to wake Jerry, who let out a fart. He lay on his side, still curled into a ball, his mouth and chin covered in drool. A pool of it drenched the pillow below.

Jerry's crusty eyes blinked open and he looked toward the living room. "Where's Dad?" He sounded angry and annoyed.

"I don't know." Josh threw up his hands. "And we've got no food again."

I could hear Jerry's stomach grumble as he sat up slowly with the blanket tight around his shoulders. It looked like a cape. I watched as the World War I airplanes that decorated its fuzzy surface folded and contorted and collided into one another. I imagined mid-air explosions all across his back. I knew they were fighter planes because Dad told us they were. He said the ones with the black crosses on the tails were Germans, the bad guys, and the ones with the blue, white, and red bull's eyes were the British, the good guys.

I loved the story of the Red Baron and always imagined myself in his three-winged plane shooting down Canadian ace Roy Brown. The Baron's plane was cooler looking than Brown's by a long shot. Both the Baron's red Fokker DR.I triplane and Brown's Sopwith Camel buzzed around Jerry's neck when he stood up and shuffled into the kitchen. He slammed the cupboard doors in frustration and collapsed on the floor crying.

"I'm hungry," he wailed repeatedly.

Josh abandoned me. "Don't cry, Jerry," he said, going to him and rubbing his back. "We're going to go over to the store and get some food, like last week." He looked over at the window I knew faced the convenience store. "With all three of us out there, we'll get all kinds of stuff. It'll be fun."

Josh went to the fridge and grabbed one of the half-drunk beers and gave it to Jerry. "Brown pop. Drink it."

Jerry dropped the blanket and took the bottle with both hands. He

Me, posing for the camera, 1980.

scrunched up his face, put the bottle to his lips, tilted his head back, and swallowed.

I pictured him drinking a magic potion. *Jerry is the toughest of us all*, I thought.

"Gross," Jerry let out. He hated brown pops and never drank them when Dad gave them to us, but he knew it would fill him up. He handed the empty back to Josh, who went to place it under the kitchen sink with the others. When he opened the door, cockroaches scurried into the darkest corner of the cupboard.

"We also got this," Josh said as he walked back to the fridge, a glimmer of enthusiasm in his voice. The turnip he pulled from the crisper was as big as his head, and the thump it made when it hit the floor shook our apartment. It sounded like a bomb went off. Josh rolled the clumsy boulder over to the edge of the warplanes, hitting Jerry's foot.

"Dad said we could eat this. I know we tried before, but we gave up too easy," Josh said.

I waddled over to the vegetable wondering how it'd fit in my mouth. Josh pulled a knife out of a drawer and sat down and began to hack at the turnip. Flecks of white and hard yellow the size of pennies flew in all directions as Josh whacked away at it. I put one of the white pieces in my mouth and bit down, but my teeth couldn't meet all the way. I chewed away. It tasted like nothing, but I swallowed anyways. I rubbed my fingers along my bottom teeth—they were covered in a waxy film.

Jerry picked up a yellow piece and chucked it in his mouth. The click of his jaw told me the yellow parts were way harder than the white ones. He folded his arms and spat the piece out onto the ground. "It's worse than brown pops. It's like a rock. I can't eat that."

Josh's blade paused a second as he took a big yellow piece and placed it in his mouth. He tried to look like he was happy eating it, but we could tell it was torture. The muscles on the side of his head flexed and bulged. He spat it out and agreed with Jerry: totally inedible.

There was a loud knock on the door.

Josh gently placed the knife on the ground and put his hands over both our mouths. "Be quiet," he mouthed and made a shush shape with his lips. The battle-scarred turnip rocked back and forth, threatening to give us away.

Another knock assaulted the door.

"Open up," a voiced boomed. "It's the police. We know you boys are in there."

Josh's eyes widened, and he grabbed my shirt and pulled me toward the wall, as if he didn't know what to do or where to go.

Jerry shot up, tossing the blanket on the floor. "Come with me," he said as he launched me and Josh into the bedroom. We skidded over to Jerry's hiding spot, a large air vent in our room that he'd discovered when we first moved in. When he showed it to Dad, he was impressed with how much room there was inside. Jerry told him how he'd used a penny to turn the screws at the corners to take off the grate, and how the shaft went straight twelve feet and then turned right.

"Smart lad," Dad said. He'd tied a string to the back of the grate. "Now, when someone comes—and I mean anyone—you all pile in here and just pull this string. It'll close the vent cover behind you. Got it?"

Jerry nodded and tried it out. The first couple times, the cover went on crooked, or sideways, or not at all. Eventually, though, with enough coaching from Dad, Jerry could pull it closed in a second or two. From the outside, it was hard to see the string or that the screws weren't holding the grate on.

Boom. Boom. Boom.

The knocks at the door turned into what sounded like powerful kicks. It was only a matter of minutes before the door gave way.

"Hurry. They're coming," Jerry said as he pulled the grate off and rammed my head through the vent opening. He kicked my bum to hurry me up. A wall of warm, dry air slammed into my face and arms as I flew down the shaft. Josh was right behind me, pressing his face into my ass. He shoved me farther down the shaft toward the darkness.

"Go—go—go," he commanded in a frantic but hushed voice. "Faster, Jesse, crawl faster."

The more we wiggled forward, the more our bodies dented the tin walls. It sounded like thunder all around my head. I began to cry. I looked back and could see Jerry pull the string closed. The grate slapped into place in one shot—perfect, just like Dad taught him. We covered our mouths to silence our breath, dust settling all around us.

Boom. Boom. BOOM!

I could hear the front door burst open and footsteps stampede into the living room. It sounded like the herds of bison stampeding that I'd seen on nature shows.

"Look at this," I heard one man say. "The kitchen is full of trash."

"Hey, look," another called out from the bathroom, his voice echoing off the tiles, "there are rigs and gear in the tub. Check it out."

One voice stood out from the rest. I could tell he was in charge. "Yep. Just like the neighbour described. Dope and children. Find them."

The violent sound of crashing cupboard doors was followed by the clanking of empty beer bottles. "Jesus," a deep voice said from near the kitchen, "they've been hacking up this turnip. They got no food."

I heard them go into Dad's room and then more noise. "Nothing in here but skin magazines."

A pair of black boots appeared in front of the vent, and someone bent down to look under the bed. It was a police officer. I could just see his uniform past Jerry and Josh's bodies. "Nothing in here," he said, as he shone his flashlight into the vent. His voice was higher and younger than the rest. "But the pillow is wet. They must've just left."

"Not possible," the voice in charge said. "The lady next door watched him leave last night at 10:30 and the kids were inside. She saw them herself when she peeked in from the door across the hall. She said they beg for food in front of the store or the arena—we checked both locations, and they weren't there. That means they're still here. Look harder."

"I don't know, Sarge. We checked everywhere. It's a tiny apartment, where else could they be?"

Jerry's arms were shaking as the pair of black boots readjusted in front of the vent. A radio chattered as Josh squirmed. The tin made a muffled knock under his arm.

"Wait a minute," the high voice said. "I think they're in here." The front of the vent shifted as he dug his fingers under the grate and tried to pull.

Jerry gritted his teeth and held it tight with all his might.

"They're in the vent. I can see them! But they've got it locked off somehow." The herd of black boots entered the room as the young officer's eye peered in to get a better look. "Yup." He smiled and put his palm up to the vent holes.

I was shaking, and I could feel Josh was, too.

"It's okay, fellas, nothing to be afraid of."

"Move outta the way," the lead voice barked and the grate was ripped off.

A huge meaty hand with hair on it reached in and pulled Jerry out, then Josh and me, my Mighty Mouse PJs ripping on a screw in the opening.

Jerry and I were shaking and crying. I couldn't speak. The string had rubbed Jerry's palms raw as it was torn from his grasp. Blue-and-red lights flashed against the ceiling of our bedroom.

Dad is going to kill us, I thought. Josh began to cry. He was probably thinking the same thing.

The officer who found us bent down and smiled. "Which one are you?" he asked Josh as he dusted the lint off my brother's shoulder and wiped his tears. Josh just glared at him and kept his mouth shut, the dust on his face now smeared back to his ear.

A kind-looking black woman with a clipboard emerged from behind the young policeman. I could smell her fruity perfume—it made me hungry. She knelt in front of Jerry. "We're going to take you somewhere safe, there's no need to be afraid."

Jerry pushed her away and crossed his arms.

She nodded to the police, and they scooped us up.

As the officer carried me out of the apartment, I looked over his shoulder and saw my blanket sitting on the kitchen floor. It half-covered the turnip and some empty bottles. I could see the edge of the Baron's triplane, and I imagined myself flying it higher and higher into the sky, up near the sun.

THE PACT

THE NICE BLACK LADY AND the young police officer took us to a large red-brick building with lots of windows.

"You boys will be safe here," she said.

She took Jerry by the hand from the squad car. Jerry didn't put up a fight, neither did Josh or I. We walked through a pair of giant steel doors that guarded the front entrance and down a long hall, into a large room with rows and rows of bunk beds. It smelled of bleach.

There were other kids there. They sat on their bunks and checked us out as we walked to three empty beds at the back of the room. Josh and Jerry got bottom beds, I got the top. I noticed two black kids and a few older boys who had dark skin and hair like us. They looked like our Indian cousins in Saskatchewan but different. The covers and sheets of the beds were done up perfectly, corners tucked tight under the mattresses, the pillows flat and smoothed out. I'd seen Mom make a bed that way before, but we'd been with Dad for months and he never did anything like that for us, and he couldn't afford these kinds of pillows.

I was relieved at the order and cleanliness of this new place, whatever it was.

"This is Children's Aid," the black lady told us.

Through the tangle of bedposts I saw a red-headed boy looking at me.

He flashed me a smile and a tiny wave. I ducked down and buried my head in the black lady's leg.

"That's Johnny," she said. "He's a nice boy. No need to be shy."

Jerry and Josh peered over, and the boy again smiled and waved. They stared at him until his hand fell by his side.

The place was way bigger than our apartment or any of the places I'd ever been.

"Where's Dad and when's he coming to get us?" Josh asked.

The black lady just gave us something to eat and then tucked us all in and left, turning the lights out.

I wasn't scared and fell asleep, my belly full. I dreamt about the black lady and wondered what her name was. When I woke in the morning the place buzzed with activity, and we were ushered in lines into a hall where we had oatmeal and bananas. I stuck by my brothers as the other kids checked us out. Josh did all the talking, telling everyone that our dad was away and that we'd be going home as soon as the police found him.

"I used to think that, too," one kid said. "But we're orphans now—don't cha know?"

I didn't know what that meant.

We became good friends with Johnny and the other kids. Jerry said Johnny was like our red-headed brother, that he was part of our tribe, too. Johnny told us that his parents couldn't afford Cheerios one day, had a big fight over it, and then dropped him off here. He said he felt like it was his fault, that he never got the chance to tell his parents that he didn't even like Cheerios and that they'd be okay without cereal.

I was sorry for him. I thought the same about why my mom and dad had left us. I'd been a bad boy and had asked for food too often. We'd eaten Dad's secret food too many times, and he'd probably gotten so mad over it that he'd up and left us. I gave Johnny a hug.

After a few days, strange things started happening.

The black lady and other people who worked in the big building started taking kids out of the large room one by one. They asked them all kinds of difficult questions. Doctors examined them for any bugs and sicknesses, checked their hair and tongue, in their underwear, and under their arms—or so we were told by the kids when they returned.

Some were taken out and never came back. That was the scariest. It was like they'd been eaten by monsters. No one knew what happened to them, but the older kids said they were the lucky ones because someone wanted them. I didn't understand that; our mom and dad wanted us, why didn't theirs want them, too?

When they came for Jerry, Josh rushed over and bit the lady on the hand and I ran and kicked her foot as hard as I could. We screamed and screamed, fought and fought, our faces getting redder than fire engines. Johnny joined in, stomping her toe until she let go. We four scurried to the back of the room and nestled in a corner. Josh grabbed hold of our necks and pulled us in close. We locked arms and brought Johnny in, too, holding tight to one another, gnashing our teeth. We did exactly as Dad had directed—protected each other from strangers.

The woman left the room to get help.

"We gotta stick together," Josh said, panting. We all nodded. We made a pact, then and there, to take care of one another no matter what. We squeezed each other with all our might and shut our eyes, sealing the deal.

Five minutes after the pact was struck, a team of workers came in and wrestled Johnny from our circle. We tried fighting back but they held us down and took away our red-headed brother—they were just too strong. We never saw Johnny again.

I thought of him when they came and got us three brothers a few weeks later.

MONSTER RESCUE

"YOU BOYS ARE LUCKY," THE black lady said to me after I'd been checked over by the doctor and placed in the hallway with my brothers. "We've found a foster home that will take all three of you."

Josh stood on defence between the front entrance and the door of the large room. Jerry milled about. He was silent, biting his nails.

"Take us?" Josh asked forcefully. "Where? What about our mom and dad?"

Jerry's face went blank and he stopped pacing. He moved behind Josh, as if to back him up.

What does "foster home" mean? I'd never heard that word before. Who is going to take us? I wasn't sure, but I knew my brothers were uneasy.

The lady hesitated, and I could tell she was thinking hard about what she was going to say next.

The doctor came into the hall and handed a clipboard to her. "They're all clear," he said, "but this one's still a little underweight." He pointed to Josh. He looked fine to me.

Josh asked more questions, but we got no answers about our dad or mom. The lady just kept telling us that we were lucky, and that our ride to our new home would be along shortly.

We were cleaned up—teeth brushed, hair combed, shoes tied—and had our belongings packed up. I had the leather Adidas bag Mom had given me before Dad took us from Saskatchewan, and Jerry and Josh had theirs, too. Our names were on them and we always kept them ready just in case we had to run at night—it was a fun game Dad played with us when we moved. The police must've brought them when we first came to the red-brick building, but they forgot to bring our old clothes.

I was glad to hold my bag again; it meant I was going somewhere new. And it was filled with better clothes now, even a brand-new Mighty Mouse T-shirt. I was excited even though I knew my brothers were worried.

We went outside, and an old man drove up and got out of his car.

He said, "Nice to see you, Gladys," to the black lady, and told us his name was Clive. He smelled like old cigars and had grease on his overalls. He was way bigger than Dad, and I thought he was at least a hundred years old, judging by his grey hair and fat belly.

Gladys shook Clive's hand then knelt down and pinched Jerry's cheek. "I'll miss you boys," she said, picking the lint off his yellow-and-brown-striped sweater. "But I'll miss you most, Jerry." I could see he almost burst into tears. They hugged while Clive loaded our bags into the trunk of his car, and with that, we were off.

The car ride to our new house took forever. We drove until nighttime, and I couldn't keep my eyes open. When we pulled up to Clive's place, a woman and girl came out to greet us. They had big smiles and balloons, and a small dog was barking its head off beside them—it was about the size of a beaver and had scraggly brown hair.

"This is my wife, Cynthia," Clive said. "And my daughter, Matilda." Cynthia looked so old to me, like Clive, and Matilda was around the same age as my cousin Suzanne back in Saskatoon—around nine years old. Her hair was curly, down to her shoulders. I could see her braces when she smiled. The dog continued to bark and sniff as we made our way inside.

My memories of the time inside that house are misty. Like a shroud of fog not yet lifted just before dawn. The wild shapes of things black and blue, bleeding into one another. The sunlight not yet strong enough to make out what lurks in the tall azure grass ahead, the line of spruce just out of view at the other end of the meadow.

What I do remember, though, is grease, pressure, that yapping dog, and wishing it would end.

I remember my brother Jerry fighting off the giant wolf that came into our room and floated over our beds and ripped him apart.

Jerry's tiny fists punched up and into the darkness, right before his little body was dug out and broken.

He would put himself between me and the Monster. He would rescue me from whatever it was that had him and Josh squealing in the next room while I cried myself to sleep.

I would turn my head and try to hide from it all, but it always found me.

Jerry and Josh changed after that. They lost their superpowers, they peed the bed every night. But they were still my protectors.

The fragments of that time blend and refract light in a way that blinds me, but I do know that one day the black lady showed up, and that before we left the house, Josh shut the door in the dog's face. Its whining is the last thing I remember from that horrible place.

THE BEAST

WE RACED BY JUTS OF rock and small Jack pines. My eyes tried to keep up with the jagged landscape, but the blurred tracers of green and black just made me feel sick.

My grandparents Cyril and Jackie Thistle looked exactly like they did in the pictures Dad used to show us. Grandpa, who was driving, had a brown moustache like Dad's, but it was trimmed neatly around his upper lip. His hair was slick and parted like Alfalfa's from *Little Rascals*, but not down the middle. Grandma had a grey-black Afro that wobbled with the motion of the van.

She leaned back to offer me a sandwich. I was hungry, so I took it.

Grandpa smiled at me in the rearview mirror. His eyes gleamed like blue sapphires, the light catching them just so through his glasses.

My grandparents didn't say much to us boys on the drive to Toronto, but I could make out that my grandmother was mad at my parents by the way she complained to Grandpa. Her fury at our dad for leaving us alone. Her anger when she talked about our mother. I didn't understand that, though. Dad had talked Mom into letting us go in Moose Jaw. It wasn't her fault the way things ended up.

As Grandma railed on, I realized there was a force in her that was more powerful than that of my grandfather. Grandpa listened and nodded, careful to watch the road, but it was clear Grandma was in charge.

In between sentences, Grandma turned to face me, and, with the taste of ham and cheese thick on my tongue, I could smell the scent of charred wood and tobacco coming from her direction. Somehow, the odour told me I could trust her enough to share my words.

"Thank you for the sandwich, Grandma."

She rubbed my leg. "You're welcome, Baby Boy." She peeled an orange, and I shared it with Jerry and Josh, who fell asleep soon after, but I remained awake, fascinated by Grandma and her campfire smell. I stared at her as she smoked her cigarettes and flicked them in an empty coffee cup she kept between her knees.

I'd later learn from my aunties that Grandma's people came from a place way up in northern Ontario called Timiskaming, and that she was part Native and part white like us boys—Algonquin and Scottish, and that her dad was from a reserve near Notre Dame du Nord in Quebec.

As I examined her features through the cigarette smoke, I recognized that Grandma was a little Indian, but her hair was all curly, not black and straight like my mom's and aunties' out west. Her skin was more tanned than my grandfather's. He had the same tone as a freshly opened cube of Spam—pink through and through—like Dad and me. Not Grandma. She was lighter than Josh, but almost looked the same beige mix as Jerry.

"Look," Grandpa said after hours of driving along what seemed like a never-ending road. We crested a hill and the landscape opened up before us. "That's Toronto—that's where our house is." He lifted his bear paw from the wheel and pointed to a cluster of buildings on the approaching horizon. The toothy jumble of grey concrete in the distance was unlike anything I'd ever seen before. Way bigger than anywhere else I'd ever been.

"You see that needle-looking structure right in the middle?" Grandpa asked. "That's the tallest building in the world—the CN Tower."

I almost fell forward off my seat trying to get a better look.

Grandpa laughed. "We live over there," he said, motioning to a smaller cluster of buildings. "In a place called Brampton. But I'll take you boys to see the tower after we're all settled in."

The houses in Brampton were set in neat little rows, with perfect lawns and freshly paved roads. Everything looked so clean, orderly, and taken care of. Blue jays and robins sang to each other in the treetops; squirrels ran everywhere collecting things; and cats walked, surefooted, along fence tops. There was so much sunlight. It comforted me to see so many parents walking with their kids. I thought of my mom and dad— but in a good way, when we were happy and together.

This new place was so beautiful.

We rounded the corner, pulled into a driveway on the coziest street I ever saw, and Grandpa declared, "We're home."

"Just be careful of Yorkie," Grandma said as we got out and made our way to the front door. "He likes to jump."

Bounding out the door came a beast of a dog. He had brown and black fur with flecks of silver down the sides, and his ears were erect like a German shepherd's. He looked like a wolf and stood as tall as the middle of my chest. His tail wagged so hard that his bum shot from side to side—even while he charged at us. He leapt at me, I fell backward, and he started licking my face until I couldn't breathe. I started to cry.

But Yorkie kept licking, yelping with glee. He was doing his best to welcome us home.

TOUCH OF HOME

"CYRIL," GRANDMA SAID TO GRANDPA. "My catalogues are missing again." Her permed hair bobbed as she lifted the chesterfield cushions. "One of the boys keeps taking them and hiding them all over the house, and I need to order something." She stood, mouth open.

"Maybe they have to order something, too, Jackie." Grandpa smirked at me and returned to his egg-and-bacon breakfast. The fork and knife looked tiny in his elevator-mechanic hands. I peered at my feet, which dangled from the chair next to him. His thumbs were about twice the size of my big toes. My eyes barely rose above the kitchen table. Grandma left to go down to the laundry room. Her slippers slapped against the hard yellow calluses on her heels, like leather against wood.

"What's the verdict, Jesse? Do you have something to order?" Before I could answer, Grandpa delivered a swift karate chop to my leg. "Hiya!"

My knee jerked. I squealed with glee as eggs spilled out of my mouth and down the front of my PJs.

"Grandpa!" I shouted, half shocked, half laughing, ketchup smeared all over my lips and chin. He just winked, looking like Popeye without his corncob pipe. His forearms were bigger than Popeye's for sure.

"Watch it, buddy," he said as he put up his dukes. I put mine up like a little fighting Irishman.

Grandma called upstairs. "Cyril, wait till you see this." I heard her heavy rhino steps, then saw her. She had the missing catalogue in her hand. "I found it behind the toy box. Look." She opened it and held it up. "Just like the last few times it went missing." She placed it in front of my grandfather and pointed. "The women's underwear section is ripped out—the whole section."

"Well, I didn't do it. Must've been one of the boys," he said and laughed. "At least they took the best part."

"Cyril!" Grandma looked disgusted.

I pushed my eggs around to avoid eye contact, but she leaned forward, crossing her arms over the damaged magazine. "Jesse. Do you know who did this?" Her brown-rimmed glasses magnified her eyes. Grandpa turned to face me.

"No, Grandma—"

Yorkie the Wonder Dog, who'd become my most trusted friend and ally, came in and pooped near the fridge, saving me from saying more. Grandpa pushed aside his breakfast, and Grandma ran over as Yorkie scurried away with a guilty-dog smile, his tail tucked between his legs.

"You see what happens when you boys don't walk him enough!" Grandma grabbed a grocery bag from under the kitchen sink and dangled it in my direction. "Come clean it up."

I usually woke up early, and often was the first one up. It was something I'd learned while living with Dad. The first one up and to the cupboards or fridge was the first one to eat. And the first one to eat was often the only one to eat. But this morning at my grandparents' I stayed in bed, cozy in my own room, buried under my blanket, not worried about breakfast. My grandparents had lots of treats, and my instinct to be the first one up was giving way to a desire to sleep in.

I awoke to find Grandma in my room.

"Jesse. Time to get up." She put an armful of clothes on the chest of drawers and began folding sweaters. "Aunt Sherry and Uncle John are coming over and we've got to get you ready."

My aunt Sherry was my grandparents' only daughter, and Grandpa's favourite child by a long shot. She was the youngest and was pretty with long flowing brown hair and beautiful hazel eyes. She always made us the best food when she came over—fried chicken, pasta with salty cheese, and chocolate cake. Uncle John, her husband, was strong like a lumberjack—he cut wood with an axe, beard and all, at their house in the country, and I imagined he was so powerful because of all the delicious foods Aunt Sherry made him.

I cleared the sleep from my eyes and sat up. Yorkie ran in, his tail wagging and tongue hanging out. He jumped on the bed to lick my face, and the sound of crunching echoed throughout the room. *Crunch, crunch, crunch, crunch, crunch.* Everywhere he put his paws on the bed, the sound resonated.

"What the hell?" Grandma said and turned to investigate the strange noise.

Stop moving, dog, I pleaded silently.

Yorkie continued to romp about. Grandma grabbed him by the scruff, threw him off the bed, then reached down and pulled my covers back. I tried raking them back up, but she'd already seen. Strewn all around me were pages and pages of the Sears catalogues. There must've been about seventy-five beautiful young underwear models nestled in my bed.

"It was you," Grandma said. "Why?"

I tried to hide. "I don't know. They . . ."

Grandma pushed the ripped pages aside and sat beside me.

"I like them," I whispered. Yorkie put his paws up on the bed again. "They remind me of my mom. They're beautiful."

Grandma's scents, curves, and soft voice had taken the place of my mother's. But they weren't the same. Mom's body was brown and lean. Grandma's was beige and chubby, with wrinkles and moles all over. I missed holding on to my mother's leg, nuzzling her breast, cuddling against her stomach. I missed feeling the strength her being possessed, the sense of warmth and protection. No matter how hard I squeezed, Grandma just wasn't home.

"Oh, baby," Grandma said and hugged me.

GODZILLA

WHEN I WALKED INTO CLASS the first day of kindergarten, I saw a kid standing alone by the tinker toys and coloured blocks in the corner near Mrs. S.'s desk. He was much shorter than me. His hair was dark brown, cut into a strange kind of bowl cut, and his nose was large and hatchet-shaped.

"My name is Leeroy," the kid said. "I'm a Newfie. My parents come from an island called Newfoundland."

I knew where that was because Grandpa came from Cape Breton. I imagined a land of Newfies with big noses, just like my new friend. I soon found out that he lived on my street, right around the corner from my house. In all, it was around fifty metres from his door to mine.

Leeroy and I got along right from the beginning. We'd jump our bikes off the curbs after school, and he was the only kid on our block who could beat me in a race. But I was tougher and could get the best of him most times—having older brothers gave me an advantage. He took me to cool spots like the gravel pit where we'd catch frogs and crayfish. Jerry would come with us, too, but it was clear Leeroy and I were best friends.

Leeroy had a big sister named Sylvia who was in Grade 2 with my brother Josh. She was twice the size of me and Leeroy.

"We need to watch out for her," Leeroy said. "She's a bully."

There was a wall that separated the kindergarten section from the older kids' playground out back. Whenever Sylvia came into our area, we'd whistle to warn each other, and then take cover behind the bushes. Most times we escaped her wrath, but sometimes she'd catch us by surprise and beat the pulp out of us. Her strength was unreal—like some real-life version of Godzilla, but with dirty-blond hair and a frilly pink dress. Her footsteps seemed to shake the very earth beneath our feet, and her nose was even larger than Leeroy's—when she'd throttle me, I thought it resembled the snout of a T. Rex, roaring and full of dinosaur teeth.

One day, Leeroy and I had had enough. We decided we were going to fire a giant wad of gum into Sylvia's hair at recess. She'd beaten and embarrassed us too many times. The moment the wet gum left the sling and slapped the side of her head, we knew we'd taken it too far.

She reached back and tried pulling it out, but that only made things worse. The gum stuck to her fingers and formed thin strands that blew back with the wind. A whole spiderweb of gum clung to the side of her face and neck. Her hair would have to be cut to get the gum out. Tears filled her eyes and she let out the most monstrous screech I'd ever heard. Her very body seemed to grow larger and larger the louder she yelled. Then she moved with lightning speed, cornered us, and began pummelling us in front of everyone.

Our classmates began screeching, "Save them, Mrs. S., Sylvia is going to murder them," as she tossed us in the air like rag dolls.

It felt like I flew five feet in one direction, Leeroy, four in the other. We knew we'd probably die if we stuck around, so we decided to make a run for it.

The playground was boxed in on one side by the school, and surrounded by fences on the others, and Sylvia blocked the way back toward the main road, so the gravel pit on the other side of the playground seemed like our only option. I signalled to Leeroy with my eyes, he did the same back, and the instant our sneakers hit the ground, we bolted. Sylvia may have been bigger and stronger than us, but we were faster, and we ran like our lives depended on it. When we thought we had a good lead, we turned to see how much earth separated us from the gum-haired Godzilla. She was about a half-kilometre away, screaming, crying, and cursing. For now, we were safe from the beast's clutches. For now, victory was ours.

From then on, Leeroy and I were inseparable.

LEEROY AND THE BROWN POP

LEEROY'S PARENTS BOTH WORKED DAYS, and he stayed in the after-school program until his mom or dad picked him up at 4:30 p.m. Sylvia also stayed after school, and Leeroy didn't like being in an enclosed space for two hours with his big sister and the other kids.

"The class breaks out into wrestling matches," he said, "and I always get the worst of it from Sylvia."

"Come play at my house," I said to him one day. Once 4:20 hit, he could walk back to school for his 4:30 pickup, like he'd never left at all. He jumped at the chance at freedom.

None of the kids usually liked coming to our house to play. Who could blame them? It was like stepping into a time machine. We had blocks of wood to play with; bits of steel my grandpa brought home from his construction job; some old dinky cars; a couple of beat-up hockey sticks from my uncles; and a few beach rocks we'd picked up in Cape Breton on our yearly trips. I knew my grandparents loved us; they just didn't have a lot of money.

We did get some good toys at Christmas, though, from our uncles and aunts, but we always destroyed them in a few days. Josh dismantled them to look inside and see how they were made and never put them back together, and Jerry and I simply abused them.

Down in our basement, I chucked a half-painted red block of wood across the concrete floor at Leeroy, trying to pretend it was Superman. It bounced and stopped dead in its tracks—definitely not Superman. Leeroy let out a sigh. Thirty minutes after reaching my house, I knew he was bored out of his mind. I began searching around for a way to keep us occupied. Then it hit me. I did have something Leeroy didn't have. Something way better than even his mountainous hoard of awesome toys.

"Leeroy," I said, so excited I just about shit myself. "Want to try something?"

"Sure," he said, unenthused.

I walked over to the fridge and yanked on the handle. The seal on the door broke and revealed a massive stack of Labatt 50 beers piled sideways, one on top of the other. They formed an odd pyramid shape that almost touched the bottom of the freezer. There must've been over three feet of them—ninety at least. The brown bodies of the bottles seemed to sweat and gleam in the neon basement light. "Brown pop," I said to Leeroy.

My dad used to give me sips of it when I lived with him in Sudbury, especially when I was crying. I remembered it tasted horrible but I drank it anyway, and the more I drank without complaining, the louder my dad and his friends laughed. They laughed loudest when Dad put me on the counter and I'd piss in the kitchen sink like they did.

Grandpa, too, loved brown pops, and it was my job to bring them to him when he came home from work every night. "Baby Boy!" he'd holler from his purple armchair in the living room. "Gimme a cold one." I would drop whatever I was doing, go grab one from the fridge, and run it upstairs. An empty bottle was always waiting for return by the side of the coffee table. If I was fast enough, and he was in a good mood, he'd give me a karate chop to the leg, then rub my hair. "That's my boy," he'd say through clenched teeth.

"I'm not sure if you've ever tried them," I said to Leeroy, "but my grandpa loves them, my dad does, too. They say it puts hair on your chest."

"Hair?"

"Yeah." I stepped back so Leeroy could look inside the fridge.

"My dad drinks these, too, so does my mom. But not this kind."

I grabbed one and shut the door. The cold glass felt nice. "This metal thing on the wall, that's the opener." Leeroy examined it.

"You just put the cap in at an angle, under the top tooth." I showed him. "Then you press the bottom of the bottle. The lid will come right off. I do it all the time for Grandpa." I could tell by the way he'd been looking at the opener that he'd never opened a bottle himself. When I pressed the bottle toward the wall, it hissed, and the cap fell and danced on the ground by our feet. Before I lost my courage, I hoisted the bottle to my lips and took a big swig. I could tell Leeroy wanted to try it, too. I gulped with all my might and almost vomited. A second later my stomach convulsed, but I said, "Ah," and wiped my mouth with the back of my hand.

"Give it to me," Leeroy demanded. He snatched the bottle. It was clear he wanted to impress me. The swill he took was bigger than mine, and his eyes bulged. He spat it out over the back of the bar. "That's disgusting."

I rescued the bottle from him before he dropped it. The brown pop still felt warm and bubbly inside my guts.

"No! I want to do it!" he yelled and yanked the bottle out of my hand. His chug was even bigger than before. This time he kept it down. *Success.* He smiled and let out a huge burp, and we both giggled.

By the end of the third bottle, I had a pressing urge to pee. I attempted to walk to the washroom, but couldn't see right, and my legs gave out halfway to the stairs. I fell in the middle of the floor and pissed myself where I lay. Leeroy, too, tried taking a few steps, but his legs buckled, and he veered off and slammed headfirst into the bar. He looked like a disoriented cat that tumbles sideways after being spun round and round. As he toppled to the ground, the bottle fell and smashed on the floor. We howled with laughter, our legs and arms writhing.

My grandmother must've heard all the commotion because before I knew it, she was standing over the two of us, hands on her hips. "What in God's name are the two of you up to now?" Her nose sniffed at the air.

We continued giggling, unable to collect ourselves, and totally unafraid. She grabbed my shoulders and hoisted me onto my feet. "Dear Lord, are you drunk, Jesse?" She let go of me. I fell toward her, grabbing her shirt for balance. She had her answer.

"Omm . . . Phurtttt . . . Haazzz . . ." I tried explaining what we'd done but nothing but bafflegab came out. Leeroy was cackling beside us, rolling dangerously close to the broken bottle. Grandma stood him up before he cut himself. She tried to scold us but started laughing until she wheezed, tears rolling out her eyes. I'd never seen her laugh so deeply over something I'd done. It made me feel good.

She got us upstairs and gave us a few drinks of water and some bread, and changed my pants. "Now get outside and walk it off," she said, shooing us away. "Like two miniature drunken sailors, you are."

We eventually fell asleep under a neighbour's tree a few houses down the street. When I woke up, Leeroy was gone.

ROBIN'S EGGS

MY FRIEND BRIAN, WHO LIVED down the street, told me he had a secret one day and that if I kept my mouth shut he'd show me. I promised not to tell a soul, and Brian showed me a robin's nest in his backyard. Every day Brian and his family put seeds beside the nest to feed the mother robin before she went foraging in the afternoon. She would leave at the same time every day—4:30 p.m. on the dot.

I remember looking at the eggs in wonder. There were three of them, and they were so beautiful—bright baby blue, tucked into the yellowed grass and mud of the nest. I imagined the eggs carefully positioned by their mother's feet, protected under her soft feathers, and guarded by her watchful eye.

Brian's mother called him in for dinner. "I'll wait for you and watch over the eggs while you eat," I said. Assured, he left. As soon as he did, I grabbed the eggs, put them in my sock, and ran home. On the way I slipped and fell and broke the eggs. Shocked at what I'd done, I threw the sock in the sewer, then hid in my grandparents' basement.

About a half-hour later Brian and his parents, Mr. and Mrs. T., showed up at our door looking for me. Mr. T. was a police officer but was kind to me and my brothers, and sometimes even played catch with us neighbourhood kids. Mrs. T. was even nicer, always baking up batches of cookies for Brian and me when we played Montezuma's Revenge on his computer—the only high-powered computer on our street.

My grandmother searched the house and found me behind a stack of boxes.

"I'm really sorry," I said when I was confronted about the eggs and told them what I'd done.

Brian cried. He was heartbroken.

"Why did you steal the eggs?" Brian's mother asked.

I broke down into a blubbering mess. The more they asked me, the more I bawled. But I didn't tell them why I did it.

My grandparents gave me the licking of my life, but I didn't break: I still didn't tell them why I stole the eggs.

When I saw Brian the next day at school he wouldn't talk to me.

The truth is, when I saw the three eggs tucked into that nest it reminded me of my brothers and me and our home in Saskatchewan. I thought of how much that mother robin loved those eggs and how well she and Brian's family took care of them, and I got jealous. The eggs had their mother, and my brothers and I didn't anymore. So I took the eggs. I thought that if I had them, in some way I'd have the same love the eggs had, and that would mean that in some way I'd have a mother's love again.

ATTABOY!

AS SOON AS I COULD hold a screwdriver and control a jigsaw—when I was about six years old—Grandpa trained me to use tools.

Grandpa believed in an honest day's work. He told us he was raised by his grandfather, Pappy Peter McKinnon, after his own father, a coal miner, passed from a heart attack. He used to say that if a man didn't have callused hands, he couldn't be trusted and didn't really work. He also said that your word was your worth, something that meant life or death when he grew up during the Depression. Because of his beliefs, I never heard Grandpa lie, never, not even if it hurt him to tell the truth.

"If a man knows how to build," Grandpa said as he wrapped my small hands around the circular saw, "he owns the world. Anything is possible. It's like large-scale Legos, just with sweat and more thinking."

Grandpa steadied the five-by-eight plywood board on the sawhorses, positioned my hips and arms, and continued with his lesson. "I built my own house, once, in Ottawa, just to see if I could do it. Nice house, too. And I had to work one of these saws all the time. After I teach you, you'll know how to do it for life."

Josh cried at first when Grandpa tried to teach him to work the saw, and almost gave up before he gritted his teeth, focused, then ran the blade straight through, winning Grandpa's admiration. Jerry flat-out refused. I assume it was because whenever Grandpa taught us any new skill it meant we'd have to use it to help him on one of his projects. Studding up the basement, ripping plywood for the skirting around the cabin down east, or building a new deck in the backyard, all were things we'd done once he'd trained us on new tools.

When Josh asked him why he made us work so hard, he said it was because his father had died when he was five years old. "That's when I became a man," he'd say. "I didn't have no childhood working in the mines. But growing up without my father made me tough, like a dried piece of salt cod left out in the sun too long. Grandpappy Peter also taught me to work up on Black Point, fishing in the dory. And I ain't letting you boys grow up without some of that hardness. Work was the only thing that pulled me and my mother out of the Depression."

Jerry always rolled his eyes when Grandpa went into his hard-done-by speeches.

As I steadied the saw, which was about the size of my torso, I imagined how hard working the way he did must've been for my grandfather.

"Just hold it straight, level, follow the line, and let the blade do the work. Most importantly, don't be afraid! I'll catch the offcut so the saw doesn't kick when it falls. And if it does buck, for God's sake don't try to grab it, just let it go," Grandpa said. "Got it?"

"Okay, Grandpa." I placed the face of the saw on the board, up against the clamped straight edge, my arms straining to keep it level. Both my brothers were looking on, and I tried my best to hide my fear from everyone. Jerry smirked and made a face. Josh joined in.

"Exactly. Now, press the trigger and let 'er rip. Like Josh did." Grandpa got into position beside me and made sure the extension cord wasn't in the way.

1, 2, 3, I counted in my head then squeezed the trigger tight. I had to fight the urge to close my eyes or run away. The whine and power of the saw frightened me at first, but I waited a second until I was comfortable pushing the machine forward. Grandpa nudged the back of my elbow and the blade moaned and bit into the wood.

"Now, easy does it, Jess. Steady."

The smell of pine filled my nostrils as sawdust kicked down onto my foot and back toward Jerry. I kept my eye on the plywood where the saw met the straight edge. Surprisingly, the saw tugged my hands and lurched forward on its own, but I pulled back against its torque, created some resistance, and kept everything balanced. Soon the blade had run through the length of the wood and the board offcut fell into my grandfather's hands. It looked like a baby delivered into the waiting arms of a doctor. He laughed out loud and his belly shook up and down behind his brown oil-stained overalls.

"That's how it's done. That's my baby boy!"

His eyes beamed with pride as he turned to face Josh and Jerry, who stood cross-armed. Both grimaced at me. I knew I'd get it from both of them later when Grandpa wasn't around. Despite the impending beating, I was proud of myself, even though it was only one piece of lumber.

"Thanks, Poppa," I said, grinning from ear to ear. "I wasn't scared at all."

"I know. Attaboy, Jess. Attaboy."

He reached over to the radio and turned up the George Jones song that crackled across the AM sound waves. He hummed to himself as he examined my cut, then lit a cigarette.

"Listen boys," he said, a plume of Du Maurier smoke swirling around his stubbled face, "I got a secret weapon. No one will have a go-cart racer like ours. Trust me—we'll never lose." He promised us we'd build a go-cart once we learned how to use the saw. He shuffled out onto the driveway, over to the side of his van, and slapped the side panel.

"A man must drive in style, boys, with a clean vehicle. That's his horse. You ever see knights riding around on scrawny, beat-up horses destined for the glue factory? Well, there's a reason for that."

Josh turned to me and said, "What the hell is he talking about? Glue factories didn't exist back when knights were around."

Jerry laughed and said, "He's trying to say that after we're finished with the go-cart we have to wash the van—again," while he pretended he was riding a horse, swinging a cowboy hat above his head, galloping around me and Josh.

Grandpa emerged from the van and caught Jerry making fun of him. "You look like a chubby version of Roy Rogers, galloping around all cock-eyed without a horse or gun."

Josh and I howled, while Jerry stood there stunned.

Grandpa never talked much while he worked, and today was no different while the four of us toiled away on the go-cart. We just kind of nodded and passed each other tools like nurses give surgeons instruments in the operating room—noiseless and quick, no mistakes. I think that's when we were closest, when we were silently working away in the garage, fixing the van, or doing other things. When the job was done, Grandpa cracked a beer, and we all drank Coke.

"It's a fine racer," Grandpa said. The go-cart was all decked out with a real car seat, two-inch-thick chassis, and rope steering, and it rode on "the fastest, most durable wheels known to man!" as he put it. Grandpa had pulled a set of four elevator wheels from the van—they were yellow and small and the same colour and texture as glycerine soap.

I just about pissed myself thinking of beating the pants off the other kids around us in the go-carts they had made with their fathers.

Jerry got the first push down the block. I figured it was because Grandpa felt bad about his comment earlier. Jerry screamed down the street, smiling and laughing, hair waving in the air. We cheered him on from the driveway, and Grandpa took a swig and hollered, "Attaboy, Jerry, attaboy!"

We all lived to hear him say those words.

LITTLE THIEF

"JESSE!" GRANDMA CALLED FROM UPSTAIRS. I could hear from the crinkle of paper and foil that she was searching through an empty pack of cigarettes on the phone stand beside her rocking chair. The terse clinks of her lighter against the side of the ashtray told me she was getting impatient. "Jesse! Hurry up! I need smokes." She broke into a fit of coughing.

Grandma without her smokes was scary. She got aggravated, which usually meant we'd get more chores. The longer she went without nicotine, the more toilets we had to wash, the more carpets we had to vacuum, and the more frequently we had to walk the dog. I ran upstairs.

"Here's the letter. John is working today. You know the kind—Du Maurier Special Mild, the tall silver box, not the short red one. Here's the money, and don't lollygag."

Going to the store was fun. I wasn't allowed to go there usually, only when Grandma sent me. It was far outside my safe terrain, two blocks farther, past the parkette, across the schoolyard, and down the street, where I didn't know anyone. Grandpa would warn me about the older boys who hung around outside the store, saying they were selling drugs and that their minds were warped by heavy metal music. He said they were just like my dad. I wondered about my father: where he was, why he wasn't around, and if he was still mad at me.

Was it my fault he took off? I questioned as I skipped down the street. *Does he miss me like I miss him?*

I rounded the corner and saw the older boys hanging out around the store pay phone, their music blaring on their silver ghetto blaster. I imagined Dad with the same kind of rocker haircut, cut-off jean jacket, and a black Ozzy Osbourne concert shirt.

"Hey, little man," Mitch, the oldest boy, said. "Come here a second, I want to ask you something." The other three boys were passing around a cigarette that smelled like a skunk, and they coughed like my grandma did when she woke up. I wondered how Mitch and his friends could squeeze through the hidden hole in the fence behind where they were standing. I'd seen them do it whenever the police pulled up to the store. My dad had run like that.

I got closer, my hand clutching the ten-dollar bill Grandma had given me. Mitch's aviator glasses glinted and blinded me for a second.

"It's cool, little man, we ain't gonna hurtcha. Relax." Mitch smiled at me. "You here to buy cigarettes for your granny?"

"Y-y-yes," I stammered, my gut churning. I searched to see if Grandpa was anywhere. He'd beat me if he caught me with Mitch and his friends.

Mitch leaned over. "Can you do us a favour?" The other boys suddenly turned and loomed over me. "Can you buy us a pack of cigarettes? John won't sell to us because our parents told him not to, but he'll sell to you because he knows your grandma."

My legs went wobbly. "Um . . . I'm not supposed to talk to you or anything. I'm just here to get her cigarettes. I'll get into trouble."

"No one will know." Mitch thrust a ten-dollar bill into my hand. "Player's king-sized—20s. Now go. I'll be here." Mitch pushed me toward the store and watched as I pulled on the glass door. I hauled away on it until my arm almost came out of its socket, it was so heavy. Each of the boys cracked a sideways smile. I didn't have a choice. They beat guys up if they didn't listen, and I was small. I smiled back and made it in. John was at the counter.

"What is it today, chief?" he said, his tanned face beaming in the dust-filled light. John's hair was curly and cut short. I once heard Grandpa say he was a half-breed like me and my brothers, but our hair and skin didn't look like his. He looked half black and half white to me.

"Here. The silver ones. For my grandma." I slapped down Grandma's letter. John turned around to select a pack from the shelf behind him, and my hand shot toward the shelf of candy bars. I grabbed as many as I could and stuffed them into my underwear—just like Josh and Jerry had taught me. I must've snatched about ten.

John turned back, cocked his head, and asked, "Is that it, chief?"

I almost shit my pants.

"No . . . sir . . . I'd like to buy another pack of cigarettes. Player's King, 20." I reached into my pocket for Mitch's ten. The ruffling noise of candy bar wrappers sounded louder to me than someone crunching up hundreds of newspaper pages. I kept my eyes on his to see if he'd notice.

"Player's?" he asked. "Your grandparents don't smoke those."

"I—I—um . . . My uncle!" I burst out. "They're for my uncle!"

He looked me up and down, then swivelled back to the shelf. I saw my opportunity and my hands darted forward, grasping about five packs of Fun Dip and six packs of Big League Chew and rammed them in my pants. I felt a chocolate bar fall to my ankle. Somehow my pants kept it there.

"I'll give them to you today," John said as he slid the Player's and change across the counter. "But next time I'll need a letter from your uncle, too."

I grinned even though it felt weird and said I'd bring the letter next time, then waddled toward the door. It sounded like I was wearing a diaper.

"Hey, wait!" John called out.

Sweat was pouring from my forehead like water from a faucet.

"Tell your grandpa I say hi. The lottery is up today. He needs to play to win!"

"Okay." I nodded and left. Before the door closed, the chocolate bar down by my ankle dropped out onto the floor. I booted it onto the sidewalk and waited for the door to close behind me. I thought for sure John had seen it, but I walked over to the pay phone to give Mitch the cigarettes, and John just stood behind the counter and watched as the older boys ran up to me. One of them, the one who appeared the slowest and sleepiest of them all, scooped the candy bar off the pavement.

Mitch's gang told me I could keep the change for the work I'd done—about $4.50. I told them John needed a letter next time.

"No problem," Mitch said as he lit a smoke. "This will be our little thing, okay?"

I agreed. Buying cigarettes for the older boys for pocket change sounded great. They were so busy swarming for cigarettes, they didn't even notice that my gotchies were filled with about a half-case of chocolate bars and gum.

When I got home, Grandma wasn't in her rocking chair in front of the veranda door like usual. Something was up. Yorkie barked, and I heard Grandma stampede down three flights of stairs—faster than I'd ever heard her move before. She charged at me. I turned to escape, but she shoved the door closed.

"John called!" she roared like a pissed-off bear, her lips gnarled back so I could see her black cigarette-stained teeth. "His candy bar shelves are bare. He also told me you bought a pack of Player's." She pulled my pants down before I knew what was happening, and my hoard fell onto the floor.

I started crying. She was having none of it and started spanking me.

"Why?" she screamed. "Why. Are. You. Stealing?" She started to weep and hit me even harder.

"I didn't steal, Grandma. Some kids gave these to me, and I stuck them in my pants."

She looked confused. "Now you lie to me on top of it! My God, Jesse. What is going on with you?" She smacked me across the mouth, then pushed me into the corner while she gathered the chocolate bars and gum.

I tried to pull them out of her hands but she was stronger than me. She slapped me again. My cheek was on fire.

"I'm not lying, Grandma. The bad kids outside of the store got me to buy them a pack of cigarettes and gave me this candy! That's what they paid me with." I knew that was something she would understand: *The bad drug-dealing kids—just like her son.* Grandpa always cursed them, and I hoped my lie would sound believable to her.

"They said they'd beat me up if I didn't." To my surprise Grandma stopped. I stared at her. I knew she was weighing the possibility of truth in my gigantic lie.

"I'm sorry, Jesse."

The lie had worked! She thought I'd been bullied. Guilt washed over me—I'd used my dad against her—but I didn't tell her the truth.

"Well, your grandfather will hear about this."

But when Grandpa returned home from work that night, nothing was said. My grandmother, I figured, didn't want to get in trouble, either.

I thought about the feeling of excitement I'd had grabbing the chocolate bars off the shelf when John had turned his back, the feeling of power. Now I had a strange and satisfying feeling of control—control I'd never had before.

I liked it.

SUPREMACY

MY BROTHERS AND I FOUGHT almost every day at school. This was my second time in Grade 2, and fighting probably had something to do with that.

If anyone too big or too strong, from say Grade 4 or 5, picked on me, I'd band together with Leeroy, and we'd annihilate them. We'd chuck rocks, throw baseball bats or whatever, trip people when they weren't looking, or pummel them right in the hallways—whatever it took. Many times, we ended up in detention or in the principal's office together. But Leeroy and I weren't bullies—we didn't go looking for it. We only reacted when we were picked on. And if Leeroy and I couldn't handle it, I'd run to my brothers—by far the strongest kids their age—who could.

We Thistle boys, plus Leeroy, formed a kind of warrior clan that dominated a section of the schoolyard near the portables and the benches. We covered about twenty square metres of terrain, but our domination over this area was contested. There were other tribes of boys, older and younger than us, vying for supremacy, always trying to take our spot. These clans were formed by friends, brothers, cousins, and, if things got intense enough, competing enemies would forge alliances to vanquish common foes.

Otis, Hershel, and the other five black kids in the school formed the strongest clan, but they were more interested in breakdancing and girls and were too old to bother with us second- and third-graders.

Next, there were the two Smith boys and their sister, Tania, along with the rest of the Simmons Street kids. They all played rep hockey, which meant they fought well as a coordinated team. They were quick with their fists and reminded me of professional NHL enforcers.

The Histon crew, on the other hand, was a handful of kids who weren't into sports at all and liked to read the Hardy Boys. James and Doug, two English-descended kids who lived near the fence, were friends with me and Josh. Sometimes, when we needed to duck out from a beat down, they'd invite us over for KD until things cooled off.

The most dangerous kids, however, were the loners. Amongst them was a Vietnamese girl named May, who was the most brutal fighter at our school even though she was tiny. Once, I pissed her off and she just about scratched my eyes out. Even the older kids wouldn't mess with May. She sent scores of tough guys home, crying, to their mothers. But May was sweet if you didn't provoke her, and she never bothered me about my missing parents or called me "Indian."

Our archenemies at school, though, were Ronald and Kurt and their sidekick, Ethan. They didn't need provoking. They'd go out of their way to kick my shins, steal my lunch, push me face down in mud on the way home from school, or embarrass me and my brothers in front of everyone. Ronald, the eldest, was in Josh's Grade 4 class. Kurt was my age but in Jerry's grade, and Ethan was a year younger and in my class. He resembled Beaver Cleaver but had the dastardly personality of Eddie Haskell. Rumour had it that Ronald and Kurt were so tough because they knew karate and had black belts.

When Leeroy and I tried ambushing Ronald and Kurt, they always outsmarted us, leaving us with bloody noses and black eyes. Even my brothers seemed powerless against the duo. You could never catch them off guard or alone. They were strong, tactical, and had backup with Ethan always close by.

Going to school was like entering a battleground full of feral gangs, chanting and scheming and beating the shit out of one another.

I hated every minute of it.

HEART ATTACK

"WHERE'S YOUR MOM AND DAD?" Mando asked. She was a pretty East Indian girl new to the school and my class. She sat in the desk in front of me and when I got frustrated I'd stare at the back of her head—the light played on her shiny black hair whenever she moved and reminded me of my mother's.

I kept my eyes on the dragon I was drawing and thickened the lines until they turned ugly. I wanted to bawl whenever I thought of my parents. My dad hadn't come home from the hospital two years ago like Grandma said would happen over Christmas. All I knew was that he was sick and that he'd be home when he was better. But he didn't show. Grandpa was furious and started spending a lot of time in the garage building and fixing stuff, drinking more brown pop than usual, and yelling at us. I got yelled at the worst, maybe because I looked like Dad the most, but Jerry got hit the most because he stood up to Grandpa.

Maybe he just stayed in the hospital? I reasoned.

Grandma started to eat and sit in front of the TV watching her soaps more. Sometimes the phone would ring in the middle of the night and she'd run downstairs to see who it was. She'd whisper, "Sonny, is that you? Is that you? Please, come home. We love you." She'd say this over and over until Grandpa came downstairs and yanked the receiver from her hand.

Sometimes the phone would ring in the middle of the day and I'd rush to answer it. I'd hear breathing but no words. Grandma usually took the phone from me before I had a chance to ask who it was, but sometimes I was on long enough to ask if it was me who made him run away. The breaths would sometimes turn into what sounded like whimpers, but never words, and never a dial tone. Someone was listening.

Grade 2 was tough on us. Josh had failed it in 1981. Jerry failed it in 1982. And I failed it in 1983. I couldn't concentrate. I kept thinking about Dad. I didn't learn how to read, write, do math, or anything. Mrs. Z., my first Grade 2 teacher, held me back. I hated that Leeroy and all my other friends were a year ahead.

I knew Mando didn't know any of the stuff about my parents, or that I was a failure. My old classmates, on the other hand, did. For a while I used to tell kids at school that my grandparents took care of us to give my mom and dad a break, that they'd come back to get us soon. I stopped when I realized that no one believed us, that our enemies loved watching us squirm. They said our parents had abandoned us because we were ugly Indians who ate from the dump. They'd ask about our missing parents to be dicks and start fights. They'd chant at us with war whoops because Josh told them we once lived in a tipi in Saskatchewan. *Idiot*, I thought.

The tip of my pencil buckled and a shard broke off, hitting Mando's sundress. She brushed it away, and I knew she was waiting for an answer.

"Go away, please," I said.

"Didn't you hear me, Jesse?" she said patiently. "I asked, 'Where are your mom and dad?' I've seen you with your grandma on parent-teacher night, but never your parents. Why?"

"If you really want to know, they're dead, and I'm an orphan," I muttered. But in my head I was yelling, *I don't fucking know where they are*. If Mando were a boy, I would've hauled off and punched her in the mouth right in the middle of class.

Mando's lip quivered as she shifted backward.

The old tipi in the hippie colony near Debden, Saskatchewan. We stayed there one summer with some of Mom's friends before our family fell apart.

I pushed my dragon drawing off the desk and watched it float to the ground.

Mando leaned over. "I'm sorry, Jesse. I didn't know." She grabbed my hand and started crying.

Her hand felt warm on top of mine, and I started crying, too. She squeezed my hand.

There was a nudge against my back.

Then another.

Then another.

"Look at the crybaby crying!"

A finger jabbed into my shoulder. I turned around and saw Ethan, Ronald and Kurt's sidekick. The freckles on his nose looked like someone shit on his face through a screen door. He was laughing and so were some of his buddies.

"Look at Jesse, crying in class. Just like a baby. Boo hoo!" Ethan pushed me and I fell forward into Mando's chair.

"What the hell is wrong with you?" she yelled.

"He's a baby," Ethan teased. "Baby, baby, baby!"

I punched Ethan square in the eye. Spit flew out of my mouth, and my head felt like it was going to explode. I flipped the desk nearest to me into the air, knocking over a few chairs and hitting a couple of people by the blackboard.

"Who's the baby now?" I yelled.

I could see Mrs. C. leaping over about five desks to try to get to us. I grabbed my pencil and lunged at Ethan, aiming for his heart. Mrs. C. tried to push me away, but I kicked and punched her. She had a tough time blocking my shots, and I think Ethan was afraid I'd murder her to get to him, cause he scuttled like a rat to the back of the room.

I couldn't breathe. My chest heaved up and down, my heart was going a thousand beats a minute. I started slamming my fists against my head. Mrs. C. grabbed my arms and placed me in the hallway. Ethan and his cronies were making war whoops as she slammed the door behind us. Mando was at the door trying to say something, but it got lost in the ruckus. Mrs. C. tried to restrain me.

"What happened?" she asked. "Why are you fighting again? Why did you try to stab Ethan?"

I could tell she was shocked. Hell, I was shocked. Ethan was lucky—I'd wanted to kill him. I would have gutted him if it weren't for Mrs. C.

"Answer me!" She put her hand under my chin and forced me to look at her. I squirmed under her gaze. I kept my mouth shut and furrowed my forehead right back at her.

"Answer me. You could have really hurt him!"

I imagined Ethan dead on his back with a pencil jutting skyward out of his chest. I grinned at the thought.

The more Mrs. C. pressed me, the more I dug in. If I was good at anything, it was keeping my mouth shut. I wasn't going to rat, not even on him. Not to her, not to the principal, and certainly not to my grandparents.

NOT A PICTURE IN SIGHT

I LOVED CHRISTMAS.

"I hope I got the new Megatron," I said to Josh as I launched myself down two flights, landing near the base of the tree. Shimmering boxes, bows, and tinsel busted out across the living room floor. The lights flickered and danced, adding to the drama.

After unwrapping half my presents, I realized, to my dismay, that I'd gotten practical items like underwear, socks, or cruddy, oversized long johns. It was, after all, Christmas with my grandparents, and they always bought us grandparent-like things.

For breakfast we had our traditional bologna, bacon, egg, hash brown, pancake, and bannock meal. I ate until I couldn't see.

"My stomach hurts," Jerry complained as he finished, adjusted his PJ bottoms, and belched.

"It's because you drank the corn syrup," Josh said. "Should have left some for the rest of us." We all laughed because it was true.

Even Grandpa was chuckling as he hummed to the Boney M. song that blasted over the old record player. Grandma was at the counter—she was already three-quarters of the way through all her prep work, but she still had lots to go.

I eyed the about fifty pounds of potatoes that needed peeling—a job she always saved for Aunt Sherry—and fired whatever leftovers I had under the table, so Yorkie could partake in the gluttony. My hand was covered in slobber, but it was his way of saying thank you, and I loved the way his tongue tickled my fingers and the *bing* sound his tail made when it banged against the table leg.

At noon, everyone began to arrive—first my aunt Sherry and uncle John; then my dad's brother uncle Ralph and his wife; Uncle Ron, who was my dad's younger brother and best friend; and all my cousins—accumulating until we were packed in like sardines.

The whole comedy roast started with my aunt Sherry's cackle. "The only thing worse than Ralph's turkey farts," she said, adjusting her apron, "are Jesse's butter-tart farts—so creamy. Can you believe a smell like that can come from such a scrawny kid?" The living room quaked with laughter, and the pile of skinned potatoes next to my aunt almost fell over from the commotion.

Each of us took a turn razzing the person next to us, and I swear my aunt turned beet red when Uncle Ron laid into her. As I sat on the couch and watched everyone bellow with laughter, I envisioned my dad at home with us, and it was like the instant I'd opened my eyes that morning, hours before everyone came, before all the jokes.

When I woke up, I'd pictured him arriving at home looking like a gentle yet rugged Marlboro man in a black overcoat, with rosy-red cheeks and a long knitted scarf like Tom Baker's from *Doctor Who*. Grandma watched *Doctor Who* in between reading her Harlequin novels and watching her soaps. She'd been a fan since the early '60s, had seen all the Doctors throughout the years, and thought Tom Baker was the best one of them all. I always figured Dad looked like him for some reason. Maybe I just wanted him to be as smart and brave as Tom Baker, as the Doctor.

I imagined Dad's grand entrance occurring at the perfect time—just as we were unwrapping our treasured gifts. He'd pause in the front alcove, scrape his boots on the doormat, brush gigantic, Hollywood-style snowflakes off his broad shoulders, then look me right in the eye and smile—all without saying a word. I'd throw aside my gifts and rush into his open arms, the presents rendered worthless compared to the prospect of grabbing hold of our long-lost dad.

Or I'd yell, "I'm mad at you!" stopping short in front of him. "You left us with nothing and all alone up in Sudbury!"

I'd kick his foot and try to stay mad, but he'd say, "I'll never leave again, Jesse," his cheeks still cold from the frost. "You have my word on it," talking his way out of it, like usual, giving me all the sweet answers I longed to hear.

I'd collapse into his arms and bury my face in his scarf, smell his cologne, and hold on for an eternity.

That was my Christmas wish, what I'd dreamt of that morning and what I was dreaming of again.

"Wake up, boy," Grandpa said. "You see this mountain of wrapping paper that needs tending?" Only his request for help taking out the trash managed to break me from my imaginings.

I knew Grandma dreamed the same dream that I did. I saw her look at the door even after everyone had arrived. I knew that every year, fuelled by hope, she over-prepared. We watched in awe as she marshalled forth a parade of food—the same way she'd done every year since 1981.

One of my cousins commented first, saying, "This is way too much food, Nana! How are we supposed to eat all this!?"

Grandma didn't answer, but kept the gravy boats and platters floating in. Plates, forks, food, and my relatives mashed together, caught up in the force of it all.

I understood what the flood of food really represented, but didn't have the courage to name it and stop its annual inundation. I sat at the dinner table watching my grandmother out of the corner of my eye. Between laughter and smiles she discreetly and periodically scanned the front door, poised to spring up at the turn of the knob.

I watched my grandfather, too, after dinner, as I played on the floor in front of the tree with my cousins. As usual, he sat glued to his armchair swilling beer, until his speech slurred. I saw him staring at the police awards Uncle Ralph had won and that he kept displayed on the living room wall beside the fireplace.

"See, Ralph," he said, pointing at them, the smell of beer now strong in the room. "That's my boy. That's a *real* Thistle. And you," he fired over at me. "You're an asshole, just like your father. Oh, I know what you've been up to," he said, flicking the snout of his beer with his thumb and making it pop. "I'm watching you, buddy."

I tried to understand what I'd done wrong, but couldn't. I stared up at the wall. It didn't have any pictures of Dad. None. In fact, there weren't any pictures of me or my brothers or my dad anywhere in the whole house.

Grandpa kept glaring at me, and I ran to the washroom looking for a place to hide. He didn't stop as I ran past, but cracked a smile. I slammed the door.

At the end of the day, Grandma collected the extra food and drink she'd laid out, embalmed it in cellophane, and then interred it in the fridge and freezer. I loomed over the unopened presents that lingered under our tree. They were addressed to "Sonny Boy." They stayed under the tree, and the tree remained up for a long time, reminders that something horrible had happened and that Dad wasn't ever going to come home.

We ate the leftovers well into February.

THE FAKE ITALIAN

LEEROY KICKED HIS LEG OVER the blue bin behind the convenience store and disappeared inside. We dove in every other week, and we'd find *Playboy* magazines, old gum, and maybe some candy bars. It was a good little after-school activity that kept us busy.

People thought Leeroy and I were brothers we were together so much, except that I looked like some awkward mix of Italian and something else, and he looked whiter than a bleached bedsheet. Derick, the small Greek kid who lived across the street from my grandparents, was with us and was the darkest kid around—darker than Josh even. I thought I looked like Derick and his father a bit.

"Score," Leeroy called out. He held a porno mag over the edge of the bin and Derick and I cheered.

"Anything else?" Derick asked.

I heard what sounded like boxes shuffle and bags rip followed by Leeroy saying, "We've hit the motherlode!" He tossed out a dusty box of Snickers and climbed out.

"Check the expiry date," I said as I searched the side and found a label: *March 1984*.

"Must be from the backroom or something," Derick said as he examined the label and ripped open the box. He had a bar unwrapped and in his mouth in a matter of seconds. As he tried to gnaw at the brown steel, the skin of the bar cracked and broke.

"That shit's three years old," I said. "Don't break a tooth."

Leeroy stood transfixed near the edge of the bin—he was gawking at the skin mag. He flipped it around and showed us a picture of a naked woman laying down in a desert. She had on feathers and leather buckskins—bits of her costume hung loose and revealed her breasts.

"Your people," he said to me, laughing. I didn't know what to say and picked up a Snickers bar and attempted to snap it in half to see if it was edible. It didn't flex a millimetre. I wasn't putting it in my mouth.

Derick giggled and moved closer to get a better look. He said, "My brother told me about Indians." His mouth was full of chocolate as he looked over at me and tossed his wrapper on the ground. "Said they're all dead."

Leeroy held the magazine up and smiled. "She's not dead." The woman in the pictures was now completely naked but was beside a painted horse and had a spear in her hand.

"It's in that Iron Maiden song," Derick said. " 'Run to the Hills.' My brother plays it all the time."

"Yeah," Leeroy added. "My sister, too—I love that song!"

Both broke out into the lyrics, Derick holding his hands in heavy metal devil horns, Leeroy headbanging his mullet. I could make out that the song was about killing Indians and selling them whiskey and destroying the buffalo. The only clear part was the chorus—same as the title. I assumed it meant that the Indians had to run away.

I thought about when Derick's brother, Moses, played that song on the ghetto blaster in front of their house. I heard the name "Cree" in the lyrics and Moses explained to me that it was about when the British Army killed a bunch of Cree Indians on the plains out west and then gave the land to white people.

"You're from out west," Moses said. "Are you a Cree?" I didn't know what to say and wondered if my mom was a Cree for a second.

"No," I blurted out. "We're Italian." The lie came from nowhere, but I thought it might keep me safe or include me somehow. "We have some Indian way back," I went on. "But my skin is dark because we have Italian in us—see." I held my arm to his.

"That's not what Josh said." He gave me a skeptical look.

I thought about my parents and all the questions that burned within me growing up, and the resentment that had taken root. I hated them; I hated myself. I hated explaining to other kids where my parents were and why my skin was darker than theirs. I felt torn between wanting to be Indian and wanting to hide in my lie—kind of how I felt standing there, listening to Derick and Leeroy thrash to that song by the dumpster with the naked woman in the magazine dressed like an Indian.

It would just make life easier, I decided, to tell people I was Italian.

FALLING APART

1988–1996

MY FABRICATED PERSONA

"Life of the party," they said
Whatever they put in front of me, I did.
Lines
Joints
Cups of straight whiskey
Chased down by false manhood

I took bits of all the Gods and mixed them together
Hendrix
Jim Morrison
Conan the Barbarian
Chavez the Native horse thief from Young Guns
And—voilà—an instant Warrior

I drank more than they could
Jumped higher
Ran faster
But nobody told me
That Indians aren't made in Hollywood
And we were never meant to be the good guys

ODDBALL

I COULDN'T READ FOR SHIT and stuttered, so I avoided reading out loud in front of everyone. I didn't understand how I'd graduated Grade 5 without really knowing how to read and write, but there I was, at a new school, in amongst a whole new crop of kids.

Leeroy was in Grade 7 and would walk to school with me every day, so I had the edge over some of the Grade Sixers who, I assumed, didn't know anyone. On our walks we often picked up butts off the ground and pretended we were smoking. We didn't have a lighter or matches because John at the store had stopped selling anything cigarette related to us kids after he found me supplying Mitch a few years back.

Leeroy's sister, Sylvia, however, smoked with her rocker friends, Mitch included. They all had big teased hair—Sylvia's hairsprayed bangs were a three-inch wave cresting on her forehead. Her nose didn't stick out so much anymore, and she'd started getting bumps and curves all over. Her makeup seemed to sparkle, the same dreamy way as the women in Grandma's soap operas, and my vision got blurry whenever I saw her sucking on a cigarette, and words—forget about it. I couldn't form a coherent thought around her.

The first time Leeroy saw me acting like an ass around Sylvia, he said, "I'll rearrange your face if you look at her that way again."

Still, I couldn't help dreaming about her and those cigarettes.

Josh went to the same school and was in Grade 8 with Sylvia, and Jerry was in Grade 7 and had made a whole new batch of friends separate from Josh and me and our street crew. His buddies were now the smart and good kids from neighbourhoods I didn't know. They didn't smoke or drink or cause any trouble that I knew of; they were awkward and read comics. But my brothers still held their ground. I felt safe with them and Leeroy around.

That left me free to explore—girls especially.

One day in October, while waiting to catch a bus for our school field trip to the Royal Ontario Museum, I noticed *her*, up on the hill in front of the arena right beside our school.

She had flaming red hair and a pair of black-and-white British Knights running shoes. I knew her name was Lucie because I'd heard a teacher call it out at an assembly during orientation week. I'd heard classmates say that she was an excellent swimmer and took classes in the swimming club, where all the elite swimmers our age took lessons. She hung out with the cool kids—my friend Brian and some rich kids.

I wasn't like them, though.

I walked around the bottom of the hill, fidgeting with my book bag. I wanted to talk to her, but my brain wasn't working properly, just like when I was around Sylvia. I could tell Lucie didn't even see me, sweating and rehearsing how to say hi. She was gossiping with two other pretty girls I also had weird feelings about. One of them was Kiley. She had long, flowy hair that made my guts do backflips. She had two sisters at the school who were into soccer, just like Kiley.

"They're a family of athlete goddesses," Leeroy said.

The other girl, a strawberry blond named Sarah, was "developed," as Leeroy would say. It drove all us boys nuts. Everyone wanted to dance with her at the seasonal Much Music dances, and when the music started up, she was like a queen bee covered in a beard of adolescent males. I once tried dancing with her but was almost trampled. I spent the rest of the night bopping in the corner all by myself, far from the hormones and chaos.

"Hi," I managed to spit out as I got about halfway up the hill, thirty feet away from the three girls. They didn't hear me. "Hi," I said again, raising the volume a decibel or two. My voice cracked under the strain. I wanted to flee but I pushed on. Still no answer. I thought they were ignoring me.

But Sarah turned and rolled her eyes. "Look, it's that nerd that hangs out with Brian. What does he want?"

Kiley laughed and looked me up and down.

Lucie was silent and scrunched up her face at Sarah.

"Hello, my name is Jesse." I extended my hand. "Is this where the class is supposed to meet to catch the bus for the school field trip?" They giggled. My hand just hung there. *Nice moves.* I squirmed. *Real smooth.*

"Does this look like a bus stop?" Sarah retorted, pushing my hand away. Her flowered sundress looked menacing in the breeze.

I had nothing left to say, no more moves, no courage.

Kiley turned her back and whispered something to Lucie and pinched her nose as if I smelled. Lucie didn't react. I flashed her a smile. She smiled back a little. But I couldn't bear to be there any longer and went to leave.

"Wait," Lucie said, as she reached for my hand and shook it. "My name is Lucie, nice to meet you."

Kiley and Sarah were dumbfounded.

JUST LIKE THE REST OF THEM

"LET'S GO TO THE MALL," I said.

Anything was better than lunch hour at school, even walking two kilometres, and there was a place called Frank's that served the best fries and gravy in the city. After, we could go to the convenience store and play Double Dragon or Time Lord on the arcade machines. Leeroy was pretty good, I sucked ass. Richard was with us. He was a small German kid with a big head who was just as mischievous as Leeroy and me. He'd been in my Grade 6 class the year before, and I'd done something with him I'd never done with Leeroy—I'd skipped school.

At the mall, Leeroy pulled five dollars out of his pocket. Richard had twenty. I, on the other hand, pulled rabbit ears, like usual. When we got to the burger stand the two of them slapped their bills on the counter, ordered "Fly Baby," and laughed.

"Fly Baby" is how Frank called orders of fries and gravy back to his wife, who manned the fry station behind the till. We kids had heard him say that a few times and started saying it ourselves. We thought it was funny. Frank usually gave us our orders without saying a word, then, once we were far enough away, he'd turn to his wife and say something in Korean.

Mrs. N., our home economics teacher, reacted the same way when I made fun of her Japanese accent during class, becoming silent. When

I didn't do my assignments—which happened all the time—it was my way to shut her down. The class loved it every time I deliberately mispronounced something and encouraged me with laughter.

For as long as I could remember, people had teased me about being a half-breed "Indian," and I hated it, but when I acted the same way toward others, nobody ever focused on who I was. Mrs. N. didn't deserve it—no wonder she failed me with the brief report card comment "Frequently unprepared for class."

After Frank handed over the two orders of fries, Richard inhaled his. He didn't share a single bite with me. I was insulted. After all, I was the one who'd asked him along and I expected him to give me at least a couple of fries in return. Leeroy, to my shock, did the exact same thing. He'd never done that before. To make matters worse, just before Leeroy finished up, Richard reached over and grabbed a fry—all dripping with gravy—and chucked it in his mouth. He grinned at me then turned to Leeroy and said, "Those were delicious, eh, buddy?" Both cackled, mouths open, fry matter visible on their tongues. I was furious. I challenged Richard to a fight after school, in the park across the street, where no teachers could interfere. He accepted. I stomped off, leaving the two of them chewing on their shitty fries.

When the school bell rang that afternoon, I bolted to the park. Word had spread quickly that the "crazy Indian" was going to scalp some poor German bastard. A pack of kids followed us across the street and formed a giant circle around Richard and me. Chants of "Go, go, go" filled the air as kids began shoving us closer and closer together. I swung first and hit Richard in the mouth. Stunned, he stood still for a moment, then hurled his book bag at me, missing my head by about a foot. I followed with a straight leg to the gut.

I was winning.

Then he said, "Figures," coughing and holding his ribs. "You're just a dirty Indian, like the rest of them."

Everyone burst into laughter, followed by loud war whoops. The rage that fuelled me drained away. Silence gripped my tongue.

"You'll probably die drinking like they all do."

The crowd shifted from my side to his, and I saw my street friends laughing and pointing at me.

They believed it, too. They all believed it.

THE MOST IMPORTANT THING

IT WAS A SATURDAY. THE summer sun was shining, the lawn mowers were humming, and the bacon was frying. It was all I could smell. I heard my grandfather's flip-flops shuffling against the worn linoleum floor in the kitchen. He was too cheap to replace it. But he was letting me sleep in, which was odd, considering he always got us up at the crack of dawn for chores, or to polish his golf clubs before he went out to the range, now that we were all of working age—thirteen, the same age he told us he'd left home and went picking potatoes in Prince Edward Island.

I heard Jerry sobbing through the wall between our bedrooms. It wasn't his usual, annoying crying. He sounded like a gentle whale plumbing the depths in some uncharted region of the Pacific, calling for a distant herd. I sat up in bed and listened as he went on for what seemed like a million years. I knew something must be wrong and wanted to hug him right through the drywall, but I dared not leave my room. I didn't want to get in trouble or find out that someone had died.

I heard Yorkie pawing at the door. I opened it. He held his head low, like he'd done something bad, and his tail wasn't wagging.

"What is it, boy?" I asked him. "What's going on?" I rustled the top of his head, and the back of his tail raised to quarter mast and batted back and forth.

"Jesus Christ!" Grandpa said after it sounded like he dropped a plate.

Yorkie bolted. Jerry continued to cry. I decided to go down and find out what was going on. I hadn't heard a peep from Grandma and wondered where she was.

When I entered the kitchen, Grandpa was clattering through forks and knives in one of the drawers and swearing.

"Do you want some goddamned eggs?" he barked.

"Sure." I waited, staring at him.

He grabbed a fork and tried to stab out a few pieces of bacon, but he fumbled and the fork fell over the edge of the skillet onto the floor. A strip of bacon teetered on the drawer next to the stove.

"Fuck," he muttered and wiped the stove with a paper towel. "Sit down, boy."

He tossed my breakfast plate on the table and pulled my chair up all in one motion. He looked frail almost, in a way I'd never seen before. To me he was invincible, with his strong, hairy arms and barrel chest. But now he was as he really was—an older, greying man.

"I've already told your brothers, and I don't like beating around the bush, so listen up." He reached over and rubbed my arm. He'd never touched me like that before.

"Your dad was never in the hospital," he said. "He got into trouble robbing some stores, went to jail. When the police found you, you lot were starving and dirty." He tapped his finger against the table like a tiny hammer trying to beat back the past. "Once we heard what went down, me and Grandma went and got you. Sonny got out and was supposed to come home but . . ." Grandpa's voice trailed off for a moment. "I guess he loved drugs and booze more. Fucking asshole." He slammed his fist on the table and his plate fired beans into the air. "Family is the most important thing, Jesse, and if I ever catch you doing drugs I'll disown you."

His face looked harder than I'd ever seen before—like steel, tungsten even. I trembled. Tears began rolling down my cheeks like an ancient levee had broken.

He pulled his hand off my arm.

"None of that," he said. "Men don't cry; you're a man now."

The smell of margarine filled the air as my grandfather slathered his browned square of toast with it and ate it, and I tried not to cry. Then I heard the sound of my grandmother's rocking chair in the next room, moving back and forth, and the sound of her crying.

CANADA GEESE

"THERE'S ONE RIGHT OVER NEAR the portable," Leeroy said as he reached down for a juicy butt. His black-and-white Mötley Crüe concert shirt, a hand-me-down from his sister, was skin-tight against his back. It looked like it'd burst open as he bent over to grab the smoke. Even tighter were his acid-washed jeans, which were rolled up and pinned at the bottom to accentuate his kicks, their tongues hanging out like overgrown dog ears. He looked like Sylvia's rocker friends, but without any style.

I didn't have the wicked threads he did. We wore Bargain Harold's crap Grandma purchased from the sale bin. Black turtlenecks were about as fashionable as I got, and the one I was wearing was covered in mustard from the lunchroom.

"Holy cow!" I said, trying to rub the stain off. "That hasn't even been smoked!" Leeroy held the cigarette up to the sun. The body of it was near perfect, it was just crooked. It had yellow moisture stains, but the Export A logo was intact.

Leeroy pulled a book of matches out of his jeans pocket and dangled them. "Look what I got," he whispered, looking back and forth for Mrs. W. or Mr. G. They were always on patrol and gave any kids they saw hanging around a tough time. We knew we could end up incarcerated in the principal's office.

"I stole them from Sylvia this morning." Leeroy grinned. He peeled open the book of matches to reveal three perfect rows. The cigarette drooped from his lips and begged for a flame. I huddled close to guard against the wind. The ember burned cherry red as he struck the match, lit the butt, and hauled in a breath. He strained to hold the smoke in, and his face turned green. He exhaled and coughed so loud it sounded like a flock of Canada geese erupting from his lungs.

"Here, your turn," he said, still convulsing.

I grabbed the smoke and pictured my grandma and grandpa yelling at me. I took a big drag and pretended to blow smoke at them. I didn't cough like Leeroy, though. I wheezed, dropped the smoke, and fell ass-backward onto the ground. I groped the grass—everything was spinning. I saw black spots dance across the blue sky. Leeroy laughed, a sound that pulled me back into this world.

"You suck." He reached over, plucked the smoke off the gravel where I'd dropped it, took another drag, and handed it back. "Just ease into it, Jess. Like me." He exhaled without coughing, then crossed his arms, oozing style.

I wanted to be as cool as him.

CHEESE SLICES

"WHO THE HELL HAS BEEN into the fridge again?" Grandma hollered. "We aren't rich—you boys know that, right? You'll eat us out of house and home!"

I looked toward the kitchen from the chesterfield and my TV program. I heard Grandma slam the fridge door, and an avalanche of something hitting the floor. All I could see was her hair wagging in the morning light, and the dog's ass bounding up the stairs. Yorkie was never one to miss the prospect of spilled food.

"I dunno," I said, shrugging. "I swear, Grandma. Wasn't me."

"The goddamned cranberry juice is nearly gone, too. I told you boys that's for Grandpa's gout." She held up a bunch of empty cheese wrappers, a near-empty package of hot dogs, and a three-quarters-empty bottle— the remaining red liquid sloshed around, angry.

I wonder how she slammed the fridge door, I thought. *With her foot?*

"I don't know what to do with you boys anymore." She dropped what she was holding and took a drag of her cigarette, smoke licking around her flustered face. I could tell she was trying to remain calm. "Go get your brothers, Jesse."

"Okay, Grandma," I said, with a feeling of dread, even though she sounded defeated, not angry anymore, kind of like everyone in our house since learning the truth about Dad. She nodded and began picking stuff off the floor.

My brothers were wrestling in the backyard; Josh beating the shit out of Jerry like usual. He had Jerry's head in a full nelson, pressing it forward into his collarbone, choking him almost unconscious. It was his signature move—I knew from experience it was impossible to escape.

"Grandma's pissed," I said, trying to catch my breath. Josh let go of Jerry, who fell to the ground clutching his neck, the pinkish colour of life replacing the purple-blue of suffocation.

"What's she on about now?" Josh asked.

"What does it matter?" Jerry shot back, as he got to his feet and made his way to the house. "The dog probably shit inside because we didn't walk him. That's your fault; you're supposed to walk him in the morning."

I bit my nail. "It's more serious than that."

Grandma was sitting on the edge of my grandfather's chair in the living room. On the coffee table were the empty cheese wrappers—a stack of around twenty. Small price tags were taped to the table right next to them.

"See," Grandma began as the three of us walked in, her nicotine-stained index finger pressing down so hard on one of the price tags her fingertip was white. "The wieners here, they cost $2—I buy the good beef kind for your grandfather. He deserves them." She flicked her butt, the ash tumbling into a puke-yellow glass ashtray. "The cheese"—she motioned to the cloudy wrappers—"that's around $3.50. Black Diamond cheddar. Again, only the best for your grandfather." The cherry on her cigarette hissed as she took another drag and moved on to the final exhibit. "And this here, that's cranberry juice, *real* cranberry juice. The doctor told me to buy it to help with your grandfather's gout. He gets it in the knee and big toe and can't work a day without a glass. That costs $5. Together, it all costs $10.50, and I just bought it yesterday. It should've lasted until next Friday when I do my groceries again."

A boa constrictor wrapped tight around my ribs. Jerry rubbed his palms down the front of his jeans.

"But it's gone. Now what am I gonna give him?"

"Wasn't me," Josh blurted, shaking like a Chihuahua with hypothermia as he pushed the bottle toward Jerry.

"Wasn't me, either, Grandma," Jerry said. "I swear!" He kept it together but looked guilty as sin. He shoved the bottle at me, not knowing I'd already been interrogated.

"Jesse already said it wasn't him, either," Grandma said as she tapped the bottle. The tiny echo boomed in my ear drums. "So, I guess you're all lying—again." Her sigh seemed to drain the life out of her. "You boys steal food and lie all the time. This time is no different than the thousands of times before. You came to us like that—broken. But, now, for once, I want a straight answer. Please tell me the truth. Who did this?"

We looked at each other, shrugging and making faces like idiots. Grandma didn't budge. Silence hung heavy around us, resting somewhere between her polyester slacks and the wads of Black Diamond cheese that lay digesting in one of our guts. A smatter of rain misted the sliding doors while we waited for someone to give. Gradually, it turned into a light patter as the wind picked up. I saw a crow perched on the fence looking in at us.

"I can't take it anymore," Grandma finally said, her voice thin and monotone behind a lungful of cigarette smoke. "I want you each to go to your rooms, pack one bag of clothes, and bring it downstairs. I'm taking you to the Children's Aid Society. Your grandfather and I have spoken about this already, and we've tried our best . . ."

Josh's mouth dropped open. Jerry's eyes were wider than Josh's mouth. Me, I felt nothing, or what I can only describe as a yawning chasm of hate—the first time I'd felt it.

"Make sure to take your boots and winter hats. You'll need them. You're old enough now to survive. Go on. Get ready." She shooed us off. "Haven't got all day."

A flash of black caught my eye—the crow had flown off. I went to my room and began packing. I couldn't stop thinking about being hungry when we were kids with my dad, that gnawing ache that haunted me every day, that made me always think we were on the brink of starving, even when we got to my grandparents with their full fridge. I could actually feel that ache in my legs.

Jerry, I knew, felt that hunger most. He'd told me how he always felt like he could never get enough food, even when he was full. It was a force that drove us to steal and lie, to eat until we destroyed every hors d'oeuvre plate at every family function my grandparents took us to. My cousins used to tease us about how we consumed everything in sight. They called us pigs, but it was something we had no control over.

I kept thinking about that hunger as I pulled out my favourite red sweater, my Batman T-shirts, my Blue Jays baseball cap, and four of my favourite jeans from my drawers. I packed them carefully in my Adidas bag, making sure to place pictures of Grandma and Grandpa between the layers. I always wished I'd had pictures of my dad to remember him by and didn't want to forget my grandparents wherever I was going. I also grabbed the old, worn-out Polaroid I had of my mom from off the dresser—one of her wearing a Russian-style fox fur hat—and put it in my back pocket for safekeeping, then made my way down to the front door.

Josh and Jerry were there, bags packed, stone-faced. Yorkie was there, too, whining and turning in circles, tail wagging faster than normal. Grandma was upstairs, we assumed searching the change drawer for taxi fare, slamming things. We didn't wait for her to walk us out. We shut the door and left. The brass door knocker clanged rudely behind us. *Good riddance*, we thought.

Before we hit the end of the driveway, we linked arms and decided to keep going as far as we could, to find homes where we could eat whatever we wanted, where we didn't have to be afraid anymore. Jerry pulled a butter tart out of the side of his suitcase—we had enough to get us to where we were going.

We made it as far as the other side of the mall where Grandma did her shopping, about five kilometres. We sat near a bush and ate the lone tart. As night set in, we got cold and hungry and decided to make our way back home. Jerry and I waited outside the house with our bags, while Josh went inside to take the heat for the missing food and for running away.

DRIVE

ONE DAY, I ASKED MY uncle Ron where Dad went. "I'm sorry, Jess," he said. "I miss him, too, but we don't know."

According to our family, Uncle Ron was the toughest of my uncles. He was like a pro wrestler, stout through the middle, the bridge of his nose was thick, and he had a gold tooth that glinted every time he talked. His body looked like he'd been attacked by wild animals. There were deep gashes, burns, and knife marks all over. The scars on his knees were the deepest—"from a shark attack back in the '70s," he said. Grandma said they were from when he'd broken his legs at work and from when his friend ran him over with a car.

He told me stories about my father, and how they'd get in trouble on the golf course they both worked at as caddies, or fight with neighbourhood boys, or chase girls and terrorize their boyfriends with firecrackers. "I even blew up your grandfather's garage playing with gasoline," he said, adding that Grandpa laid the smack down so hard for that, Ron saw stars for several weeks.

Grandpa and Uncle Ron had a strange relationship. Grandpa tried to keep him out of the house, but always let him back in, I think because he loved him. There were times that Uncle Ron went to jail for months. When he came home, Grandma always hugged him and made him a big meal, and everyone was happy and joking. But when Grandpa got home and saw him, he gave him a tough time. Everyone went silent. Uncle Ron just smiled and didn't say anything. I thought it strange he would allow himself to be treated that way, but I understood why he never quipped off to Grandpa. Respect was important in our home.

When me and my brothers first arrived at our grandparents', it was Uncle Ron who greeted us and made us feel at home. There was something about him. Dogs and kids loved him, but everyone else was scared. My older cousins were terrified of him. They fetched him beers and cigarettes whenever he was around—he'd just motion to the cooler or a pack and they'd run. But I loved him. He lived around the corner from us and he'd come and put me on his shoulders, take me to the park, and swing me on a swing until I laughed so hard I got dizzy. He was a father to me in many ways.

"Come on, Jess," Uncle Ron said, punching his cinder-block fist into my shoulder and bringing me back to the moment. "You wanna come on a delivery downtown tonight? I gotta see a few people on Yonge Street. It'll be fun." He was a flower delivery man and good at his job—he collected money and no one was ever late on a payment. He'd pull up, and men would run into the shops and come out with wads of money. His gold tooth glimmered between his lips, inviting me to join him.

"I guess . . ." I twisted my foot on the ground as if putting out a cigarette, trying to decide if I wanted to feel sorry for myself in my room or go out and cheer up.

"You don't have to look so morose, you know." He punched my arm again, and I struggled to smile through the pain. "I'll be here at four—be ready or else." He winked.

When he screeched into the driveway that afternoon in a red convertible Mustang, I was waiting on the balcony. I had no idea where he'd gotten his new ride, but it was nicer than the beat-up work van he usually drove. I had on a white muscle shirt and a jean jacket with the sleeves ripped off. I thought the frayed strands that dangled over my shoulders made me look tough, like one of the characters from *The Outsiders*. Like Uncle Ron. My fake Ray-Bans added to my persona.

"Get a load of those pipes," Uncle Ron said. I knew he wasn't making fun of my arms, he was trying to make me feel confident. A field of zits covered the whole of my face, and my arms and legs looked like stretched hot dogs as I'd shot up nearly a foot in the past few months. I put on my best bodybuilder pose, curling my fists and biceps inward as hard as I could. It felt good.

"You'll get there, kid," he said as he stood up in the driver's seat and returned my flex with his own double guns. "Just gotta start liftin'." His arms looked like Hulk Hogan's as he rotated his head and kissed the bicep-crest of each arm. They were bigger whenever he returned from jail.

"Now let's ride," he hollered as he sat down, tooted the horn twice, and combed back his hair, looking in the rearview as if he were a 1950s greaser. "We haven't got all day, Schwarzenegger." I launched myself off the balcony, down ten feet, hopped over the passenger door, and we were off.

A mix of Foghat, Deep Purple, and Steppenwolf blasted out of the car speakers as we drove, announcing to the world that two badasses were in the vicinity. The wind blew through my hair as Uncle Ron drummed on the steering wheel, reminding me of my dad. When we got downtown, people gawked as we went by. I got excited when I saw women looking at us, but they weren't checking me out. Uncle Ron, I knew, caught all the eyes.

"You see that, Jess?" he said as he smiled back at a blond woman coming out of a store. "It's all in how confident you are." He flexed his left arm, twirled a toothpick between his front teeth, then held it erect in the sunlight.

I rolled my eyes.

"Just try it," he said. "Be the rooster." He bobbed his head back and forth to the beat of the music.

"What does that even mean?" I asked, adjusting my vest.

"You know, cock of the walk. Own it; feel the music. Like this." He curled his lip up, revealing his gold tooth; it reminded me of a jailhouse Elvis.

I tried bobbing my head and smiling at the ladies on the sidewalk, just like he told me to. But I knew I was more like a malnourished chicken, and every girl I grooved at stared right through me over to Uncle Ron and his muscles.

He laughed. "Just give it time, it gets easier. I promise."

I laughed back. I was glad to be hanging out with my favourite uncle, making him happy, the sun beaming down on my face.

We stopped in all the cool spots to collect money, eat ice cream and French fries, and listen to street performers. The men we stopped to talk to, though, were terrified, just like my cousins. I'd see the look of relief on their faces in the side mirror as we pulled away. I'd heard that my dad and Ron were in business together years ago and wondered if it was delivering flowers.

Uncle Ron also introduced me to other guys, his friends, as "Sonny's boy," and they all looked like Uncle Ron, muscle-bound and tough, and all of them were super excited to meet me. They had scars and tattoos and toothpicks, and they talked about my dad like he was a legend. The stories washed over me. Not one person had a bad word to say about him—not like Grandpa. It was nice to hear. I'd never been proud to be my father's son before.

On our way out of one of the shops on Yonge Street, we came across a guy bumming change in front of Sam the Record Man. He was thin and looked much older than Uncle Ron, with long, greasy hair and a matted grey-and-brown beard. In front of him were a woollen blanket, a few plastic bags, and a paper coffee cup. Not many people ventured near him, veering close to the storefronts instead and turning their heads. I was compelled to do the same.

Uncle Ron, though, walked right up to him and put a twenty in his cup. The man smiled a toothy smile and said thank you, but Uncle Ron just stared at him. The man looked at him, then over at me. I could tell he was trying to assess what was going on, but then Uncle Ron said, "Don't mention it, brother." Before we rounded the corner to where we were parked, Uncle Ron turned back, but the homeless man was gone.

"I always think," he said, "that it could be Sonny."

BIRDSONG

MRS. R., THE FRENCH TEACHER, walked up to my desk and handed back my report card with its proof of signature. She peered over her glasses at the report card and me, and said, "We need to talk after class."

I could have sworn a black cloud hung low around her calf muscles and knee-length skirt as she turned and walked back to the front of the class. She was stern, powerful, and in control, and the clomp of her high heels thundered through my brain.

Whispers from my classmates came from all directions. My friend Renee, who'd sometimes help me when I didn't understand things, turned around and mouthed, "You're dead meat, Thistle."

I gulped. Mrs. R. wasn't to be trifled with—she screamed in our faces if we did something wrong. In the worst cases, she'd get so mad that she'd cry-yell and make you do consecutive detention for a couple of weeks.

I glanced down at my grade: 35 percent—a big fat F. Worse than F, more like K. The comment beside it read: "Jesse is frequently unprepared for class. A more consistent effort is required." Brutal and bleak. I was two-thirds of the way through the year and sure to fail at this rate.

Aside from taking away our hard-won Nintendo and go-cart and grounding me, I knew Grandpa would whip me so hard I wouldn't be able to sit straight. Like the way he lashed Josh with the red rod—an unbreakable half-inch fiberglass golf flagpole—when Josh had thrown that rock in the park and it ricocheted off the fence and broke that Sikh man's window. It wasn't Josh's fault. I was there—the rock simply bounced, redirected itself off the fence post, then smash! But that didn't matter. A window was shattered, it cost Grandpa $200 to fix it, and Josh had to be punished. The strips Grandpa tore off his backside were purple and puffy, and Josh had to lie on his side while they healed but they still left stripe-like welts. He looked like a zebra.

Grandpa's anger that day wasn't usual—it was the same rage I saw when he warned me about doing drugs after he told me about Dad's disappearance—and it scared me so much that I bawled in my room as Josh received the beating of his life. I lay on my bed and covered my ears with my pillow to hide from the sound of the rod thrashing through the air. In my head, I begged for Josh to cry out, but he kept it together somehow. I knew it was to show he was a man the way Grandpa liked, but that only made things worse. After what sounded like thirty more blows, Josh finally bellowed out in agony. It was a sound so sad it penetrated right to where I was hiding, right through the concrete foundation of our house.

Grandma once told me that Grandpa was that "way" with discipline because his pappy was that "way" with him, and that he got it worse than us. Grandpa was only five when his father died from a heart attack in 1938, and he had to move two hundred kilometres, out to the sticks of Cape Breton, to live with Pappy. There, he'd worked hauling wood, picking rocks, and fishing on the dory like a grown man—he never got to have a childhood like us. I always wondered if that was why Grandpa took us in, because he knew what it was like to have no one, to lose his family.

Whatever the reasons for the way Grandpa was, the scream Josh let out that day sounded like he was being killed, and I questioned how Grandpa's childhood beatings could have been worse.

Mrs. R. rapped the blackboard with her pointer and trained her eyes on me. "Some students"—she cleared her throat—"didn't come with their report card proofs signed by their parents. I've already spoken with most of you, but I'll see those of you who didn't after class."

After class!

I started to chew my thumbnail. I spit a bit out and it landed in the hair of the girl who sat ahead of me, but she didn't notice. The clock hands seemed to beat forward with incredible speed, and each tick sounded like an explosion.

Tick!

I only had four minutes until the bell rang, and I'd have to answer for what I'd done.

Tick!

I stared at the French vocabulary signs that adorned the room, searching for a way out. The stupid French toad with the *à bientôt* word bubble above its head; the picture of that annoying little girl waving *au revoir* to nobody; the huge picture of those bright, obnoxious yellow daffodils that screamed *le printemps*. I imagined them all piled on a bonfire with Mrs. R.'s head roasting on a stick.

TICK!

The minute hand surged forward—two minutes left—reminding me that I was trapped.

Shit!

I knew why Mrs. R. had singled me out. It was in the way she'd looked at me after she'd peered down at my grandmother's signature and handed me back my report card. The edges of my grandma's name were shaky and didn't flow right.

When I'd received my grades before the Christmas break and saw my F, I panicked. I couldn't let my grandparents see how poorly I was doing. It didn't take much to set Grandpa off these days. I didn't want to end up like Josh. I told Leeroy on our walk home, and he told me about a guy in one of his classes who'd forged his parent's signature on a report card and gotten away with it.

The idea sounded plausible—genius even—so I went home and traced over an existing signature Grandma had written on a permission slip for a field trip I'd taken in another class. The practice signatures all looked great. But then I messed up. I only had one report card, one shot, and I failed miserably. When I handed the report card in, I'd done it quickly, tossing it on Mrs. R.'s desk underneath everyone else's report cards, hoping she'd be lazy and would just hand them in that way. But she didn't. She'd checked each one and discovered my crime, and now I had to pay for it.

Ring, ring, ring! The bell went off.

What the hell happened to the time?

As I lurched toward Mrs. R., I straightened my cardigan and kept my eyes down. I somehow thought that if I didn't look at her, I could still hide and maybe everything would be okay. She ushered the class out and paused before shutting the door and asking me to sit in the seat adjacent to her desk. It was known as the hot seat.

"I taught your brothers," she said. "They were good students, Josh especially." She took the forged document from my hands and fingered my sloppy fraud. "I've seen a lot of faked signatures over the years, but this one has to be the worst." Her words were like weights dragging me to the bottom of the ocean.

"You know I have to report you to the principal. He'll contact your grandparents."

I expected her to yell like she always did—cry-yell even—but she didn't. She just kept looking at me. I started squirming.

"This is a very poor start to life. Fraud is a real crime," she continued. "Why did you do this?"

I thought of Josh and the punishments we got. I couldn't breathe.

"You don't know how it is," I said. "You don't know how it is for me." I began to sob.

"How what is?"

I rocked in my chair.

"I can't go home with a report card like this. You don't know what will happen," I couldn't feel my face but I was crying. "It's not his fault. He was raised that way."

Mrs. R. didn't say anything, just sat there, rubbing my back.

I couldn't hear the clock anymore, just Mrs. R.'s soft breath and the sound of a robin singing outside.

JACK HIM

"FUCK *FAMILY TIES*," I GROWLED and changed the channel. I couldn't stand to see Michael J. Fox get hugged by his stupid-looking, bearded father after he'd apologized for taking speed and redeemed himself. If I got caught with even a cigarette I'd be practically tarred, feathered, beaten, and grounded for a year.

"Dude," Leeroy cried. "Now we'll never know what happened. Put it back on!"

"It's bullshit. Bloody Alex P. Keaton." I flicked through a few stations then launched the remote across the room. Bits of brown and green plastic exploded all over the concrete floor. Leeroy let out a goonish laugh, the kind of sound we made when either of us started shit.

I didn't care that my grandparents would be upset. *Fuck them, too*, I thought. *I'll just blame it on Jerry*. Putting it on my brother was a diversion strategy that worked most times. He was a horrible liar; so bad, in fact, that when other people did stuff—stuff he was totally innocent of—and he tried explaining to my grandparents what had happened, he looked guilty just talking. The poor bastard had taken so many of my thrashings I'd lost count.

"We could drink some beer?" I half asked, half offered. I walked over and opened the fridge but saw tumbleweeds. Leeroy searched the empties; nothing there, either. Black-and-white static on the TV rolled and buzzed like a hive of angry bees. The set was stuck on channel 81, the late-Saturday-night porn station, and even if we could hear what was going on, we'd be lucky to see a nipple. It made it difficult to mastur-bate, chasing phantom nipples. I pulled out my pocket knife, stuck it in the broken rotary dial on the left of the screen, and jiggled it. The vise grips we usually used were gone, taken by Josh no doubt in one of his fits of backyard engineering, and my little Swiss Army knife wasn't strong enough. I pulled the plug on the TV with a grunt.

"I think I'm going home," Leeroy said, rubbing his stomach beneath his Maple Leafs jersey. It was hours past dinnertime and we both hadn't eaten. Grandma made fish cakes earlier, but neither of us liked them, so we passed on her offer. It was the only meal I could say no to. I hated the huge raw onions packed into the patties. When I was around five my grandparents caught me one night after I'd stuffed my cheeks until I looked like Dizzy Gillespie and excused myself from the dinner table repeatedly. I was spitting my cargo in the toilet. Grandpa thought it was clever of me—his little puking chipmunk. Grandma wasn't as impressed. They tried to force me to eat them over the years, but I never did.

"Okay, I'll walk you over." I put on my shoes. The smell of fish and oil spilled onto the street as we left. The night air was cool for September. Street lights flickered in the park, surrounded by a blanket of blackness. I kicked a pop can and it rolled over a storm grate and stood motionless at the base of the curb. Leeroy kicked it, sending it up across the boulevard and onto the sidewalk.

As we rounded the corner, we saw Ivan, a blond Polish kid about four years younger than us who lived ten houses down from Leeroy, playing on his front lawn. I thought it was strange that he'd be out at this hour all by himself. To us, he was spoiled beyond belief. He had toys galore, and I often saw him at the convenience store with his dad buying chips and gum and whatever else his little heart desired. His dad usually gave him the leftover change, and sometimes he'd share with me if I was hanging around with my friends. It was hard to see him with his dad, all happy and eating candy, holding hands, and playing hockey together out in front of his house every Saturday. Grandpa never did anything like that with me.

"You thinking what I'm thinking?" I asked as I turned to Leeroy.

"What? No!" The expression on Leeroy's face told me he knew exactly what I was thinking. "That's too much, even for us."

I stopped in the middle of the street and grabbed his arm. "The kid is loaded. We can jack his money and run away. It's dark. He won't know what hit him." My Swiss Army knife burned in my back pocket, begging me to take control of the situation, to follow through so for once I'd have some goddamned lunch money and could buy my own goddamned fries.

"Don't be crazy." Leeroy ripped his arm away. "I live right down the street; I can't." He stood his ground. He wasn't going to cross the line, not now, not tonight, not on his street. Just then Ivan stood up at the end of his lawn and waved over to us.

Leeroy is right, I would get caught, somehow, like everyone gets caught on all the police shows. No one gets away.

"See," Leeroy said with a look of relief, knowing I was backing down. "That's the Jesse I know. Just chill." He smiled at Ivan.

We'd gotten in lots of trouble before, and Leeroy had never put his foot down about anything, but here he was chickening out and telling me what to do. I was humiliated. My knife weighed down the back pocket of my jeans, and I put my hand over it to hide its imprint from the night sky. Leeroy walked backward toward his house and told me he'd see me in the morning on our walk to school. Then he went inside.

I was out there alone with Ivan and my knife.

Without a thought, I walked over to him, thrust my knife in his face, and robbed him. He cried for his dad, then ran into his house when I let him go. I fled into the dark, holding the change I'd ripped from his pockets. I was shocked at what I'd done. I wondered if my grandfather would forgive me like fathers did with their sons on TV.

A NEW FAMILY

THE NIGHT BEFORE CHRISTMAS EVE, Grandma surprised us.

"Your mother moved from Saskatoon to Ottawa," she said. "She's coming to see you tomorrow."

Grandpa grunted and slammed back his chicken and potatoes, barely looking at anyone. Josh, Jerry, and I excused ourselves from the dinner table and retreated to our rooms; it was the first time we'd all left food on our plates before.

I wondered if Mom would still look as beautiful as she did the last time we'd seen her, and I couldn't sleep that night waiting for her. I stared out my window looking at the stars, trying to think of the right words to say, but they all jumbled together. I pictured her laughing face on the surface of the moon, the light of it dimming with each passing cloud. My throat closed as I tried to swallow.

I finally got up and pulled my best Chip & Pepper T-shirt, my nicest black slacks, and my penny loafers out of my closet. I laid all of them on the floor in front of my bed, methodically picked lint off both garments, then applied shoe polish to the loafers until they shined like mirrors. I tried to figure out how I'd comb my hair—down the middle, spiked up, or off to the side. I couldn't decide. I wanted to look good, to show Mom how much I'd grown.

From across the hall the deep rumbles of my grandfather's snores were followed by the squeaky squirrel noises Grandma made to wake him up and keep him from suffocating to death from the sleep apnea he had. They weren't conferencing about me for once, and that made me happy. Often at night, I could hear them talking about me, even though their voices were hushed—as though I was in a different kind of trouble than usual.

Perhaps they know about the things I've done, I'd worry. *Perhaps they're going to take me to the Children's Aid Society after all.*

Finally, morning hit, and Yorkie's bark announced Mom's arrival. I ran downstairs as fast as I could, hair gelled to one side, and flung the door open so hard the door handle punched a hole in the wood paneling. Yorkie was running around in circles behind me.

"Hi, Jesse!" Mom shouted with a huge, beaming smile, her arms stretched out.

She was wearing the Russian hat from my picture tilted to the side. The cold December air froze puffs of breath around her head so they looked like smoke caught amongst the fox fur. Her hair was shorter and browner now, not the black flowy locks I remembered, but she still looked the same to me. Beside her were two gym bags and a little coal-haired boy, around six years old. Mom looked toward a man rummaging in a grey car across the street, who waved over to us, then she turned back to me, waiting for her hug. I had a sudden urge to go and hide in the boot box. The little boy tugged at Mom's leg.

"Hug her, you idiot," I could hear Josh say from behind me. His words snapped me out of my daze. He pushed me aside and embraced Mom. I fell against the wall, my hand finding purchase in the newly created hole. Deep growls of joy emanated from Josh and Mom, warming me somewhat. Josh rubbed the boy's head and introduced himself. The boy said his name was Daniel.

"He's your little brother," Mom said.

A surge of jealousy ran cold up my spine.

Jerry trailed along the hallway leading to the door. Each step was strained and reminded me of when Grandma forced him to walk the dog on Sunday mornings. He had a sneer across his face, and his arms were crossed.

"I can't find my wallet," the man from the car hollered over to Mom. "I think I left it at the gas station near Kingston."

"I have it here in my purse, George," Mom said. "Now get over here and meet my boys!" The man nodded and made his way to us, a small skip in his step. Daniel stuck his hand out to shake mine, but I batted it away and stuck my tongue out at him. Mom didn't see. She was focused on George.

"That's not nice," the man said as he grabbed their luggage and placed it inside the house beside where I was standing. "He's your little brother— my son. His name is Daniel and mine's George. Nice to meet you." He, too, stuck his hand out. I kept mine down by my side.

"It may take some time," Mom said to him as she pushed Daniel and me closer together. We did eventually embrace, but the whole thing seemed wrong. I wanted to bear hug him until he couldn't breathe, crush his ribs, then stomp his tiny head on the driveway right in front of George.

Jerry sighed and went back upstairs without saying hello. I figured he was just as upset as me about Daniel. Josh and Yorkie, however, were wagging their arses like fools at their new friends.

Fucking traitors, I thought. But I forced myself to be nice to Mom and George and helped them with their stuff.

The last time we'd seen Mom was in 1985, when I was ten. She'd bussed out by Greyhound from Saskatchewan—it took her three days to get to Toronto. When she arrived, I'd just stood in the doorway clutching a dream catcher I'd made for her at school, my mouth open. She looked exactly like she did in my faded Polaroid. The photograph was yellowed at the corners and curling inward, but she remained untouched in the centre, standing gracefully in front of some snow-peaked mountains. She looked like a real-life Indian in that photo, one from the movies, not like me and my snotty brothers.

I ran and hid in the boot box, a giant wooden cabinet Grandpa had made beside the downstairs doors, until he yanked me out to say hello. I couldn't muster a sound, just handed her the dream catcher. She laugh-cried and hugged me tight, lost for words herself, holding my gift.

During her visit, Grandma only let us out of her sight a couple of times: once when Mom took us to catch a Saturday matinee of *The Jungle Book*. I thought Grandma was crying as we drove off, but it was hard to tell through the back window of the taxi. The other time was when Grandma went to bed early after dinner one night and we snuck down to the basement to watch TV with Mom. Grandpa saw us tiptoe past his armchair and waved us downstairs like he was landing a plane.

"Go, go," he said, with a grin. He had a soft spot for my mom. He told her she was a good person, that none of it was her fault, and that we'd go back to her once we'd grown up and left home.

Mom was sitting cross-legged on the couch, reading a comic. She had a stack of them she'd brought with her. Josh and I knelt in front of her, while Jerry sat across from us on the wood stove under the window, as silent as ever.

"Josh, I want you to have these before I go back home tomorrow morning." She waved her hand at the comics. "Conan's a fighter like you."

The first time our mother came to visit us at our grandparents', in 1985. I'm on the left; Josh is on the right.

"Cool!" Josh cried out, his eyes lighting up as he rifled through his hoard of newfound treasure.

I strained to imagine my brother wielding a massive broadsword and lopping off the heads of demons, like Conan was doing on the cover of the comic in my mother's hand. Conan's muscles rippled, and his shiny black hair made him look like an Indian, like my uncle Ron, but certainly not like Josh.

Josh splayed the comics across the floor and lost himself in them, turning the pages faster than any human eyes could read.

"And you, Jerry," Mom said, remaining on the couch and respecting the distance between them. "I'll always keep the picture you drew for me. I won't ever fold it or lose it or anything. I promise. Will you do the same with the one I gave you?" The roar of the water heater filled the basement as she waited for an answer. Jerry just shifted his ass around on the stove, then nodded while looking at Josh freaking out.

Mom smiled, then turned to me, and I shifted my knees closer to her.

"And for you, my little pumpkin head, I have something special." She reached down under her ashtray and handed me a glossy photograph. It was of her. Her hair was wet and sticking out all over the place and she was lying on a bed holding a baby.

"That's your younger brother, Daniel," she said.

"What?" the three of us asked in unison.

"You have a brother," she said as she took a drag of her smoke and leaned in close to point to the baby. "I want you to have this picture of us, Jesse." She looked so happy. "I met a kind man a couple of years ago and this is our son. I wanted to tell you before I left and waited for the right moment."

I fell back, the air sucked out of my lungs, but I managed to squeak something out. "I wish we had a sister instead."

Mom looked hurt and confused. I knew she was waiting for me to say something more, but Josh spoke first.

"I think it's wonderful. Now I'll have three younger brothers I can beat up."

Mom didn't laugh, nor did Jerry, and I just stared at the picture, wondering how my mom could start over without us, and what Dad would think.

After Mom left, Grandma took us to a drugstore. We were told it was for something called the Kids Identification Sign Up and it was because strangers in our city had murdered and killed children our age and we had to watch out that we weren't stolen from right under our parents' noses.

During the fingerprinting and mug shot process, the workers briefed us on child sexual abuse, stranger danger, street proofing, and how to call the police, and we were told that we should memorize where our home was on a map. Grandma gave them our dental and health records, blood types, and known allergies. I didn't understand much of what I was told, or why I had to promise to keep my eyes out for trouble—trouble that wanted to kill me. I'd never thought about dying or going missing before, and both scenarios scared the shit out of me.

After, Grandpa told us it was because Grandma loved us so much and was trying to protect us.

From what? I thought.

I don't know what I did with that picture Mom gave me. I certainly didn't have it when she, George, and Daniel showed up at our door on Christmas Eve. It was like my memory of it had blacked out.

I had a hard time getting used to seeing myself as a middle brother—it meant I was like goony Jerry all of a sudden, with his middling spot as neither oldest nor youngest. No special responsibilities like Josh had as the oldest to take care of business and teach us younger boys about life or protect us. And Jerry didn't get away with stuff like I did as the youngest because I was too small to understand anything. I was now just an invisible middle child like him.

My grandparents' cottage in Bay St. Lawrence, Cape Breton. We all got to smoke cigars that summer.

The whole time Mom was visiting with Daniel and George, I tried my best to reclaim my status as the "baby boy." I acted younger than I was, purposefully messing up my grammar and asking her to cut my meat at dinner, like she did with Daniel. She ignored me and Grandma swooped in with her mother cape to do it, ruining the whole thing. I showed Mom a photo of when I was five smoking a cigar with Grandpa at the cottage in Nova Scotia—everyone else loved that photo of us, but she barely glanced at it. I tried to remind her that I was the youngest Thistle boy, not Daniel—Daniel was just some latecomer. Turned out he also somehow had our father's name, but he clearly wasn't his son, he was George what-ever-the-fuck's son.

It was all to no avail. Daniel was the centre of her affection—he was her new "baby boy." She let him rest on her lap like an infant in front of everyone, she got him dressed every morning, she made sure he was always with us. I wanted to vomit whenever he was around.

Grandpa, though, was nice during their visit. He went out of his way to make them feel at home, even making George and Daniel baked beans and bannock twice—a record, considering he'd only ever made those staples of the Cape Breton diet for us three times in ten years! He also made them his "special" sugar-glazed apples. "When I was a boy, molten apples were like golden candy," he said. "Everyone lost their minds whenever they got them."

If they're so special, I sneered as Grandpa, Daniel, and George devoured them in front of me in the kitchen, *why don't you stick 'em up your ass.*

Grandpa and George even had a few private heart to hearts in the living room while watching the Leafs play, and I could tell from my vantage point on the stairs that Grandpa was sizing him up. He watched the way George drank his beers, how fast or slow they went down, and if he requested another once the last was done. Grandpa said you could tell a lot about a man by how fast he drinks, how he holds himself during conversation, how he asks for things, and how firmly he shakes your hand. I was sure George had no idea he was under my grandfather's microscope.

Grandma barely spoke with George, Mom, or Daniel. She'd acted the same way when Mom had come before. Just plenty of flybys and quick, probing questions, like, What's going on? Where're you going? Why're you here? What do you want? She was like a patrol helicopter looking for a bank robber. Josh told me it was because she was scared—of what I don't know. Wherever we were with Mom, Grandma was close by, pacing, silent, breathing heavy. She didn't even read any of her Harlequin novels, which was odd considering she did that obsessively any other time. Josh even found her with her ear up to the wall once, listening to our conversations with Mom.

"I'm keeping an eye out for mice," she'd said.

We knew that was bullshit because she kept the house crumb-free and spotless.

One day before New Year's, Mom made me my favourite lunch. Spaghetti and meatballs—she remembered.

"Of course I remember," she said as she placed my plate in front of me. "You're my little pumpkin head." I was happy that I still had a special place in her heart.

Josh and Jerry were outside playing hockey, Grandma was in the living room, the theme to *General Hospital* was blaring, and Daniel and George sat across from me watching Mom serve us.

There was what sounded like an avalanche of two-by-fours outside. Grandpa started swearing. He'd come back from the hardware store with framing wood and I thought maybe I should be outside helping him.

I dug into a meatball and George spoke.

"Look here."

He pulled out a black-and-white picture of a strange man from his wallet. He had on a black robe with a huge cross draped over his shoulder. He was like Friar Tuck from the *Rocket Robin Hood* cartoon: bald on top with a long, unkempt beard. There was a severe look about him. I twirled my noodles around my fork and tried to ignore George and the picture.

"This is Gregory XVII," George said. He yanked a similar photo from the other side of his billfold. Mom placed George's lunch in front of him—I think she was trying to get him to keep quiet.

"He's the real Pope," George went on.

I glanced over at the picture; he didn't look like Pope John Paul II to me.

"A long time ago," George said. "The Catholic Church lost its way. It became decadent and stopped following the true way." Mom's left eyelid twitched.

"That's when Pope Clement XV—the order's first Pope—decided to split from Rome and form the Apostles of Infinite Love out in Quebec, about two hours from where we live in Ottawa."

Daniel sat up straight at his father's words.

"It's nice there," Daniel said, a noodle hanging out of his mouth. "I lived there with the brothers for a few months." He smiled.

Grandma stormed into the room—the strong scent of tobacco trailing behind, which was odd because she was out of smokes. She scowled at George and Mom like a mama bear defending her cub. George stuffed his pictures away. Mom smiled.

"No religion in this house," Grandma barked as she slammed some dishes in the sink. I felt that awesome power in her again, the same as when she got us years before.

I didn't know what to make of George or his picture, but it was creepy.

Mom, George, and Daniel left later that week. I asked Grandma and Grandpa if Mom was okay. They didn't seem too concerned. But Mom and Daniel kind of disappeared after that, no phone calls or anything.

TRADITION

"THIS ONE HERE LOOKS NICE, try it on." Grandma handed me a preppy white button-up shirt to go with the black slacks she'd pulled from the good section of the Hudson's Bay men's department, over near the Polo clothes. The shirt fit slim around my torso and snug around my neck when she buttoned it up. She turned me to look in the mirror, but before she did, she licked her fingers and slicked my eyebrows into place.

Spiffy.

"Well, look at you! My baby boy all grown up and ready for work!"

I fixed my collar and stuck my chin up slightly. I knew this was a special occasion because Grandma usually took me to Bargain Harold's or Zellers, and we'd go to the Skillet Restaurant and eat hot dogs in a basket afterward. Not today, though.

I thought of those Skillet hot dogs as I admired myself, and said, "But, Grandma, these pants and shirt are nearly $200. We can't afford that."

She wagged her head and scoffed. "You better believe we can. When it comes to work you gotta knock 'em dead."

I'd never seen her so excited or generous before, except when it came to Grandpa's work boots and overalls. He always had the best. Even his lunch pail and thermos. Work was important to the Thistles, and Grandma made sure her man looked good and was well-fed when he made our family its money.

Grandpa, too, had acted differently since he'd gone across the street a month ago to talk with our neighbour, Mr. Q . He'd come back whistling, Yorkie by his side, and the dog appeared just as gleeful as he did.

"Good news, Jess," he said with a huge smile. "You've got a job." Mr. Q. was a manager at the produce department at the grocery store in the biggest mall in town, and Grandpa told me I'd start in a few weeks. "You'll be a produce clerk. $3.75 an hour."

He walked past me into the house to announce the good news to Grandma, who was watching a soap opera. She gasped with joy—I could actually hear it through the screen door, from where I was on the driveway. As I pulled out the lawn mower, she waved to me from the balcony. Like those old pictures of when men went off to war on battleships or trains and their women saw them off. I could feel my face flush, and I flashed a smile at her. I knew it looked weird. Grandpa didn't drink that day, and I caught him singing to himself later in the garage as he organized his bits and bobs for his job on Monday.

I examined myself in the mirror. I was now receiving the same treatment as Grandpa, and I smiled. Grandma hiked my pants up, exposing my socks and squaring my nuts in the process. "They fit nice," she said, "but up here, around your waist. I don't want to see you with them hanging low around your ass like you do with your jeans, that godawful rap style."

I thought I looked like Urkel on *Family Matters*, and I grimaced but somehow managed to keep my smile.

Grandma pivoted, grabbing one paisley and one striped tie from the shelf beside me. I covertly pulled my pants back down. *Relief.*

The ties in Grandma's hand weren't the wide-bottomed ones Grandpa wore to the elevator awards once a year that were the worst shades of brown and green, putrid remnants of the 1960s that he refused to replace. The same colours as those hippy flowers on the bath tiles in the upstairs bathroom. No. These ties were royal blue and black, thin at the bottom—actually fashionable.

"Calvin Kleins," she said as she turned them over to show me the labels. She lassoed one around my neck and had it bound up before I could say go, pulling it tight. My eyes bulged in the mirror and she patted my bum. "A lady killer, you are. Tall, dark, and handsome."

I looked at myself in the mirror with doubt. I was tall, but lanky as a daddy-long-legs, and still covered in zits.

But I had just started Grade 9, and Leeroy and I were taking a drama class, and, to our surprise, discovered it was filled with beautiful girls who found us funny. And in one of the photography classes I took, a girl named Heather asked to take my headshot. She had a crush on me, or so I'd heard from classmates.

"Sure," I said. "As long as I get a copy."

She made a bunch of prints and posted them on a wall near the gym—I saw them when I walked past. By the end of the day all the girls at school had stolen them. I knew because they'd been waving them at me in class. I couldn't be angry—I was more flattered than anything.

"No facial hair, though," Grandma said. She rubbed the back of her hand against my cheek and then pinched it hard. I pulled away, rubbing it with my fingers.

"Toughen up, sunshine!" She waved it off like it was nothing. "Native men don't get hair the same as others," she added. "Maybe you'll be lucky and never have to shave, like me." She hiked up her fuchsia slacks, exposing her leg. "It just didn't grow. That's the Algonquin in me."

The thought of never shaving upset me for a brief second. I pictured Grandpa dipping his razor in the sink before work every morning. I loved watching him shave when I was small. Sometimes, he'd lather up my face and we'd shave together. It was serious business. The silence between us was only broken by our laughter when he slapped on aftershave and screamed from the sting.

"Your granddad is as hairy as a Scottish musk ox," Grandma said, as though she could sense what I was thinking. "He hates shaving every day." Not wasting time, she wrangled a black leather belt from over by the till and fastened it around my waist. It fit perfectly, its chrome buckle reflecting light into the mirror. I felt like a millionaire.

"That's it," Grandma said. "That's your uniform."

We stood admiring the ensemble, Grandma holding my shoulders. I loved her so much at that moment—she was a good grandma, I knew that. I leaned over and gave her a big hug. I did look good, in a grown-up kind of way. My new job represented a real step toward adulthood. Most of my friends, like Derick down the street, only had paper routes. But here I was with a real-deal outfit and, soon, a real-deal paycheque. I suddenly felt confident and handsome.

When we got to the front desk to pay, Grandma turned to me.

"Grandma Clara King, my grandmother you met last year that's over one hundred. Her grandpa was a chief factor of the Hudson's Bay Company up on Lake Timiskaming during the fur trade one hundred and fifty years ago. He ran that fort. Our family built this country, Jesse."

The teller scanned the goods, and the total of $374.87 popped up on the register. My heart jumped. Grandma opened her ancient purse and handed over her credit card.

"That's why we shop at the Bay. Tradition is important—remember that."

Grandpa was running the van just by the store entrance. He had "El Paso" by Marty Robbins blasting on the radio when we got in, exhaust fumes flooding around us as we buckled in. Grandma promptly blazed up a Du Maurier and sucked in a massive drag. I coughed, waving my hand in front of my face, but I took in what smoke I could—I needed a cigarette myself. Grandpa leaned over into Grandma's cloud of death, peeking inside the bags.

"What you got there, little lady?" he asked.

"Never you mind, Cyril!" Grandma snapped. She snatched up the receipt, pushing his hairy paws aside, and folding it into the wad of other receipts in her purse. He let out a loud yelp, and they both laughed. "The boy looks like a million bucks."

TROUBLEMAKER

AFTER WORD GOT OUT THAT I had a steady job at the grocery store, my stature at school elevated further.

I had my own cash to buy pizza and cigarettes at a store across the street during lunch, and soon I made friends with older kids at my school and other high schools across the area. I continued to hang with my local street buddies—Brian, Derick, Leeroy—but my new friends drank and slept with younger girls and went to all the best parties. Some weren't in school at all. They had their own apartments, cars, and jobs. We formed a gang. We called ourselves the Bud Boys because Budweiser was our beer and we put Bud beer caps on our baseball hats. The caps helped identify who was who when we brawled at parties or in school parking lots.

By the middle of Grade 10, my grades were plummeting. I was scrapping by with 50s and 60s and still couldn't read or write very well. Math was the only grade I was keeping steady, but even that began to sink after I started skipping class all the time.

I was branded a brash troublemaker by school authorities after the stereo in the drama classroom was lifted in a break-in one Friday night. Leeroy's long arms didn't have any trouble reaching the window into the classroom. I climbed him like a ladder and tossed out the audio equipment. We took it to a Vietnamese kid who was waiting in a townhouse nearby. His cousin bought it for $200. Leeroy and I got $100, and we split that. I was questioned by the police, teacher, and principal, but they didn't have enough evidence to lay any charges.

The authorities threatened to expel me if things didn't turn around, but I didn't give a shit. Grandpa didn't seem interested in me anymore. Sure, he drove me to work here and there, at six a.m. on my weekend shifts, but I expected him to punch me out when he found out about the stereo, and he didn't.

"You're just like your dad," he said instead.

One lunch period near the end of the school year, I wandered over to the Chinese market on the other side of the parking lot where they kept the school buses during the day. I noticed a group of kids out back huddled behind a dumpster, so I decided to check it out.

Balpreet was there—a tough Sikh kid we called Ballpeen because he hit like a ball-peen hammer. I'd known him since Grade 3. He stood in the middle of everyone holding a bottle full of smoke with a backward cigarette sticking out of the bottom. He called me over, and everyone shifted to make room for me.

"Indian," Balpreet said. "You ever smoke hash before?" He held the bottle up in my direction.

"No," I said. "Never."

I looked closer and saw a little brown stone cooking on the end of the cigarette in the bottle. Smoke circled round and round within it and left a cream-coloured stain on the clear plastic side. I thought of Irish coffee.

Balpreet uncorked the lid, pulled the cigarette out, then thrust the bottle full of smoke in my face. "Suck and hold," he said. A wisp of smoke floated up under the bill of his Blue Jays hat. It smelled like burnt earth.

I put the open nozzle to my mouth and sucked as directed. The smoke shot into my lungs.

Raunchy.

I almost coughed it out, but held it for about a minute until my ribs convulsed and I dropped my cigarette, then I spewed a plume of grey air up into the clouds—it was too thin to call it smoke. Still no coughing. A feeling of euphoria hit me, and I wobbled and leaned on the dumpster.

Balpreet said something in Punjabi and laughed. I noticed there was a line of tiny hash balls strewn out on the edge of the dumpster. He cracked a sideways smile and dabbed his cigarette on the next toke then slid it in the bottle. He reminded me of Clint Eastwood after he gunned someone down. I broke out in laughter.

That was my first encounter with drugs.

The next week I was buying a gram of hash from a friend behind the pizza place across from the school when squad cars rolled up. My friend, who had a leg in a cast, crushed the dope on the ground with the end of his crutch and it stuck to the bottom of the rubber tip. The cops searched everywhere—on the roof, in the garbage cans, in our mouths—but couldn't figure out what we'd done with the drugs.

"We know you have some," one cop yelled. "We saw the transaction."

We emerged with only a warning, and my reputation solidified. Older kids, and not just the ones I already hung out with, began showing me respect.

A few months later I was selling acid by the sheet and sniffing speed in the washroom before class every day.

THE STRONGEST BROTHER

JERRY MADE A CHOKER OUT of chicken bones and coloured wooden beads. He was a creative guy and drew things like dragons and elves and played Dungeons & Dragons with his nerd friends at his new high school, an arts school way out in the country. For as long as I could remember, too, he'd been proud of being what he called "Native" and found creative ways to express it. I made fun of him and his friends, but I secretly played D&D with them and always had a blast. They were genuine in a way that my cool friends weren't.

"Look," he said with a big smile. "Isn't it beautiful?"

The bone necklace was kind of alright. I thought it made him look strong and proud.

"It's last night's dinner," I said, deadpan.

"Why do you always do that, Jesse? Why do you shit on our heritage like that?"

I knew he was being sincere. He remembered more of Saskatchewan than I did, and had recently gone on a school trip near Regina and learned stuff about our mother's people and started making pipes out of soapstone, burning herbs, and wearing beads out in public. He started lifting weights after that, taking care of his health, and I even heard a drum bump ever so softly in his room sometimes. He said he was singing

Indian songs. I didn't care. I stole the tobacco he got out west, not concerned about what ceremonial "Indian" uses he had for it.

Heritage be damned, I just wanted a smoke. I looked at him and the necklace.

"Because it looks awful. Why do you and Josh play Indians? Fuck, we're from Brampton and never practiced that stuff. It's embarrassing."

Jerry quietly asked me to leave his bedroom and shut the door as I left. I heard his drum that night, and the next day he wore his choker to school.

I was jealous of Josh when we were little, and I was jealous of Jerry now.

CHOICE

MR. T.'S MUG HAD A blue police emblem on it. He took a sip and placed it on his kitchen table and asked me if I wanted Earl Grey or orange pekoe.

"Doesn't matter," I answered. I wondered why he'd called me over to his house for a chat. He'd never done that before—phoned my grandparents' house and asked me over. I thought maybe Brian was sick. Or worse, that Mr. T. had heard at police headquarters some of the stuff I'd been involved with lately, him being the deputy chief of a police division and all.

He plopped a bag of pekoe in my cup, poured in some boiling water, and then gave it to me. The bag drifted around, releasing a stain that was more brown than orange. He took a seat across from me and slid a stoneware container of sugar my way.

I helped myself.

"Jesse," he began. "I know you're a good kid."

I added another lump to my tea and thought, *Here we go*. I had a hard time not rolling my eyes.

"Since the time you stole our robins' eggs, I knew you had it rough—orphan, no mom and dad." He took a sip and continued: "I grew up without a father; my mother did it all on her own." He pulled a leather photo album that was older than dirt from the counter next to him and opened it. "See here? That's me." He pointed to a picture of a guy around my age doing a layup shot. The picture was black and white, and in it he was clean-cut, thin, and athletic, with hairy legs. The socks and shorts he was wearing were both too high to be fashionable. There were other basketball pictures and a photo of him and a woman he said was his mother outside an old tenement building. She had on a long trench coat, and he told me how she used it to smuggle him into their building as a child because single mothers were looked down upon back then.

"I found basketball and the force," he said and closed the album. "It saved my life."

I poured a bit of milk into my cup and the tea churned in a grey tornado.

"My poor mother," he went on. "She just couldn't show me how to be a man."

I was uneasy hearing Mr. T. speak this way. It was the most any adult had spoken to me in months. I started to respond, but he lifted both hands slightly off the table and said, "Just listen, please," and then planted his elbows down in front of him.

I gave my teacup a turn. I wasn't ready for a lecture.

Brian lit my cigarette with his Zippo and asked me to watch for ashes because they could burn the upholstery of his new car, a used Renault his parents got him for his seventeenth birthday.

"I have something cool to show you," he said as he pulled into the parking lot of the local park. He turned his headlights off, hopped out, and grabbed some beers from the trunk. I got out, and we both sat on a bench.

"See here?" Brian held out one hand. His fingers peeled back to reveal his silver Zippo.

"Yeah. So?"

"And in this hand"—he held up his other hand—"I have the car keys. I want you to pick."

I reached for the beers and yanked one off the rings. "I want one of these. Fuck your lighter and keys." I laughed and pulled the tab and it hissed open. I took a swig and belched.

"No, serious, bro. Pick. It's a lesson I learned at Landmark."

Landmark was a series of empowerment workshops his uncle had gotten him for Christmas the year before. After he'd attended a few sessions, Brian would spout off about how we had to face ourselves, how we had to live our best lives, and how truth was subjective because everyone's truth is true or some shit like that. None of us really paid attention to it.

"Easy, Socrates," I said. "Can't we just drink without all your philosophy bullshit?" I really hoped my comment would diffuse his little life lesson, but he persisted.

"Pick—lighter or keys. There is only one right answer."

"If I must. Keys."

"Why? Explain why."

"What the fuck you mean, explain?"

"Tell me why you chose that over the lighter."

"I don't know. Because I can drive away in it." I took another swig, the beer fizzing in my throat.

"Wrong!" he yelled, sounding like a game-show host. "Pick again."

I was confused but gave it another go.

"Okay, I pick the lighter this time."

"Explain why." Brian flicked the Zippo and twirled it around his knuckles like a leprechaun twirling a gold coin. I snatched it from him.

"Because you said the keys were wrong and I need the light for this blunt." I pulled out the joint I had in my pack of smokes and lit it with the Zippo. I took a big toke, thinking I had the right answer this time.

"No. Wrong again."

"Fuck this game, yo." I took another huge drag and passed the joint over, but Brian declined. He really wanted me to keep guessing, so I did for about ten goes till I had enough of his stupid game.

"I asked you to choose the lighter or the keys. And you rightfully chose one or the other like I asked." He put the lighter and keys on the bench between us and cracked a beer. "And when I asked you to explain why you chose it, you said something about how you'd use it or how it looked—how you could drive it, light it, its colour—anything. That's wrong."

The weed hit me, and I got really interested in what he was saying. "Then? What's the right answer?"

"The right answer is that you chose because you chose. That's it. All the explanations you gave to justify your choice are just excuses your mind made up after the fact."

A gong bonged over my head. I couldn't tell if it was the beer I'd drank and the kush I'd smoked, or the power of his crackerjack philosophy.

"So that's the big reveal?" I said. "I chose it because I chose?"

"Yeah. And when you know that you can just choose to do anything you want."

"Get the fuck outta here," I said. I grabbed another beer, flicked my ash on the grass, and stared up at the stars.

There'd been too many lectures lately, not enough talking with me. But it seemed Mr. T. was determined to give me another.

"Love is an important thing," he said. "And I don't see that in your life too much."

His words lingered around the ceiling fixture and then crept down the walls into my brain. *How dare he.* My fists clenched around my teacup and near scalded under the pressure of my grip.

"I take Brian to basketball, to soccer, to canoe in Algonquin Park, and I help him with his paper route. I do it because I love him. He's my son."

The words dropped like a cold stone in my belly. I remembered all the times Mr. T. had invited me to attend Brian's soccer and basketball games, and how I went out with them on Sundays to deliver newspapers.

He'd always included me throughout the years, bought me snacks at Brian's games when we cheered him on from the sidelines, taught me how to shoot a jumpshot when he taught Brian, showed me how to study for one hour a day, and told me how that added up and made a world of difference in Brian's reading.

I searched my mind for any recollection of my grandfather making time for me like that but couldn't remember anything, except work. There was never any hockey or basketball practice for me or my brothers, no swimming lessons, no canoe trips in the woods, no paper routes, no study time, no interest. We did go to judo for a few months when I was ten, but that was because we got beat up so badly at school, and he rarely stayed to watch us practice. And there were our yearly Cape Breton vacations, but that was mainly about Grandpa, his lobster, and drinking—not us boys.

Then I thought of my father and wanted to run away.

Mr. T. dropped another sugar cube in his tea and slowly stirred.

"For me," he said finally, "it all changed when I realized I had choice. Choice is the human ability to go one way or the other." He opened the album again, but this time to a picture of when he must have been in his thirties, in a police uniform, around when I first met him. His wife was beside him with little Brian in front. He paused a second, then turned until he landed on an older photo of himself in what appeared to be his early twenties taking a shot on a billiards table.

He slammed his finger onto the photo, and I flinched at the force of it. "I was a hustler, Jesse. Was good at it, too. Thought it was all I was worth." He turned the album upright and pushed it toward me, knocking it into my tea. It was a great photo—his hair was greased back, and the bottom of his jeans were rolled up, exposing ankle socks and loafers. He looked cool.

"I had to make a choice," he said. "Live this way"—he flipped to the police pictures—"or this way"—he flipped back to the greaser photo.

"So, how'd you do it?" I asked, truly curious.

"I realized it was all on me and no one could save me—not Mom or anyone. I had to choose to do the work of bettering myself, just like I chose to hustle in pool halls all day. It was that simple." Mr. T. scratched his chin and admired himself in the pool hall shot.

I thought he'd offer me more wisdom, but he offered me more tea.

PREMONITION

"THERE JOSH GOES WITH HIS feather and that shit he keeps burning and waving everywhere," I said to Leeroy and my friends out in the high school smoking pit. Rows of yellow school buses hid us from the view of the teachers who routinely scanned the parking lot for students doing drugs. We blazed about three joints and got away scot-free as always.

"What is it?" Leeroy asked, as he put the roach in his cigarette pack with the rest of the day's smoked roaches.

"Some Indian herbs or something. Sage." I flicked my after-joint cigarette and watched it ricochet off the ground, sending burning ash into the air. I smacked my lips and the taste of cheap cigarettes mingled with the smooth, expensive flavour of Afghan blond hash. "Who the fuck knows, as long as Tonto ain't waving it at me. He's gone Indian. Just like my other brother." I rolled my eyes and popped my jean jacket collar, even as I wondered, *What was it?*

Leeroy laughed and agreed that my brother looked ridiculous.

Later that same week, I was surprised to see Josh come out of the side door of the school. I was skipping off like I always did, but Josh was such a goody two-shoes. Why wasn't he in class like he always was?

"Hey, Josh," I yelled from the smoking pit. "Get to class, you brown-noser!"

Me and my stoner friends giggled as I took another pull of the hash joint. When my toke was finished, I looked up at Josh, but he didn't respond.

"He looks like he's crying," one of the girls, Sarah, said. "Why?"

"What? Josh don't cry. He's a beast," Leeroy said, his eyes bloodshot and nearly closed.

Leeroy was correct, my brother was a beast. He was 240 pounds in Grade 11 and had shattered the long-standing bench-press and leg-press records at our school. He was also one of the biggest and fastest rugby players in the district and struck fear in the hearts of many of his opponents. He could also fight better than anyone at our school if he got pissed off enough, but he had a gentleness about him and only fought when provoked.

"No, seriously, Jesse. He's crying."

Just as Sarah finished saying that, I saw one of the teachers, Mrs. M., burst out the side door. She tried to grab Josh from behind but he collapsed on the ground before she could reach him. I dropped my empty book bag and ran to his side.

"What's wrong, yo? Josh, what's wrong?"

When he looked up I saw his eyes were wide and red.

"I . . . ," he mustered, unable to catch his breath. "You . . ."

"Back up," Mrs. M. said with the force of a lioness. "Something happened in class and he needs air."

I was confused. Had someone died? Had someone said something hurtful to him? Had someone done this?

"I saw . . . I saw you," he said. "I had a vision and . . . It was horr . . ."

A scrum of teachers came out of nowhere and pushed me aside before he could finish his thought. They sat him up and kept anyone—including me—from talking with him. An ambulance came. High off my tree, I soon lost interest and turned my back on him, drifting over to my friends in the smoking pit.

"What the hell happened?" Leeroy asked.

"I don't know. He said something about a vision, like he's a mystic Indian or something."

Leeroy and the gang snickered and talked about the feathers we'd seen Josh with earlier. "You're alright, though, Jesse," Leeroy added.

"Yeah, you're not into that Indian shit. I remember at public school when you used to say you were Italian," someone else said and laughed some more.

I joined in.

BERRIES

IT WAS THE HOUSE PARTY of the century, and in walked a young girl with a Tupperware container.

"Does anyone want muffins?" she asked, her mouth full of braces.

I was sitting by the fireplace sucking on a cigarette and watched the guys in the gang make fun of her. But she persisted, bubbly and friendly, walking around the room. When she offered me a muffin, I took it and just stared at her. Her smile was angelic despite the dental hardware.

As I ate the best blueberry muffin of my life, I was perplexed—by the taste, by our encounter, by everything. There were lots of other girls there, but this odd girl with the muffins captivated me. I mean, who does that? Who brings baked goods to a party with piles of cocaine, weed, and speed? She was like a walking loaf of wholesome Wonder Bread amid a torrent of hard candy. That pure goodness attracted me to her. I followed her into the kitchen and introduced myself and asked for another muffin.

"Sure," she said and gave me the largest one, blueberries popping out all over. The music in the house was pounding louder than a rock concert, and when she handed it to me I had a hard time hearing, but she batted her eyes—they were huge and blue. I almost dropped the muffin.

"Thank you," I said, trying to figure out what she was all about.

"Anytime," she mouthed.

Icebergs cracked and fell away inside me.

A month later we were going steady and were in love. Her name was Karen and she was eighteen, old for those braces.

I was afraid to tell Karen I was half Native at first, but she said, "I think it's wonderful. You should be proud of who you are."

I just about cried.

When Karen took me home to meet her family, I got to talking with her father, and he told me that they were Scottish and Dutch and had settled near Toronto after the Toronto Purchase of 1805 between the British Crown and Mississauga Indians. Their family received a swath of land that they'd farmed ever since. Karen had worked on the family farm since she was young, and she was comfortable doing manual labour. We had that in common.

And when I told Mr. A. about my Scottish side, he asked me all sorts of questions and I could tell he really was interested, just as Karen was, even though I couldn't answer most of them. He was even more interested when I told him about my Native family. He wondered if I was still in touch with anyone. "I read up on history quite a bit, about Canada, the prairies," he said. "And I'm curious: Do you know if your mother's people were Cree or Métis? If they hunted bison? You said they were from Saskatchewan, right?"

"Yes, she's from there, but I wish I knew more, Mr. A.," I said. "She wasn't really around to tell me about that stuff."

The three of us decided to go canoeing one day down the Credit River. It was the end of March and the ice had almost thawed.

I sat at the back of the canoe, Karen in the middle, and Mr. A. was up front.

The river ran fast underneath us, bending wildly down twists and turns. Shelves of ice broke off as our bow slammed headfirst into them—I wasn't good at steering and couldn't get the craft to turn when I wanted it to. There were spots on straightaways where it seemed like I knew what I was doing, but they always gave way to turbulence when we hit a bend. Karen still cheered me on and held on to the sides, laughing and sending up clouds of frozen breath in front of me, but it was hard to deny I was shit at canoeing. Mr. A., though, knew what he was doing and tried to compensate, pulling us forward with his paddle and powerful farmer's arms.

"Watch the corner," I heard him yell as we hurled into a sharp turn. I thrust my paddle into the water and we broadsided the bank. The canoe shifted, Karen's blond hair flew in the wind, and the winter water slammed into my chest.

My ribs ached as I drifted down and down, my arms and legs quickly became heavy and lethargic. I gasped twice and sucked in mouthfuls of water. The heavy cotton and wool of my winter clothing tangled around my body like dead weight as I settled onto the riverbed. I saw a paddle drift by. I screamed for help, releasing a muffled burst of bubbles; then, silence.

I noticed a lock of Karen's hair swaying gently like seaweed as her body writhed above me, the current pulling her downstream in the frozen water. Her movements were slow and getting slower. Her leg kicked, and her boot came loose.

I don't know what came over me then, or how I managed to shift myself. But I ripped off my jacket, kicked off my boots, and swam upward. In a few strokes I was with her. She was already above water, though, gasping for air. She grabbed my arm and pulled me to shore, where we collapsed beside one another.

We shivered and held each other for warmth. She smiled, then her expression froze.

"Where's my father?" she asked.

"I don't know," I said. I raised my head and right away saw him laughing about twenty feet down shore.

"That's how I know you love each other," he shouted and waved. "You didn't even think of dear old dad."

Karen and I went everywhere together.

"You're always with that girl," Leeroy complained. "You're never around anymore."

It was true. We had busy schedules, and spending time with Leeroy interfered with my time with Karen. I worked nights after school, and Karen helped on the farm until I finished at around ten p.m., then she would pick me up in one of her father's old trucks. It smelled like cow shit, but I didn't mind—it was our love shack on wheels.

We'd drive out into the country and talk until dawn, or we'd take off to a rave together and dance until our legs just about fell off. When the beat dropped, and she was grooving right there in front of me, with a huge smile beaming light and love, I was so free and happy.

OPENING UP

THE SIDE DOOR OF KAREN'S truck was open, letting in the cool midnight breeze. We lay side by side on the seat, heads hanging out, staring up at the sky. We were parked out front of my old elementary school, where Leeroy and I had thrown gum in Sylvia's hair. Our friends had wanted to drink and cause pandemonium as usual; we just wanted quiet and each other's company. There was a stillness between us broken only by the rustle of the leaves in the wind.

"Look at that one," I said as I pointed to the North Star. "That's the star Indians used to hunt by; they'd follow it and know where to go." I let the mystic nature of my comment linger in the night air.

"Bullshit," Karen said. She laughed, but I could tell she was halfway convinced.

I took a drag of my cigarette and blew the smoke up and watched it dissipate. The stars grew lighter the longer I stared.

Karen shifted. "Move, you beast, my arm is asleep." She giggled and pushed me over to the gas pedal, right where the scent of cow shit was strongest. I gasped and held my throat, and we both laughed, then wiggled out of the truck.

Once we were settled on a nice spot on the grass next to the playground, Karen said, "Can I ask you something?"

"Sure. Shoot." I wrapped my arm around her shoulder.

"You never talk about why you live with your grandparents." She picked a blade of grass and twirled it.

It was odd for her not to look me in the eye. I searched for the right words. There'd never been boundaries between Karen and me, and I wanted to tell her the truth.

"Sometimes life just tears people from one another. That happened with my family when I was young." I paused and sat up so Karen would look at me, and she did. "Dad had a lot of issues—drugs and violence and other things . . ."

A million years of silence followed. Stars flickered and extinguished one by one, civilizations rose and fell, great pyramids were built and crumbled, yet she kept looking at me. And the wall, a thousand miles high, that I kept between me and the rest of the world didn't exist—not a brick anywhere in sight.

Memories of Josh peeing himself by the bathroom, the hornet by the tub, and the sweet smell of Saskatoon berries along the road allowance with my mushoom and kokum filled my soul. As did the blue bruises along my mother's face. I breathed in and exhaled the rest of my truth.

"My mom had to do what she had to do." I looked up and saw a comet soar by and fall off into the horizon. I thought of Mom standing in front of the mountains in the Polaroid and wondered where she was. "When she left, it all fell apart."

Karen pulled me close.

"I understand," she said. She reached up and knocked off my baseball cap.

I was staying out of trouble for the first time in my life. I stopped stealing and lying, and had saved up lots of cash, around five thousand dollars. I was taking care of my health, too, cutting back on drugs and alcohol.

My grandparents saw the change in me and came to like Karen even more than when they first met her. I would chance to say that they came to love her. They asked her over for dinner every other week, and she always came, blueberry muffins in hand. My grandfather loved those muffins almost as much as I did, and sometimes he'd pick them over Grandma's butter tarts—Grandma didn't like that, but she still had a soft spot for Karen.

Grandpa even sat me down one afternoon and said that if I broke her heart he'd find me and neuter me. "You don't find girls like her every day," he said. "She's special."

I should have listened to the old man.

PRIDE

I CLEARED THE SLEEP OUT of my eyes. It was 5:45 a.m., and Grandpa was driving me to my morning shift at the grocery store. My head pounded, the sour smell of whiskey strong on my breath, the after-effects of a buddy's birthday. It was a reasonable enough occasion to fall off the wagon.

"Grandpa," I announced, "I want to buy a car."

He rolled down his driver-side window and the cold morning air hit my face.

"You will not," he barked.

"But you taught Josh how to drive at sixteen. And I'm nineteen now and you never taught me."

He turned down the Hank Williams song on the radio as we rounded the corner and gunned it. It looked like we entered warp speed as we hit a wall of snowflakes illuminated by the headlights.

"You're wild—always were. You'll kill yourself driving drunk."

I heard the wheels squeal. "But—"

"I said no." He pounded the steering wheel.

I thought the column might break under the force. I kicked my feet and muttered out my window, "I work hard. It's my fucking money." I'd never sworn in front of the old man before, and I recoiled as soon as the words left my mouth.

He slammed on the brakes and the load of tools in the back of the van shifted. "If I ever catch you talking like that again," he said, "I'll snap your neck."

—————

I went to the bank ATM and withdrew the last $2,000 I'd saved. The wad was thick in my hand as I looked at the receipt—*$0*. It was all gone.

Leeroy waited in the car, jungle music pounding, weed smoke pouring out the window. It was our last stop on our way to the rave.

I'd run through my savings in little under two months since the argument with Grandpa, buying everyone drinks, smokes, and endless amounts of drugs. Destroying my future was my way of getting back at the old man.

—————

"Jesse, please," Karen had pleaded. "How are you going to afford college now?"

"College? Are you fucking kidding me—I got kicked out of school last semester."

I never believed post-secondary education was attainable for me, like it was for my friends, whose parents had saved for their education since they were born. Getting kicked out of school and having a car denied me were the final straws.

"Don't talk to me about school, Karen." I hissed. "You're rich—it's different for you." She looked stunned, but I was furious. Leeroy and the other guys never questioned me about my spending. I tried to avoid her after that.

—————

"Wicked," Leeroy said as he opened the passenger-side door of his father's Pontiac 6000. I was waving my cash around like Diamond Jim, the last of the Gilded Age big spenders.

"Let's get there before the line gets too big," I said and hopped in.

I lost Leeroy two hours into the party. I'd picked up a bag of purple Es and a couple ounces of weed from one of my dealers when I first arrived and kept it in my front jean jacket pocket with my roll of money while I tripped about. The Es were so strong I had a difficult time training my eyes on anything for more than a few seconds, so it was inevitable I'd lose him. Every six hours, I dosed another E and puffed another joint hoping Leeroy would show up.

The rhythm of the ragga jungle pounded through me as the night wore on. I danced myself into a deep trance. My throat burned with thirst

Me, nineteen and high on opium.

STEFAN KNIGHT

as sweat poured down my face and neck. I must've drunk ten bottles of water. My sneakers darted nimble on the slick floor, and I grooved with speed like a hummingbird. Shouts and cheers roared with each move, and soon a circle formed around me—women in miniskirts, combat gear, and baseball hats; B-boys and B-girls breakdancing in Adidas tracksuits; dudes with their shirts off pumping their fists in the air; and a horde of other ravers blowing their whistles to the beat. They all looked as high as me. I closed my eyes and kept dancing harder and faster with everyone, the drugs now completely in control of my body and mind.

There was a silence that came over my spirit, followed by what sounded like a gust of wind. The noise of the rave receded into the background, and I heard something emerge from inside my core. My eyes pressed shut, I focused inward on that sound. There was a distant drum—louder, louder, louder still, until it vibrated every molecule in my being. The beautiful cry of Indian drummers rang aloud in every direction—from the north, south, east, west, up, down, over, under, within, and without. I opened my eyes and saw I was dancing alone on the flatness of the great plains. I was dressed in a plume of feathers, deerskins, a bustle, beads, moccasins, a rattle, and tassels. My legs rushed in perfect coordination over top of the grass, pressing and tamping it down, as vast fields undulated before me. The sun hung low as red clouds of dust were kicked up by my feet, filling the air. I danced and danced, moving this way and that, until my thirst for water and the rave seemed but distant memories of a life I once lived.

Only the blinding morning warehouse lights snapped me out of my trance, the music turned to half power, throbbing some mix of break-beats and house. My jacket, my money, my drugs, and most of the rave attendees were gone, and my white muscle shirt had spots of blood the size of cookies on it. There was one girl still dancing next to me, her eyes as wide as some starry universe. The bottoms of her pants were grim and black with cigarette ash and trampled innocence.

"How long have we been dancing?" I asked, disoriented and shaky.

"Two days," she said. Her jaw muscles flexed and clenched as she continued to gyrate, glow sticks dim in both hands. She pointed to the blood stains. "That happened to me once."

I peered inside my shirt and saw that the ends of my nipples were open wounds, like they'd been hit with a belt sander.

"Rubbed them raw against my shirt," she added. "Happens to marathon runners, too."

I never did find Leeroy.

BANANA SPLIT

A WOMAN NAMED SUE SHOWED up at my work one night. "Call me," she mouthed, holding a banana to her ear like she was on the phone.

I was stacking Florida oranges near the lettuce wet case. She put the banana down and pointed to it, then glided toward the cashier to pay for her groceries. I walked over and saw that she had scrawled her number on the side of the banana and had planted a bright red lipstick kiss over top.

That's creative, I thought.

Sue hung around with some of the guys I partied with. She was nice looking, around my age, and had her own car, but I'd never spoken with her before. I placed the banana in my pocket and went to the backroom and got busy with the rest of my work.

I never called.

A few weeks after the banana incident, my buddy Jeff was having a house party, since his father was away on business.

"No girlfriends," he ordered. "Just bring drugs and booze."

"Roger that," I said.

I asked Karen if it was okay for me to go. "It'll give you the chance to hang out with your girlfriends," I said. She was more than happy to do that.

When I got to Jeff's the windows were rattling to a base line so loud I thought they might shatter when the beat dropped. One of my buddies was spinning the turntables, people were grooving in the kitchen and living room, and I saw a few people out back giving each other massages in the hot tub. I could tell everyone was high on coke and E by the size of their pupils and how confident they were in their conversations.

There were a bunch of girls I'd never seen before, but Sue was there. She came over right away.

"Why didn't you call me?"

I didn't know what to say.

"No worries," she said. Her jaw was grinding and I knew it must be from a recently consumed E. She disappeared into the kitchen and re-emerged with a beer and placed it in front of me as I took off my shoes. "My little produce boy." She tapped my bum.

I jumped and smiled awkwardly then moseyed my way over to my friends. Sue melted into the crowd.

By four a.m. I was blitzed off my face and out back trying to cool down. The drugs were super powerful; my skin was goosebumped and sensitive to the touch, and my hair stood on end. I gulped a mouthful of water, poured the rest over my head, and sat down on a garden bench to let the night breeze do its work.

Sue appeared from around the garage and sat next to me. It was clear she was tripping hard, her eyes two pools of India ink. She nudged close and ran her fingers up my spine and through my wet hair, sending shockwaves of pleasure to my toes. Before I knew it, we were upstairs in bed together.

When I emerged from the bedroom, I was ashamed, because I'd betrayed Karen. She was the one person who'd loved and trusted me—the only person I'd ever opened up to. I didn't talk to anyone as I put my shoes on, gathered my things, and caught a taxi back to Brampton.

When I got home, Grandma was up. She handed me a note from Karen, asking me to call so we could have brunch that morning, and asked, "What's wrong, Jesse? You don't look well."

I couldn't look her in the eye. "Nothing," I said, pulling away. I dropped my hoodie and went to call Karen.

She answered, "Hi, baby," her voice so sweet I almost died.

Without a pause, I said, "Karen. It's over. I'm breaking up with you."

There was no noise at first, then a terrible, "No!" She said it over and over, then started saying, "Why, why, why?"

I could hear her crying. I'd never heard someone cry like that before. I swear I heard her heart break right then. I was so ashamed, and I couldn't even tell her why it was over.

I hung up and tried to catch my breath. Grandma cracked the door and came into my bedroom with soft moccasin steps.

"You're making a big mistake," she said. "Karen's a wonderful girl." She shook her head and placed my hoodie on the dresser. A little baggie of coke tumbled out onto the carpet near her feet. I looked down and she gasped. She knew instantly what it was.

"Cyril," she called, panic in her voice. "You better come up."

He rushed upstairs.

When he saw the bag he yelled, "You're just a fucking asshole like Sonny, to shit all over love like that."

I backed up into the corner.

"Pack your things. You can't stay here anymore."

I saw how hurt the old man was and tried to speak.

"But—"

"No. You knew the rules."

I realized then that he'd meant what he'd said all along about drugs.

I remember leaving that night with my stuff in four black garbage bags, frightened of what the future held.

I remember a week later losing my job at the grocery store.

I remember catching a ride out west with one of my buddies.

I remember asking Josh if I could stay with him.

The rest is a blur.

THE STOLEN STREETS

1997–2008

WINDIGO

the long dark winter is ever-consuming
defrost the cold hunger with firewater and skin

meat is scarce on the trap line
but, still, i hunt these alleys.

my fingers claw at the glass
and peel away the label.

i imagine icy northern lakes
abundant with pike
but these fish escape me too.

starvation sets in.
breath freezes
in january's wind.

lost and alone,
wandering.
i swill back the pain; it burns and it belches
rage and despair
leaving only a windigo
who cannibalizes himself.

ADRIFT

LEEROY DROVE DOWN HASTINGS STREET looking for a safe place to park. He'd come out west a few weeks after I did. He just showed up looking all desperate, with no money, just his father's Pontiac 6000. Josh took pity on him and let him crash on his couch until he found a job, but things went south fast—two days fast—as they often did when we were together.

Rain doused the windshield, and the wipers moaned back and forth, the friction hypnotizing me. Grey clouds obstructed the sky above. It had been raining since I'd arrived a month earlier, and I wondered if the city ever saw blue skies or the warmth of the winter sun, or if the mountains that ringed Vancouver were only a myth—I had a hard time believing they were there.

Hordes of homeless junkies slinked down the street, their skin greyer than the clouds and concrete cityscape. They moved like zombies, half-dead, lurching, and hungry. One bag lady pulled down her pants and pissed right there on the side of the road. No one seemed to care, but Leeroy laughed.

"What the fuck?" he said. "Where are we?"

I tried to laugh but a feeling of dread came over me as she lost her balance and fell over in her own urine. A scrum of people congregated on the corner of Main and Hastings—they darted their heads about and

I knew they must be engaged in some sort of drug deal. One of the men yelled and shook his fist, clutching something. His voice was guttural, it sounded torn to shreds, like he'd just drunk a bottle of Drano. His clothes hung off his body, more rags than anything. Another man hollered and the group pounced, arms and legs flailing wildly. The rough-voiced man was consumed by the swarm of violence. I rolled down my window to get a better look and the group scattered, leaving him prostrate on the sidewalk.

"Where the fuck are we is right," I said, squinting to see if he was still breathing. I noticed a pool of blood spreading near his face, a blankness across his eyes. He looked dead, but they all appeared dead in their own way, and the majority of them looked Indian. I'd never seen so many Indians in one spot before, except when I was a kid. I'd also never seen such squalor and despair; in suburban Brampton, places like this didn't exist.

"We've got to pick a spot soon," Leeroy said. "We're gonna blow through all the gas and we ain't got no money left." His left leg was bouncing up and down and he kept glancing in and adjusting the rearview mirror. I chewed my knuckle down to the flesh. Josh hadn't warned us of any of this when he'd kicked us out.

"I should arrest you both," he'd screamed. He'd come home early one night from his shift and found me and Leeroy smoking pot. "I'm fucking RCMP! What's everyone going to think?" He charged into the room and wheel-kicked my face, sending the joint flying and an explosion of ash and embers into the air. He moved like a black belt after years of tae kwon do. Leeroy cowered beside me on the couch.

It'd never really dawned on me that my older brother was an officer of the law and that I shouldn't be getting high at his place. Even his red Mountie uniform hadn't convinced me. To me he was just Josh—I acted as I always had, stealing his clothes and disrespecting him like the little brother I was. I'd even nicked his badge on occasion and went around telling everyone I was a cop so I could get on public transit free of charge, pick up chicks, and eat complimentary meals at local restaurants after I assured them that I'd protect them personally.

When Josh found out, he wanted to arrest me for impersonating an officer, but I talked my way out of it somehow. But stupid me, I kept pushing the limit. No wonder he went Jackie Chan on me for the pot.

Leeroy pulled into a lot near a river and turned off the car. The engine sputtered, followed by a hiss and a cloud of steam from under the hood. I thought it was the radiator. Leeroy reached into the glovebox and pulled out a map of the Lower Mainland that I'd pinched at a gas station.

"This car isn't in good shape," he said as he spread the map out across the dash. "I borrowed it before my dad had the chance to get it serviced."

"I heard him yell at you when you phoned home last week. He sounded upset that you borrowed it."

Leeroy glared at me. I thought he might hit me, but he furrowed his brow and busied himself with the map.

I kept pressing. "You must've done something pretty serious." I waited for his answer, but he ignored me. He turned over the ignition and it clicked a few times. The interior lights dimmed and flickered, then went black. The car battery was dead, that much I knew. We were stranded.

"Fuck," Leeroy yelled, his voice raising high.

I decided not to enquire further about the trouble he'd fled. "Where are we?" I asked, surveying for street signs. I could make out a couple, plus there was a huge white bridge off to the left. I grabbed the map and searched, trying to pinpoint our locale. Leeroy stared out his window and lit one of our last smokes.

"Here we are," I said. "New Westminster and that's the Fraser River. I think that's the Pattullo Bridge." I glanced over to see Leeroy was crying. He turned his head when he noticed me.

"Yeah," I said, peering out over the river. "At least we found a good spot."

By the third day, food had become a major problem. Every store we went into had floor walkers who followed Leeroy and me whenever we tried to steal even one bag of ramen noodles. We figured it was because of all the addicts who tried to do the same—stores in BC had way better security than out east. I got caught at the Army & Navy and was issued a promise to appear by a policeman, which I tore up the instant I got released.

"We've got to think of something quick," Leeroy said as I emerged. "I'm literally starving."

I examined his face. His eyes were sunken, and the metallic, sweet smell of starvation wafted off his breath. The taste on my tongue told me that I emitted that same odor.

Leeroy's solution was to call home. We ducked into a nearby phone booth, and he went first.

"Hi, Dad," he said. "I need help. I'm homeless in Vancouver and have no food." He sounded pitiful.

I could hear his father's voice booming. Leeroy's shoulders slumped and he hung up. "He told me to figure it out on my own. You try."

I dialled home. It rang a few times before someone picked up.

"You have a collect call from Jesse Thistle," the automatic operator voice said.

The line clicked and my grandmother answered. "Jesse," she said. "Don't ever call here again."

"But, Grandma—"

"No. Your grandfather was clear: you're not welcome."

I couldn't believe what she was saying.

"But I'm starv—"

"You are on your own now—this isn't your home anymore." Her voice was shaky like it was when Yorkie died, and she'd bawled in the kitchen.

I heard my grandfather's gravel yell in the background. "Is that the asshole?"

There was a muffled sound, then his voice blasted in my ear.

"Don't ever call here. Don't ever come here. Don't even think of here. Josh told me what happened—you are not part of this family." He slammed the receiver into the cradle. I slid down the side of the phone booth and hid my face in my knees. Leeroy didn't say a word.

The second week sleeping in the car with no food, I started to panic. Home would never be there again for me, nor would Karen—I still loved her beyond words. The dual losses were like my rudder had snapped off, without warning. I was adrift somewhere in the middle of the ocean and there was no search party coming.

Sleep was impossible. I was overheating, even when I took my clothes off and kept the car windows down in the zero-Celsius winter air. Leeroy complained of the same intense heat.

One of the local street kids told us we were overheating because we were in ketoacidosis—our bodies were too acidic and were digesting themselves, muscles and all.

"You could die from it," he said. And that it was impossible to steal in Vancouver because we looked like "starving crackheads, like all the street people." It didn't help that I was Indian, he added.

The kid's name was Troy. Leeroy got along with him right away and invited him to stay with us in our car. To my dread, Troy slept in the back seat with me, a space already too cramped. Dude smelled like a sewer, and when I complained, he said I smelled even worse. I found that hard to believe.

Troy knew more about the street than we did. He was like Leeroy and never spoke about what he'd done. I knew not to ask. The other good thing he brought was his knowledge of where to sell stuff—clothes, primarily. He had a connection at a local pawnshop. I'd purchased stylish stuff with my produce job money, and piece by piece we sold my clothes and bought food—it lasted maybe three weeks until I had nothing left but one T-shirt I wore, a pair of pants, my sneakers, and a Canada soccer jersey.

Troy introduced us to job agencies and cheque-cashing places, two things I didn't even know existed, and we were always the first, along with the other immigrants and newcomers, at the job agency counter at five a.m. to get general labour jobs. We dug ditches, packed shipping containers, moved furniture, and whatever other shitty hard tasks most Canadians didn't want to do. When we got our cheques—$25 each for eight to ten hours—we'd cash them in.

"To work like a slave only to have the temp agency take half," Leeroy complained, counting out his dough and eating our regular bag of fast food, "then the cheque place gouges us even more. Where's the security?"

"That's how it is for young guys with no education in Canada," Troy said. "They made it this way—our greedy parents. Next, all the jobs will be temp."

We soon learned of a better spot where we could get picked up and toil for the day for better money. The work was much more dangerous— moving heavy cabinets that weighed nearly a thousand pounds each and took four men to move. When Troy lost his grip and one came crashing down on me on a stairway, I quit on the spot. We never did get paid for that job.

We moved on to demolitions of old homes. We got no masks, respirators, or protective gear of any kind. At the end of one day, after weeks ripping down plaster walls at various different places, my chest hurt. I coughed into a tissue and noticed a splash of blood and some yellow stuff that looked like booger cornflakes. The immigrants I worked with said they coughed it, too, said it was from all the asbestos.

"What's asbestos?" I asked. No one told me.

At the end of the three weeks, the job was done, but the employer didn't show up. We didn't get paid.

That was tough. We were trying our hardest, but we were getting ripped off, getting little sleep, rest, or comfort in the car, and we were still wasting away. Soon we gave up getting up for work and just sat in the car.

Leeroy began to cough at night. Troy, too. Greyish phlegm that smelled like dirty honey shot out all over, and they both got a rash that spread up their necks and over their lips and face—red, bumpy, with peeling scales. Leeroy didn't look right. The emaciated skin over his face started to appear translucent, his green veins turned a bluish purple, his eyes pressed way back into his bones till they looked like they rested on the front of his brain. When he smiled his dimples folded into a hundred tiny creases, like he was centuries old and had lived in the desert all his life.

Troy coughed on me a couple times. I never got as sick as they did, but a few weeks later, my hair began falling out in clumps, and so did theirs, like shedding cats in spring. The cap on my front tooth broke off. It took a brittle piece of the bone under my nose with it, leaving me with a grey-and-black jagged-toothed smile. I never realized how important my smile was until then—the loss seemed to suck the joy out of interacting with anyone, more than even the starving situation did. I just couldn't smile without feeling horrible about my already dishevelled appearance.

I stopped smiling altogether.

END OF A FRIENDSHIP

LEEROY AND I WENT OUT begging. Troy had fled the week before, down to the East Side where there were food banks, churches, and shelter beds. But there were also all those zombies and hard drugs, and street people were dying there. We'd decided never to venture down there—we had a difficult enough time staying alive where we were. We'd been homeless for just over four months and were barely hanging on.

We returned to the car defeated, with no money, to find the back window shattered, glass peppered all over my sleeping spot. Night was falling and it was particularly cold for May. The intense heat of ketoacidosis had given way to an intense chill. I cleaned the glass away and tried to go to sleep, but my spine and hips were bending and shattering like layers of ice smashing up on a lake shore. I prayed for morning and the sun to warm me—I waited and waited. When light started appearing on the horizon, I sat up and peered out over the Fraser River. A bunch of logs drifted by, the movement rhythmic and silent as they floated off to their destination.

I looked down at Leeroy, his torso tucked under the steering wheel and legs stretched across the front seats. I knew then that it wasn't my place to stay in the car anymore—I don't know how I knew, but I did. Maybe it was the thought of my mortality that pulled me away, or maybe I didn't know anything other than abandonment, one of the earliest lessons my dad had left me with.

Childhood memories of my times with Leeroy filled me as the sun crested up over the mountains and called for me to let go of our friendship. I'd earned the sunlight, it was mine, and mine alone. I crept out of the car and shut the door gently, careful to not wake him.

As I rounded the corner of the parking lot onto the street, I looked back at the car and saw Leeroy's head appear, turn side to side, then disappear back down. Perhaps he thought I'd gone to the washroom. I said goodbye in my heart and wished him well and then made my way to the Trans-Canada Highway for the long hitchhike back home to Ontario.

ROU GAROUS

I hitchhiked home in early spring.
The mountains, then prairies, swollen lakes, the thickness of forests—all
    was uneventful.
But on the Trans-Canada Highway, somewhere east of the prairies
I was picked up by some farm boys around my age.
They said I looked rough and wanted to feed me, to give me a place to
    rest
So in their car I went.

We drove some distance off the main route
Down some obscure dirt road, far out of the way to an abandoned
    building.
I smelled smoke when I got out; a loon called in the distance.
The driver was kind and asked me to carve my name on a tree.
There were other names carved in too.
"Other hitchhikers," they said. "Others running, trying to get home."

As my blade cut into the trunk, I felt a fist slam into the back of my head.
Stars upon stars; I didn't see it coming.
The one boy tackled me and tried to bring me to the ground.
But my thick skull and strong spirit, they held me up.
I staggered and stumbled, arms outstretched, trying to regain my
    senses.
I ran disoriented into the forest toward where I hoped the highway was.

Warm blood poured out of my head.

It wasn't a fist they'd hit me with, I figured. It must've been a rock or hammer.

They stalked close behind me through the brush; I ran with all my might.

My chest burning and legs barely under me,

Weakened by months of no food.

I almost gave in.

But my relatives, the trees, saw my trouble.

"Hide within us, nephew," they rustled. "Our leaves will darken their way."

Their branches bent and covered my passage; they arched over to save me.

Deeper into the poplars, cedars, and oaks I fled,

A good three miles.

My attackers' footsteps fell silent, their voices trailed off.

In time, I chanced upon good old Highway One.

It felt safe,

Like some mighty river of asphalt that had the current to carry me home.

I stood there all night with my thumb out, begging to be picked up.

I waved my arms at each passing vehicle but no one stopped.

Or even slowed down.

NEVER THE SAME

"THAT GIRL DANCING NEAR THE base bin is fine," Rex said as he tilted his rum and Coke toward the stage of the nightclub.

I barely had my legs under me, still reeling from the long hitchhike to Toronto and malnutrition. When I got back home, friends commented that I looked like I was dying of starvation. Some were afraid to talk to me. Perhaps they just didn't want to think about how far my addictions had taken me, or that they were headed there, too.

"She fine," I agreed. But my eyes were more interested in Rex's drink than the girl, its ice glistened with each strobe of the lights. House music shook the empty glasses splayed out over the bar, left there by a bartender who, I knew, was too busy doing rails of coke to properly serve customers. Rex had a hell of a time getting his first drink, yelling four or five times before he finally got her attention. My stomach growled, a mixture of hunger and cravings. The memory of the taste of whiskey welled up, reminding me that I had no money and no business being in a club.

"I love this song," Rex said, pumping his hand in the air. The DJ had mixed in the latest track from Chicago—the mecca of house music—and Rex, in his excitement, spilled some of his drink on the man in front of us. Neither noticed. I watched and waited for the ecstasy pill I'd just taken to kick in. I lived for that Chicago sound, an amalgam of gritty four-and-four house beats, old-school funk, and gospel lyrics. No one did it better. No one.

"I'm waiting for my E to kick in," I hollered over to Rex, trying to be heard over top of the throbbing baseline. "Can you buy me a drink?" The beat finally dropped and the crowd went wild, asses gyrating everywhere. "Can you spot me for a drink?" I yelled one more time. Rex didn't hear and continued to thrust his drink in the air, watering the crowd in front of him. I tried again. "Bro!" I yelled and grabbed his arm. "I'm fucking dying over here—I need a drink."

Rex turned to me and said, "You should have said something sooner," his jaw chattering, his pupils wide open. His E had taken effect.

Lucky bastard, I thought. I wondered why I wasn't feeling anything.

"Hey!" he screamed over to the barkeep. "Gimme two rum and Cokes." She heard him right away and fired two tumblers down the bar. Rex dropped a twenty-dollar bill on the bar and she snatched it up without offering change. He handed me my drink.

"Cheers," he said, and we clinked our glasses together and looked out over the crowd of gorgeous women. I again noticed the woman near the base bin—she was beautiful. My belly warmed as the rum settled under my ribs, sending a rush of ecstasy up my spine. A swell of spectacular pins and needles broke over the top of my scalp. My eyelids fluttered, and I braced myself against the bar, waiting for the impeding tsunami of rapture. My knees buckled.

"There he goes," Rex said. His eyes looked like a shark's eyes right before the kill—completely black. I tried to smile back at him but my jaw took on a life of its own, chattering up and down. It was good E—the best kind—the kind that slams into your gut and impregnates you with a cloud of migrating monarchs, fluttering your intestines into a writhing swarm of uncontrollable pleasure.

We'd scored our E earlier from our dealer, a trustworthy guy named Island. He sold primarily to the underground gay clubs on Church Street that always had the best drugs and newest music. My friends had found that out early on, that's how we met Island, and that's how we got high as fuck on $40 Es. Most other dealers sold Es at $10 or $20, but they weren't really methylenedioxymethamphetamine (MDMA), just a mix of cheap crystal meth, caffeine, and maybe a little heroin for euphoric effect. But Island took care of us proper.

"These Es are killer," Rex said. He placed his empty glass on the bar, then rifled through his pockets. I thought he was going to give me another pill, but he pulled out a wad of bills, leafed off $40, and handed it to me. "I know you're broke. I'm just glad you're here, safe. Not hitchhiking across the continent, starving and shit."

I took the money, at a loss for words. I could barely make out Rex's face, the visual vibration was so jarring. "I love you, dude," I said, the words gurgled up out of my throat in a moment of euphoria. I heard them, but hadn't wanted to say them. Sweat poured down my face, dripped off my chin.

"I know that, guy," Rex said as he wiped my face. "We're brothers. One love."

He dapped my hand as the throb of the house music picked up.

We did love each other. It was a camaraderie, a closeness, a fellowship. A connection with the universe that's hard to explain but that happens with E—almost like you turn into Jesus, Gandhi, and Mother Teresa all rolled into one, not a problem in the world, caring for all things at once, a connection you never forget and always yearn for after you've sobered up, and when you mix it with sex, it was even more powerful.

"Listen," Rex said as he grabbed my hand and pulled me back from total ecstasy. "Someone's paged and I gotta go over to Spadina. Meet me there at four a.m." He slapped my cheek to get my attention. I retrained my sights on his face, but had trouble focusing. He was melting, blurring, fading into another dimension. A wall of colours filled my vision: a kaleidoscope of disco-ball refractions. He was somewhere in there.

"Yeah. Got it. Buzz. See you there." I held on to the bar for dear life. His shape was coming in clearer, but still wasn't quite there yet.

"I ordered another drink for you," Rex said before leaving. "It should be along shortly." He winked at the bartender, and she fired another rum and Coke down the bar. It landed in front of me, leaving tracers in its wake. I needed toothpicks to prop my eyes open, and my stomach flipped as the liquid splashed and swirled down.

Was there something different about these E pills, or was it the drink I'd left unattended in my stupor? It was hard to tell. My feet were two hot-air balloons floating high above the Paris fairgrounds, simultaneously lighter than air and heavier than the compressed core of a star for twenty minutes after Rex left. Finding purchase on the ground was nearly impossible. Flashes of black blinded me as I stumbled forward onto the dance floor. I pleaded for help. The other partiers just backed away and shot me expressions of disgust. I stumbled and fell, dropping my drink, the tumbler shattering. My mind was confused, groggy, dark. I thought maybe if I found some coke or speed I might be able to perk up, shake off whatever was happening. I thought I saw Island near the stage and so made my way toward it. I staggered, zigzagging, as far as the base bin where the beautiful girl was dancing, then collapsed.

When I awoke I was on the other side of the club near the washrooms, some forty feet away. The floor was still packed, the music was louder, people were dancing faster, and the bar was closed but decorated with drunk girls giving strip shows, and everyone was way more fucked up. I was still disoriented.

As I pushed myself up the wall off the floor, I noticed that my belt was undone, and my pants were open and hanging off my waist. My underwear was gone. I knew I'd been wearing underwear when I got to the club.

There was a deep pain in my intestines, radiating from my rectum, down across my testicles and penis. I panicked and hobbled over into the washroom and one of the stalls. I wadded up a pad of toilet paper and wiped it across my anus. A dark stain of fresh blood appeared on it. I couldn't believe what I was seeing. I ran my fingers over my bum and discovered that I had what appeared to be hemorrhoids. I tried pushing them in but they hurt more than anything I'd ever experienced—I touched them gently again. I'd never had hemorrhoids before, or whatever these were. I tried to understand what had happened, who was around me before I fell unconscious, why I woke up near the washroom, or why what appeared to be my intestines were hanging out of my bum.

I can't remember how I got home, or even where I actually went—there was nothing but a dense black fog in my memory. I saw nothing but darkness, confusion.

A deep feeling of shame shrouded my soul.

A GUST OF MOLECULES

THE PHONE RINGING PIERCED THE night calm. I rolled off the couch and went into the kitchen to pick it up.

It was Uncle Ralph. "Jesse. Go get Ronald." The urgency in his voice was unnerving.

I ran to Uncle Ron's room, Solomon, my uncle's Rhodesian ridgeback, trotting behind me to investigate the commotion. "Ralph's on the phone," I said as I pushed on Uncle Ron's foot. "Wake up."

He shifted and squinted at the alarm clock—3:40 a.m.—then shot out of bed and into the kitchen.

"What's wrong?" he barked into the receiver. He cleared the sleep from his eyes and waved me away. "Everything okay?"

I moved into the sunroom to eavesdrop but could only hear the static of Ralph's voice and Uncle Ron's "Uh-huh, uh-huh." I stared out the window at the treetops bending in the nighttime wind and hoped the call wasn't about Grandpa or Grandma.

Uncle Ron said, "I'll be right there," and then hung up and bolted out to the car without a word. I watched the car's tail lights disappear into the darkness. I placed a chair next to the window. My adrenaline would keep me awake. Solomon sat by my side.

Uncle Ron had been living in Port Hope with his daughter, who was just sixteen, since she started getting into trouble in Toronto. He figured she'd stay out of trouble out in the country. I thought it was a smart move on his part.

I'd been with them for five months. Uncle Ron got word that I was sleeping at the airport and couch surfing with friends, slipping further into addiction.

The assault at the club left me struggling, grabbing nothing but sand. One never thinks it will happen to them until it does. You are never the same and it's always there.

I had managed to sober up while I'd been in Port Hope with Uncle Ron, somehow, but I was still smoking weed trying to sort through everything that had happened. Uncle Ron represented safety to me, even though I couldn't bring myself to tell him what had happened.

At 7:30 a.m. the next day, Uncle Ron pulled back into the driveway. I was still staring out the window, after downing pot after pot of coffee and smoking cigarette after cigarette. My teeth buzzed like I'd eaten a hive of bees. Uncle Ron slumped over the steering wheel. The car was still running but the car stereo was off—and he always drove with '70s rock blaring.

He finally got out of the car and made his way to the house. I heard the grind of gravel with each step. I poured a cup of coffee and left it on the table. The floorboards creaked as he found his way upstairs and sat down. It appeared he'd been crying, which was odd to me, since he was so powerful, so full of male bravado—I didn't know he could cry.

I was afraid to ask what had happened and went back into the sunroom to my chair by the window. A stand of trees caught my eye, the tops of the birch branches dancing in the wind, the sun tangled up in their rusty leaves. The clink of Uncle Ron's spoon against the sides of his mug sounded out like a chorus of sledgehammers striking railway ties. He cleared his throat and asked me to join him.

"I don't know how to say it," he said, not looking at me, another oddity. I pulled up a chair to the table, as silent as I could be.

"Grandma got a call last night," he began. "From 22 Division in Etobicoke. The police picked up a homeless man last night—he said his name was Ron Thistle—but that's me. The homeless guy knew everything about me—my birthdate, what hospital I was born in, my arrest record, everything about Grandma and Grandpa, my siblings' names and birthdates." Uncle Ron pulled a joint from his pack of smokes and lit it, careful not to singe his hair. He took a moment before he spoke.

"Grandma told them I was out here in Port Hope."

He released a cloud of smoke into the air, then broke into a fit of coughing and handed the spliff my way. We had that between us—weed as a balm to dull the sharp edges of the world, weed as a crutch against addiction. I took a huge draw and held it in, my attention focused on him.

"Mom knew it was Sonny, your dad," he said. "Mother's intuition."

I passed the joint back and waited for him to finish.

"Only Sonny knows all my stuff," he said. His eyes were a little redder now. It was hard to tell if it was the weed.

I watched a tendril of white smoke twist from the head of the blunt. It reminded me of when Uncle Ron took me out on his collections back when I was a kid. I pictured us in his red convertible singing and bopping our heads as he smoked weed—I didn't know then that that was what he was smoking. An image of my dad begging out on Yonge Street came to me. His hands and mind slowed by winter lethargy, his clothes loose and hanging off his wasted body. I thought of Vancouver, of Leeroy's car, of the Fraser River, of sleeping with nowhere to go.

Uncle Ron rolled the end of the joint in the bottom of the glass ashtray, knocking off the excess ash, and handed it back me. It sat idle in my index and middle fingers, digits yellowed from constant use.

"Mom phoned Ralph because he's a cop," Uncle Ron said. "She wanted him to identify the man at 22, but he couldn't leave work, so he called me."

I flicked the joint and watched the ember glow red. I kept looking down, afraid of what Uncle Ron would say next.

He reached over and grabbed my free hand. "They let the guy go before I could get there." His voice wavered.

I could feel my hand going numb.

"The officer said it was because of shift change—they clear the drunks out of the bullpen at five a.m. before the day officers come in. I got there at 5:15. Fifteen minutes too late. I'm so sorry, Jesse."

I tried to follow Uncle Ron's words, but it was as if his lips were moving in slow motion. Dad was gone. He didn't care enough to stay. He didn't want to come back home.

Nothing mattered. It was as if an atomic blast followed. The stand of trees was sucked forward, then blown back with such force they were obliterated. The citizens of Port Hope were vaporized into carbon imprints on the broken cityscape. An old man walking with his cane, a mother holding her baby, a little girl playing in the park—all were transformed into shadows of daily life atomically scorched onto the concrete of sidewalks and roadways, and I was now one of those shadow people. I gazed down at my hand and saw nothing but Uncle Ron grasping a carbon handprint fused onto the table's surface.

It's pointless, I thought, *my destruction is complete.*

The next week I left Port Hope and began drifting again.

SUBURBAN WASTELANDS

MOST OF MY FRIENDS HAD moved on. Brian had gone to university, Leeroy was still out west, Derick was with a new crew, some had moved downtown for jobs. Others just didn't want me around when I got back from Port Hope. I showed up pleading for help and they literally shut the door in my face.

I tripped around for a few months, staying in bus shelters, sleeping in the mall during the day, and staying nights at the top of apartment building staircases. Many times, like a beat-up piece of old driftwood, I washed up on the doorstep of Olive, a church lady who believed in the word of Jesus Christ. Olive was the mother of a friend from high school. She wasn't like the usual hypocrites in church, though, she actually lived it in her daily life. She'd take in youths and make them feel loved, feeding and clothing them, giving them shelter when needed, and she let me in, then tried whittling me into something that resembled a human being. I hated listening to her preach, but she did make the Bible something I could understand.

I couldn't stay at Olive's all the time, though. I discovered that Brampton had emergency shelters. I tried a men's shelter first. It was a converted old fire hall, a rough place that reeked of old feet and broken dreams. The intake worker told me I was too young to stay there. "The women's shelter is safer for you," he said. "Here are a few bus tickets. I'll call so they know you're coming."

When I got to the Sally Ann, I got my own room—small, private, with a bed, dresser, bathroom, and full access to a kitchen—and a fresh change of clothes. I lay on the bed, listening to the creak of the plastic protecting the mattress sounding sweeter than an angel's voice, and thought, *I'm in heaven.* But things didn't stay heavenly for long.

"Who is that *man* making himself a Pop-Tart in the toaster? I don't feel safe with him here!" one lady complained to the frontline staff.

"He's been kicked out of his home," he said. But she kept on. It was clear I was unwanted, so I left.

I begged for money at a strip mall and made my way downtown. I paid the ten- or fifteen-dollar admissions at after-hours raves, clubs, or booze cans, doing drugs and dancing, and ended up sleeping in a corner for a few hours every couple days. New drugs—crystal meth and ketamine—were around, and I started to do and sell both in small batches, gathering enough money to buy food and admission to the next club. They were cheaper than cocaine. I tried to stay away from ketamine, though, because of its sedative effects—the dreaded "K-hole" that left you defenceless and comatose but awake somehow.

The assault was always in the back of my mind.

There was an underground club or rave every day of the week in Toronto, always a place to go to next. There was a whole community of young castaways like me. I liked being around them—they didn't give a shit that I was half Indian, had darker skin, and didn't have a clue who I was or where I was going—and all of us slowly became hooked on meth. I developed sores all over, my nostrils became red and inflamed, and my waistline shrank and shrank. I spent hours picking away at what I believed were bugs burrowing under my skin. It would escalate the longer I was awake—sometimes up to 124 hours at a time. I'd see worms wriggle on my feet, on my forearms, or near my crotch, and I'd scratch at them until my nails ripped the skin open and pulled out my veins. Then I'd repick those scabs, convinced the bugs were still there. My stomach was digesting my intestines. My breath smelled like rotten blood and juicy trash boiled in acid, and it hurt to swallow.

The state of things terrified me, and I took off back to Brampton. I stayed with a buddy for a month, but he had the same problems I had, so I moved on and knocked on Jerry's door. He had an apartment of his own he rented with one of his friends.

"I don't even recognize you," he said when he answered. "What happened?"

"I just can't stop," I said.

I recall him grabbing me and barricading me in his room. I shivered and sweated and thought I was going crazy as the drugs left my system. Every time I tried to leave, he tackled and restrained me and stuck me back in the room and re-bolted the door. Sometimes the door would crack open and a sub sandwich would fly into the middle of the room and land by my feet. I'd eat it and then pass out and have the worst nightmares—zombies eating themselves, the farm boys smashing my skull in, Clive's head exploding in his blue house, Yorkie running backward up the wall like he was possessed by demons.

As I emerged from my chemical haze, there were days when I sat with my ear glued to the wall while Jerry battled with his friends in the living room, negotiating a spot for me to stay on the couch after I sobered up. No one was keen on letting me live there.

When I could, I collected my things in a garbage bag and left.

FAMILY WEDDING

"KEEP SIX," I WHISPERED TO my little brother, Daniel, who stood near the mirror in the Value Village Clothing store in Vancouver. I ducked down and pivoted, blocking the line of sight to the cashier. I grabbed a sports blazer, a pair of black slacks, a white button-up shirt, a belt, a pair of dress shoes, and a skinny black tie and stuffed them in my plastic grocery bag.

"She's coming, she's coming," Daniel said, a note of panic in his voice. I glanced in the mirror and saw a lady in a red employee's smock. She'd been pricing men's shoes two aisles over. I threw the bag under the rack and stood up to greet her. She yanked the bag out, opened it, and threatened to call the police. Daniel and I backpedalled, and then ran out the front door and down the street.

She'd fallen for the ruse. I'd gone in behind Daniel and changed into a suit, tie, and shoes before anyone noticed, then told Daniel to keep an eye out. He had amateur written all over his face. He gawked around like he was doing something wrong, pacing back and forth, while I stuffed the decoy bag full of things—which caught the attention of the store employee who focused on the bag instead of the suit I was wearing. It was an old trick I'd learned.

"How'd you learn to steal like that?" Daniel asked.

"That was nothing." To me, it was just another day at the office. I picked a butt off the ground and lit it. The truth was I didn't know, it just came naturally, kind of like breathing.

It was the first time I'd seen my little brother since he and Mom had disappeared with George years before. When Josh phoned Jerry and invited me to his September wedding, he said we'd put aside our differences and be cordial on his big day, and that he'd pay for my flight out west if I could just get it together long enough to look human. He said it'd be the first time all us brothers would be together again—that it was important I be there.

I jumped at the chance to see my baby brother, and to witness Josh and his fiancée, Margaret, get married. I was lucky to have caught the call—I circled back to Jerry's just to check in or crash periodically—but I was glad I did. I wouldn't have missed the wedding for the world. The suit I'd just nicked was too tight. I bent over and polished my shoes with some spit. They, too, weren't my size. But it would all have to do.

Daniel picked a ball of lint off my blazer and brushed my shoulder. He had features so much like mine, but he was better and healthier looking.

We'd met up earlier that day at the church and got along right away. Mom was there, too, and we'd kissed and all that good stuff, like reunited long-lost mother and son, which is what we were, then I'd pulled Daniel aside.

"Dude, I can't go dressed like this." I pointed at my clothes. They weren't that bad, street garb, just not dressy enough for my brother's wedding. I informed him that I needed a wingman.

Daniel said he'd help right away. I think he wanted to hang out with me. My reputation preceded me, I guessed.

"What happened to you?" I asked him as we headed back to the chapel, fearful that the ass crack in my pants might split wide open. "You and Mom just kind of fell off the map."

"We had to run away."

I could hear the tension in his voice as we crossed the street and picked up the pace.

"There'd be spit flying everywhere," Daniel said about George's fits of rage. "One day, Mom had enough. She pulled me from school and we went to Saskatoon. We left so fast, Mom only had one shoe and I didn't have a coat. I'm sorry we didn't call."

"It's okay, Daniel. I've been messed up. I wouldn't have had much to say."

I sat outside the reception hall for a lot of the night, smoking. The place was crowded with out-of-uniform RCMP officers, Josh's colleagues, and their presence made me jumpy. Grandpa was there, too, and he gave me cut eye so bad I'm sure he was casting a malevolent spell on me. When I tried to speak to him during the photo shoot, he walked away. Jerry told me I was only attending because Josh had gone to bat for me.

I bumped into Grandma on the way to the washroom, though, and she said, "You look good," pinching my cheeks, and slipping a $100 bill in my pocket. "Now smarten up!" It was the only contact we had.

Mom's family was there, as well, my aunts and about seven cousins my age from Saskatchewan. They sat in a section off to the side by themselves but were super friendly, mingling, laughing, drinking, and carrying on—they were the best dancers in the joint—but I didn't really interact with them. Jerry stuck by my side, going inside to dance when a song he liked came on, and we shared bottle after bottle until the world spun around us.

Mom came out to join us about halfway through the festivities.

"Look at you," she said to me, a cigarette in one hand, a glass of red wine in the other. She swayed a little and sat between me and Jerry. Jerry pulled back.

"I hear you're a little troublemaker." She smiled. She was half in the bag, but still very much alert. I wondered if it was her way of mustering up the courage to talk to us. "That's okay," she said. "I still love you no matter what." She hugged me close and the awkwardness fled. It'd been years since we embraced.

"Here," my aunt Cecile said, "a whore's breakfast." She thrust an empty plate with two aspirins on it at me, and then handed me an open beer. I swallowed the pills and took a few chugs to wash them down. I handed back the empty bottle, and she winked and clicked her teeth. A few minutes later the pounding in my head stopped. My hangover was gone.

The smell of eggs and bacon was strong in the kitchen. We'd spent the night after the wedding at my auntie's place. She shuffled around the stove with a cigarette hanging out of her mouth as my other relatives squirmed about, still trying to sleep out on the dining room floor. Their names escaped me, but they all looked familiar. One guy looked like Josh but was slimmer. I recognized my aunt Yvonne, who sat on the couch reading a magazine.

"*Chi garçon, mon bébé*," she said to me, and then a bunch of stuff that sounded French but not quite.

"He doesn't have a clue, *Pedour*," Aunt Cecile said. "He's been gone for *vingt ans*."

"*Mon dieu!*" Aunt Yvonne bellowed. "You can't speak Michif anymore?"

Michif, I thought. *What's that?*

Aunt Cecile said something as my mom came out of the bedroom. She had a big smile on her face, like she'd already consumed Aunt Cecile's special breakfast. She said something back, and my aunties started laughing.

"I spoke Michif?" I asked.

"God, yes." Mom chuckled. "You didn't say a word until you were three, but then we couldn't shut you up!"

Aunt Cecile howled in the kitchen and my mom started to laugh so hard I thought she might pee herself.

One of my cousins sat up and said, "Yeah, and you covered everything in shit when you got upset. Dirty little bugger." Her accent was thicker than Aunt Yvonne's. *"Li Shicock.* Gross!"

Again, the room busted up.

"Never mind them," Mom said. "You were a clean boy. My boy."

"We're just playing," Aunt Yvonne brayed. "It's so good to see you." She got up and squeezed me, and her arms were like powerful bear arms. I hugged back but she was way stronger than me.

Aunt Cecile put a plate of eggs on the counter. "This is mine. All you *chyins* have to fend for yourselves." She laughed and started eating. "But there's tea made." She motioned to the kitchen table, where a teapot squatted on a lace doily.

I sat down and poured myself a cup, and Mom pulled up the chair next to me. It was hard to make eye contact without alcohol coursing through my veins. She was a complete stranger. Her sisters were hovering around like bees pollinating flowers.

"I know you've been all over," she said. She twiddled her thumbs and drew in a deep breath.

There was a jar of jam beside the teapot—"Saskatoons," it read. I focused on that. I thought of Kokum Nancy and her Coke-bottle glasses and her walking stick.

"How would you like to come home with me?"

Aunt Yvonne moved behind me and placed her hands on my shoulders.

"Mom, it's been years . . ." I could hear the tick of the clock and Aunt Cecile's breathing—she sounded like she was having a heart attack.

"It wouldn't have to be forever, Jesse," Aunt Yvonne jumped in. "Just try it out. Saskatoon is a wonderful little city."

"Um . . . I don't think so. I live in Toronto—all my friends are there. Jerry, too."

Aunt Cecile swung open the back door, and I heard something smash.

"There's work and lots of Métis girls for a handsome young man like yourself," Aunt Yvonne said, this time in my ear.

"But my home is Toronto." I felt like I had to defend my point. "I'm sorry." It was like they'd been waiting for me to wake up just to ask me this question. *Did Josh and Jerry set this up to get rid of me?* I started getting angry. I was certain my brothers were behind this.

Mom stood up, called Daniel, grabbed her keys, and marched downstairs. She and Daniel loaded up her car. Daniel asked me to reconsider, and I could tell he was trying to defuse the tension; she was hurt.

I think she really expected me to accept.

CRACK

FOUR OF US WERE HUDDLED around the coffee table in my buddy's Brampton apartment. We poked holes in our pop cans, near the base, the thumbtacks moaning as they bit through the aluminum. The resulting circle of about twenty holes was around the size of a dime. I had mine done in seconds.

"The ash goes on there." My buddy flicked his cigarette so ash covered the holes and flattened the burnt carbon with his thumb, and then waited for us to do the same. Then he pulled a little white rock from his sock and took the plastic wrap off it.

"I've got a chicken here—seven grams." He held up the walnut-sized piece of drywall-looking drug. "Costs a lot, but I'm serving you all free. Just remember to come to me afterward. Enjoy, boys." He broke the piece in quarters and handed one to each of us. "Just watch what I do." He snapped a little fragment off his quarter and placed it on his can, in the centre of the ashes. His fingers shook a little like he was holding a precious jewel. We followed his lead.

I put a particularly large piece on my can.

Ready.

He flicked his lighter and held the open flame over his crack toke and it melted into the ash. It sizzled a bit, like a tiny skillet cooking bacon. He put his mouth to the opening of his pop can and sucked in, gently pulling the flame down. The wet spot where the melted rock was sizzled louder, then collapsed in upon itself. He held in the smoke for a minute and then exhaled. It smelled like burnt cotton candy mixed with fried plastic—sweet but chemical. His chin started wagging and a line of drool rolled over his lip onto the carpet. He tried to speak but a moan came out. The rest of us lit up.

When I released my lungful of crack like a dragon blasting a plume of fire on some medieval castle, the most intense feeling vibrated my brain. I could hear the loudest ringing I've ever heard, like a locomotive train rushing by an inch from my ear. I placed my can down and the void within was filled to overflowing. I felt like a god, superhuman. Like a hundred thousand roman candles were going off in my soul. When that initial high dissipated, I did it again, and again, and again until my little quarter section was gone.

Then I got down on all fours to search the carpet for any remnants that might have fallen.

My buddies did the same.

We kept searching.

I was hooked.

CANADIAN STREETS GREASY WITH INDIGENOUS FAT

The secret history tells us
Once, a blue wolf arose from the soil.
He took as his mate a fallow deer.
There, at the head of the sea
A son was born.

Descendants of that son
Travelled light upon the grasslands
Using speed and surprise.
They learned to own nothing, to adapt to all conditions
And burning dry dung for warmth.

From out of the eastern sunrise, these homeless nomads rode.
On horseback they came,
Setting everything ablaze.
They littered the stolen streets with their bodies
And left them greasy with their own fat.

CAUGHT UP

IT WAS THE TURN OF the millennium, but the day after Y2K was odd—no crash, no power outages, no blood or violence in the streets, no Armageddon. The only thing that seemed out of place was the red University of Nevada, Las Vegas (UNLV) basketball jersey I was wearing. It was new, with the university team's fighting southern rebel mascot in the middle.

I didn't have much these days. I was with Uncle Ron drinking beer at his apartment—he'd moved back in with Jerry after his daughter had graduated high school and had moved back to the city herself. I'd begged him and Jerry for a place to stay after most of my stuff had been stolen from a local shelter, and was lucky they'd agreed. Ron and I were watching *The Saint*, starring Val Kilmer. Random farts from Solomon perfumed the stale air, reminding me that I shouldn't have fed him wet food.

I'd spent the previous night, New Year's Eve, at a friend's party. We drank ourselves into oblivion, singing and wearing those stupid Y2K glasses. As the clock edged close to midnight we congregated in the hot tub and blazed a series of fat joints, then waited for the subsequent hellfire to rip apart our lives. The girl next to me pulled down her bikini top and showed me her breasts—their fleshy presence complemented the celebratory cheers and horns that resounded throughout the house. I grabbed her and gave her a sloppy kiss to welcome in the new millennium. I think she appreciated the distraction because her tongue darted around in my mouth. There was no magic between us—we were just two young people trying to forget about the impending calamity, the emotionless kiss just an available tool of diversion.

After we unhinged our faces, I grabbed my bag of blow and cut two shoelace-sized lines on the edge of the tub. Drugs helped me forget everything I didn't want to think about and made me feel good about myself. I snorted mine first, she followed and then rubbed the leftover residue across her gums with her finger and brayed like a horse. The coke kept us up for another few hours, but there was no sex, even though we did try in the bedroom upstairs—I just couldn't get it up. Hard liquor and blow had that effect on me.

Then the music faded, conversations died out, people bid their farewells, and it was time to go. I thought of her tits as I stumbled home, and was mad at myself for not being a man, for not capitalizing. When I reached Uncle Ron's I was still wired. I leered at myself in the bathroom mirror, and my eyes looked like two piss holes in the snow.

Sleep is impossible tonight, I concluded.

I decided to go farther down the road, to see if anyone was still up over at Olive's, the church lady, where, unknown to her, our crew had our headquarters. When I got there, Olive's son Frank was up watching TV. He told me that the new hang-abouts, Stefan and Mike, two neighbourhood street kids who had no real home like me, had left a few hours before to go out on a "mission."

"What kind of a mission? Deliver drugs, shoplift at the drug store, sell shit—what?"

"I don't know." Frank shrugged.

I could tell he wanted me to leave. I couldn't blame the kid. His house had a revolving door. Olive's Christian mission sometimes left her family crowded in their own home and often without food. Frank, who was just sixteen, had done more mission work, I figured, than many pastors had done over decades in Africa. He was the same as his mom—kind, giving, and open to a fault—even if he wasn't religious. He never raised his voice around any of us, and we'd become good friends.

"Do they have dope?" I asked as I slipped my shoes back on.

"Naw. They smoked it all before they left." Frank got up. "You don't have to go," he grumbled as he shuffled past me to the washroom. "We got PB and J and bread in the cupboard, and you're welcome to it if you want."

If Jesus was like anyone, I believe he was like Frank, but without the Mohawk hairdo, facial piercings, and torn-to-shreds punk attire. But the thought of a sweet sandwich made my stomach turn, the liquor and coke sloshing around all toxic.

"Where's Tim?" I asked. He was Frank's brother. He was eighteen, looked like Alice Cooper when Cooper was young and scary—black eyeliner, black clothes, black hair shaved up the sides—and he was the opposite of his younger sibling. The constant cavalcade of homeless people in the house had hardened him, made him into what can only be described as a pure metal hell spawn who slaughtered daily goodwill by blasting Marilyn Manson and Slipknot over top of the sound of the church organ Olive had in the living room.

I'm sure that eerie mix of gospel hymns and hard-core thrash traumatized me, but Tim's reaction to all the commotion and Christian indoctrination was strange considering that most of the transient guests were *his* friends—teenaged goth misfits from group homes and juvenile detention centres who had been disowned by their families or had fled domestic abuse situations. It left me wondering if it was all some big act Tim put on as a defence against the biblical-level chaos going on around him.

"He's not here," Frank said. The sound of piss echoed in the toilet bowl. "Been gone for a couple of days." I heard the toilet flush, then he returned to his chair to flip through the channels.

I left and went back up the road to Uncle Ron's to catch some sleep.

I awoke around nine a.m. to Solomon licking my face—I was on my makeshift bed in the middle of the sunroom floor and that was his sign he needed a walk. I could hear Uncle Ron and Jerry groaning in their rooms, and a ten-dollar bill magically appeared from under my brother's door.

"Take him out, Jess," Jerry said, his voice as raspy as a desert toad.

"My fucking head's pounding." The place was filled with vodka bottles and ashtrays overflowing with joint roaches. Zig-Zag rolling papers were strewn across the sofa, looking like a trail leading up to a mountain of cigarette butts cascading over the edge of the coffee table.

Must've been one helluva scorcher, I chuckled to myself as I snatched up the money and took the dog out for his shit.

Armed with a little cash for dope, I returned Solomon to the apartment and again made my way down to Olive's. It was eleven a.m. and Mike and Stefan were in the middle of the kitchen throwing dice. Mike dressed like a flashy Puff Daddy crossed with Eminem. He looked Scottish or something, but it was hard to tell. Stefan easily pegged as Italian—olive skin and a Roman nose, and he talked with his hands and said things like "forget about it" and "mangia cake." He was much harder around the edges than anyone in our hood. He dressed like a professional weed dealer and his hair was tied up in a ponytail and was covered in a do-rag, and he had a Yankees hat perched perfectly atop his head. He'd once told me that he'd come to Canada from the United States after he'd gotten into some serious trouble down there. He towered over me and Mike and anyone else at Olive's.

Their friend, Stan, a black kid, was behind the circle of dice players holding the day's winnings. He was born with a club foot and had a severe limp and some cognitive challenges, and it was his job to dish out the round's payout to whoever threw sevens or elevens. Stan was trustworthy and always treated everyone with whatever he had—dope, food, booze, which was rare around us younger street people. I liked Stan, even if I didn't understand what he said half the time, his stutter was so bad.

There were a few other kids I didn't know rifling through the fridge.

"Y-yo, J-Jesse," Stan stuttered. "You-you w-wanna p-play?"

"I can't. I only have ten bucks," I said, "and I want to smoke a dube." I yanked out my lone bill and dangled it mid-air, hoping someone would step up and break open their weed sack and let me have a gram.

Stan smiled. "I'm a-all out-t, b-buddy."

Stefan reached into his pocket and hauled out a lean fold of bills. "I'm a-all o-out, bu-buddy." He curled up his arm and held it like a little T. Rex arm, then contorted his face. The room exploded in laugher. Stan froze and stuttered but no words came out. They all sounded like a wild pack of hyenas, and I wanted to fucking punch Stefan in the head.

Stefan peeled back the layers of his billfold, counting out his cash like he was Tony Montana in *Scarface*. He only had around $100, but to us it was like having a fortune, and he knew it.

"We had a good night," he said. He grinned and punched Mike's shoulder.

"Yeah, good night." Mike's voice petered out and he gazed a thousand-mile stare down at the linoleum floor.

Olive's music started up in the next room, so I knew she hadn't gone to church. The sound of her singing psalms cut through the tension. I expected Tim's music to soon drown her out, but he still wasn't home, apparently. I saw Frank get up from the sofa to go into his bedroom, and he waved to me on his way.

"Number one rule," Stefan went on, raising his voice above Olive's melodic petition of David. "Don't rat." The room fell silent.

What Stefan said was true: We were bound by a code—the code of silence. You only talked about what you did with those you did it with—it was better to not know than to know and have a secret that could eventually find its way out. That was our only protection.

Stefan repeated the sentiment slowly, this time running his thumb across his throat. I'd seen lots of guys warn dudes to keep their mouths shut before, but the way Stan cowered made my skin crawl.

One of the kids near the fridge stepped forward to put a glass on the table and fill it with juice. He took a swig and then said, "I got a gram," and flicked a little green baggy my way. It bounced and landed square in front of me. He either didn't care about Stefan and his warning or was too daft to listen.

"Thanks." I opened it, rolled up a pregnant spliff, and invited the room out. Only Stefan, Mike, and Stan accepted and we went out to our spot at the side of the building. Stan trailed behind me. Mike and Stefan shifted from corner to corner, staying in the shadows.

"I don't want to be out here too long," Mike said, ducking behind the cement wall blocking the view of the building next to us. Stefan joined him and kept his eyes on the pathway near the road. Stan and I held our ground out in the open as we blazed up the joint and each took a toke. Sirens in the distance moaned and whined, a familiar sound in the hood. They were much too far away to catch us, but I kept my eyes peeled regardless. Stan took another drag, then passed it off to Stefan. He, then Mike, took a short, almost non-drag then passed it back to me.

"T-that's b-boy d-dem," Stan said, his eyes trained on mine. "L-lots of squad c-cars 'round here l-last night—t-they even had the g-ghetto bird in the air." He made the noise of a helicopter and pretended to duck low. He nudged my arm. "C-careful, J-Jess."

Mike and Stefan fell dead silent watching Stan, then cackled, only softer and more sinister than in the kitchen.

Stan whispered again, so only I could hear. "Be careful."

Mike stopped laughing. "Yo, blood, I see you got some bunk clothes, homeless motherfucker. You like my jersey?" He pointed down to his UNLV shirt, pulling at the bottom to make the team's logo more visible. It was this season's. I couldn't afford something that nice.

"Yeah, dog, it's fresh," I said. "I wish I was dipped out like that, but I'm jus—"

"You can have it," Stefan interrupted, "if you can help us out."

His offer hung in the air as I took another drag.

"Sure," I said, releasing the smoke. "What do you want?"

Stan started shaking his head, his lips pursed shut. Mike walked in front of him.

"Two things," Stefan continued. "We're trying to go out west tonight and know you have connections—can you link us with a place to go? Maybe even a ride?"

I took another puff. Seemed reasonable—ride, place to stay, no problem.

"And we hungry as fuck," Stefan said, rubbing his belly and smiling. "Can you do us a solid and order us a pizza? I ain't no good at it and don't like talking on the phone neither. Plus, we'll give you a whole pizza on your own for doing it."

"Order you pizza? What the fuck is wrong with you?" I laughed and coughed on smoke, the pressure burning my throat and chest. I noticed Stan was gone. He must've slipped in through the side door, didn't even stay to finish the blunt.

"Okay. Give me the jersey right now and I'll do it." As long as I didn't have to do anything sexual or pay out money to get clothed and fed, I was game to do whatever they were asking.

Mike pulled the jersey off and gave it to me and I slipped it on.

"One more thing," Stefan said. "Just ask for the ride—don't say who it's for."

"Whatever," I said as I admired my new dips—it fit snug around my waist and looked crisp as it hung over my frame.

When we got indoors, I got on the phone with my buddy Shawn, a friend I'd hitchhiked and gone to high school with. Shawn said he could hook up a place to stay in Calgary, but that the ride would be harder to find. I knew he was puzzled by my request—I knew how to travel long distance, I knew how to hitchhike, and I already knew people to stay with in Calgary any time. Before I got off the phone, I made a mistake: I let it slip that the ride wasn't for me. But I wasn't clear who it was for.

"That makes a little more sense," Shawn said as he hung up. "I was wondering if you'd banged your head somewhere."

Next, I ordered three large pizzas, and tailored my very own just the way I liked it: ground beef, pepperoni, and extra cheese.

Fucking beautiful.

When the pizza dude arrived, Stefan and Mike told me to tip him extra. I gave him a twenty.

"Thanks, buddy," he said. "Best tip all night!"

I went home to Uncle Ron's thinking it was the simplest work I'd ever done. I was grateful to my new friends that I'd started the new millennium in such a positive way.

"*The Saint*'s a remake, you know," Uncle Ron said as the credits rolled at the end. "I like the original better." He flicked his thumb in his beer and it made a blopping noise, like a stone dropped down a well. Solomon cut another fart. "Jesus," Uncle Ron said, "I'm suffocating over here." The dog lifted his head as if he knew we were talking about him.

Just then the eleven p.m. news flash came across the TV. A cab driver had been murdered, New Year's Eve, near the Gateway Six movie theatre in Brampton. The reporter went on to say that police were looking for two suspects—a tall man with black hair in a ponytail and a shorter man with blond hair, both in their late teens or early twenties.

"If anyone has any information, they are encouraged to contact Peel Police," the reporter said. A picture of the murdered cabbie flashed across the screen, and Uncle Ron went to change the channel.

"No," I said, knocking the remote out of his hand. I stared at the name of the cabbie—Baljinder Singh Rai, 48, father of two.

It was Toronto's first murder of 2000. I swear I heard a helicopter and Stan stammering. Stan lowering his head in silence while Stefan pulled out his roll of bills like a big shot. Everyone in the kitchen laughing. How Stefan and Mike had moved to avoid unwanted attention, watching their angles and lines of sight, like we all did when we shoplifted or ran from the police.

"C-careful, J-Jess," Stan had said.

I stood up, my legs trembled underneath me, and I fell backward onto Uncle Ron.

"What the fuck?" he said. The room started spinning, and I ran to the bathroom to throw up, but I missed the toilet bowl and hit the sides of the sink and tub and got vomit on the front of my shirt.

Uncle Ron ran in. "Jesse. What's going on?"

I wiped my mouth with my shirt then realized it was the jersey—my nice new gift from my nice new friend Mike. I fell back onto my ass, up against the towel rack. The shirt, the pizza, the ride out west, the "mission" from the night before—I fell for everything. I was caught up in something huge.

I didn't even have an alibi for the time of the murder on New Year's—I was with that drunk chick doing blow, trying to score. I'd made all the phone calls, gave the pizza guy the cash, talked with the pizza place and given my name, and had the shirt Mike was likely wearing when the crime was committed.

I vomited again. The small black pubic hair I could see on the bowl's edge seemed immense, the smell of urine dominated my nostrils, nauseating me further, my uncle's breathing behind me sounded like the bellows in a blacksmith's forge. He was scared, I could tell, and the sound of my own blood coursing through my ears thundered louder than a jet engine. I sat down on the tub, clutching the edge. I ripped off the jersey and threw it onto the floor. I wanted to take a shower all of a sudden, but knew nothing could wash off the filth of what they'd done or the trouble I was in.

Uncle Ron looked at the shirt. "What?"

He had no clue.

"They did it," I shouted. "They fucking killed that taxi guy and gave me this shirt!" A stream of tears rolled down my cheeks but I wasn't crying. It was a mix of fear and rage and confusion. I was under a giant's thumb, and it was pressing me further and further through the bathroom floor into hell, crushing every bone in my body.

"Don't you say a word," Uncle Ron said, bending down to me. "Just shut the fuck up. You don't want trouble, if I think you're saying what I think you're saying."

I backed up against the shower wall, shocked. "You don't understand," I said. "I'm involved. I can't shut up."

He shook his head and scrunched up his face like he did when someone fucked around with his money. He was like me—a street person—we weren't supposed to talk. Not now, not ever, no matter the circumstances or the trouble. He was someone who'd done time, was solid, would solve problems at the drop of a hat.

He grabbed my arm and hauled me to my feet. "Snap out of it," he shouted. "You've gotta think." His lunchbox hands squeezed my shoulders. "I love you, Jesse. I'm trying to protect you. Burn the shirt." He picked it up and handed it to me.

I stared at it, wishing the nightmare would end.

He closed my fist around the shirt, holding my hand in his. "Your life's on the line."

I knew what that meant. I ran out of the apartment and down to the dumpster out back, and started gathering paper and sticks. I laid the jersey on my collection of kindling and sprayed the wood pile with the lighter accelerant Jerry kept in the apartment for his Zippo, but just before I struck a match, a sobering thought came to me. I knew Frank had seen me the night before—twice in fact. I'd stopped by Olive's at nine p.m. before I went to the Y2K party, and again at around three a.m. when it was over, and he'd told me that Mike and Stefan had gone out. He was also there, today, right before I got the jersey from Mike, so he would've seen Mike with it on earlier, and then me leaving with it later on after I'd eaten the pizza.

I put my match back in my pocket, rescued the jersey from its funeral pyre, and hightailed it to Olive's. When I got there, I peered through the sliding glass doors. It was dark. I banged on the window a few times but no one answered. Olive's two cats pawed at the glass.

"Frank!" I yelled into the night sky, then at the cats, hoping to conjure him up from thin air. The crickets stopped chirping, though, and a neighbour told me to shut the fuck up. I slumped against the doors, shirt in hand. I considered burning it again. Then a light came on in the kitchen, and I saw a hooded figure shuffling around inside. It was Frank, making himself a peanut butter sandwich. I banged on the glass even harder and held the jersey up against it, finally catching his attention. He made his way to the doors and opened them, wiping crust out of his eyes.

"Dude, fuck. I'm sleeping. Calm your shit." He squinted. "Do you need to crash or something? Come in—but shut the fuck up."

"No, no. It's more serious," I blurted out. "It's about this jersey and Mike and Stefan and the pizza and—"

"Whoa. Slow down. I'm barely awake," he said and rammed a slice of PB and J into his mouth.

"See this?" I shoved the jersey in front of his face. "That's Mike's. I made a few calls and ordered food and they gave it to me for doing them a favour—remember?"

"Yeah, so?"

"You saw him with this on yesterday and earlier today, right?"

"Yeah. Why?"

"They did something terrible," I said and glanced around, scared someone else might hear. "They tried to frame me by giving it to me and making me make phone calls for rides out west and pizza. I need you to be my witness."

Frank's eyes widened.

"The shirt is his, not mine. I'm going to call the cops and explain it all." I put the shirt in Frank's hands and asked him to leave it on the couch or give it back to Mike when he saw him. I could tell he was having a hard time understanding what I was doing, why I'd rat them out.

"Listen," I said. "They killed someone. I don't believe in hurting people like that. Selling dope and stealing is one thing, but murdering is another."

Frank shook his head, threw the jersey on the sofa, and shut the glass doors.

He'd never done that before, closed the door in my face. I wasn't sure he'd help me.

RAT

"I'D LIKE TO REPORT A murder," I said. "The cabbie from yesterday—Baljinder Singh Rai."

The line was silent, then I heard a click and the 911 operator say, "Murder? Where? Be specific."

"Brampton. New Year's Eve. Gateway Six," I said and rubbed the sweat off my free hand onto the arm of the couch. I tried lighting a cigarette but my thumb shook so violently I couldn't strike the wheel to create a spark. I flicked it a few more times—nothing.

"Okay, sir. Where are you?" Her voice sounded firmer, more focused.

I told her the address. I was still at Uncle Ron's place.

"What's your name?"

"Me? I'm Jesse Thistle. Two guys I know did it. Stefan and Mike. I don't know their last names."

She told me to stay on the line. Ten seconds passed, maybe, and I looked around for Uncle Ron. *He must've locked himself in his room*, I thought. *He doesn't want to see me become Judas.* I again tried to light my cigarette, but, again, I failed.

The 911 operator came back on the line. "I've dispatched officers to your location. Do not leave." I heard a chorus of radio chatter in the background, a barrage of police lingo I didn't understand.

Before I knew it, someone was pounding on the door. If it was the police, I had no idea how they'd bypassed lobby security. It'd literally taken them one minute to come—I was still on the phone. I hung up and peered through the peephole and saw two huge men in uniform, although they must've left their jackets in the squad car. Early twenties, their hands hovering over their firearms. My stomach dropped. They weren't fucking around.

This is it. Go time.

I panicked a bit and scanned the apartment for an exit—over near Solomon's bed, then over to Jerry's door, then the sunroom—and considered jumping out the window two stories to the ground below. Running away was my way of dealing with life, my solution when things got hairy, and was something ingrained in me since my days with Dad and travelling with my old Adidas bag. And it always seemed to work. But there was nowhere on Earth I could run to avoid this mega-sized clusterfuck.

"Mr. Thistle. Jesse," a voice thundered. "We know you're in there. We just got a call from dispatch." He hammered on the door so it shook in its frame, and I swear loosened a few marbles in my skull. His radio was going berserk, but I could make out that more officers were en route. I heard sirens screaming outside. They were getting closer and sounded like they were coming from every direction. The idea of a swarm of cops frightened me, but running was impossible now. I opened the door as Uncle Ron came out of his room. His hands were clenched.

One police officer's arms were the size of cement pillars, all veiny and tanned; the left was covered in tribal tattoos. His bulging muscles looked constricted by his tiny blue shirt. His partner was shorter, more refined, with a uniform that actually fit his torso.

The second guy did all the talking.

"Jesse? We've come to escort you to 21 Division. We need your statement."

The elevator doors in the hallway opened and more police appeared.

"Let me get my jacket and shoes," I said, my head spinning.

"No problem. Take your time."

Uncle Ron came up behind me, slipped a pack of smokes in my pocket, and told me to be strong. I can't remember if he said anything to the officers before they ushered me out of the building, but I thought of him the whole ride to the station.

I was surprised at how nice the officers were. They cracked jokes about their jobs and some of the stuff they'd seen earlier that day. They even asked if I was hungry or needed anything before we reached the station.

I blurted out, "Not hungry, but this is like being in a real-life episode of *Law and Order*, eh?" I saw the big guy nudge his partner. He was too stupid to play games, and too stupid to pretend he was my friend.

When we arrived and got out of the car, but before we entered the station, they cuffed me, saying it was for my own safety, and for the safety of the officers inside. The cuffs bit into my wrists as the bigger officer hoisted my arms up behind my back, pushing me forward, parading me past clerical officers toiling at their desks. They acknowledged Mr. Muscles, but none made eye contact with me. It was as if I was a criminal, or some trophy prize they'd dragged home to momma.

The interrogation room had one table with two chairs facing each other. There was a video camera in the corner, and on the desk were two coffees, an empty ashtray, and a pad of paper and a pen.

"Tell us everything you know," the smart officer said. He lit a smoke and pushed the coffee my way. "Don't be afraid." He motioned to his buddy, who unlocked the cuffs, then left us alone. I took a sip of coffee, and the red light on the camera went on.

I told him everything: about the jersey, the pizza, the Y2K party, the drunk girl, the call to Shawn, Frank as my witness to it all—everything. He jotted down things and let me speak freely. At times I felt like he wasn't paying attention. Every so often he'd offer me a new coffee and the big guy would come in and take away the old cup and give me a new one. They did the same with the cigarette butts after I'd smoked—always returning with a fresh new ashtray and a lone cigarette.

"I think we have some evidence," the officer said after a couple hours, as he nodded to the camera, "but not enough to charge anyone." The big officer came back into the room with his own chair and sat beside his partner on the other side of the table. "Did you see any weapons on Mike or Stefan?" the smart one asked.

The steel of the chair was cold against my back as I shifted for comfort. Then it came to me. "I don't know, but Stefan has a big knife. It's about nine inches long with a pearl handle. Serious knife." The two officers turned to face one another.

"Draw it," the big guy said, and tore notes off the pad of paper, leaving a blank page exposed. "As much as you can."

The smart officer bit the nail of his index finger and started shaking his left knee up and down. I glanced and saw that the light on the camera was still on. The lens made me feel like a tiny ant getting roasted under a giant magnifying glass in the sun. I wiped away the sweat drenching my brow and sketched out the knife—a long, sharp blade with a well-formed grip and hilt. The picture was crappy but it conveyed the vital data.

"How do you know he had this knife?" the smart officer asked. His intense stare told me this was the most important piece of information I had to offer. The hum of the neon light above us sounded like a cloud of road-allowance black flies.

"Because I taught him how to scam welfare three weeks ago."

They looked at each other, puzzled.

"Stefan's homeless and Olive was sick of having him around the house eating all the food, so I felt sorry for him and told him to go to the shelter to see the emergency social service worker who cuts cheques. All you need is a rental letter and a phone number."

Both officers leaned in, and I could tell they were having a hard time following.

"They give out $1,000 for start-up if you have that. It's to get you set up in a place with food and clothes—all that shit. But most people just scam it for money and stay at a friend's house. I do it all the time—forge rental documents so I have some money—"

"What does that have to do with the knife?" the smart guy interrupted. He pushed the drawing into the centre of the table, then flicked his butt, blowing smoke up toward the light, where it swirled around the bulb then was sucked up through the ceiling vent.

"When Stefan scammed welfare he bought a knife and some white baseball gloves. I thought it was a waste of money, but, hey, that's what he did. I hear he and Mike are back living at the shelter now. They just go to Olive's during the day."

The officers sat back, and a third, much older, officer came in and said they had what they needed. Then they took all the items out of the room except my chair and the table, and left me sitting there for a couple of hours. After, I was taken down to the holding cells. I got a single cell with an iron waffle bed—the kind they make drunk people sleep on until they sober up.

I awoke to find a perfectly bald detective in a grey suit standing on the other side of the bars. He didn't waste time with introductions, he just opened the door and instructed me to follow him. There were no handcuffs this time, but I knew not to fuck around. Out back of the station, there was an armada of black SUVs. A massive black cop was driving the one I got into with the detective. They didn't say a word to each other—not hi, nothing, they didn't even nod to one another.

The black fella scared the shit out of me—he looked like a Navy SEAL, but was dressed in what appeared to me to be a thousand-dollar suit, and was wearing a pair of black sunglasses. His knuckles were scarred, and he had cauliflower ears. I'd seen ears, scars, and knuckles like that before, on professional boxers and rugby players, but never on cops. I tried not to stare at him but he caught me in the rearview mirror. He turned up the chatter crackling over their walkie-talkies.

With sirens blazing on the lead car, our SUVs blew through a series of red lights—an ominous caravan of justice speeding mercilessly toward its destination. The morning sun didn't penetrate the tinted windows of our vehicle; it spilled in only briefly through the windshield as we turned and drove east a spell before we met another gang of trucks parked behind an abandoned warehouse.

The detective and black guy told me to stay put and jumped out to meet a crew of bigger, even scarier men armed with guns. A few were dressed in black-and-grey-camouflage commando gear, utility belts, and bulletproof vests covered in what looked like ammo magazines. I heard dogs barking in the back of one of their trucks. It was the Peel SWAT and K9 units. They formed a half-circle around the detective, who clapped his hands at every order he gave. The men jumped at his commands, checked their gear, then separated into groups of three and got in six different vehicles.

"The shelter," the black guy said to the detective as he got into the driver's seat. "We're going to apprehend them there." The detective slapped the dashboard. I saw then that he had two handguns—one under his suit jacket under his arm in a holster, and one strapped to his leg—I could see the impression under his pants. He rubbed his hand over his bald head. "After we get them," he said to me, "we're gonna take you up to the Major Crime Unit on Courtney Park. We need more info from you."

"I'll tell you whatever I know," I said, fearful of the power I knew he wielded.

Outside the shelter we saw four homeless men emerge near the smoking pit. The SUVs circled round the building, reminding me of a well-coordinated pack of wolves stalking prey. The sound of truck tires on gravel was the only sound they made; the men in the smoking pit created more noise as they shivered and complained in the cold January dawn.

I heard the black guy unclick the safety on his gun. He motioned to the lead detective, who ordered the others to wait until they had confirmation. The men in the SUV to our right, fifty metres away, were prepping their guns. They stood in position, behind their doors, which were now splayed open for protection. There we waited and waited. Ten minutes went by, until over the radio I heard a voice that said, "Negative on the suspects. Staff says they didn't stay here last night. Stand down." The black cop clicked the safety back on his gun, and before I knew it the pack of SUVs was driving off again.

When we got to the Major Crime Unit building, about a thirty-minute drive from the shelter, I was placed in a room with plush couches and a TV that didn't work. They told me I had to stay there until they apprehended Mike and Stefan. I asked for a phone call and they denied me. There I languished—for twenty hours.

It was the next evening when they finally came and got me. I'd stretched my shirt up around my head and tucked my arms in for warmth and was sleeping when the bald detective arrived. He seemed happy.

"We got them at three p.m., Jess," he said. "They were at Olive's."

I was relieved at the thought of them getting arrested, but I wasn't happy to hear they'd been at Olive's. I thought of Frank, Tim, and Olive and wondered where they had been when it'd happened. I hoped they weren't home.

The cops never did ask me any more questions. They simply drove me home and told me I'd be okay because they'd protect my status as an informer.

No more than six hours passed before I started hearing that I was a dead man walking.

AFTERMATH

I WAS TERRIFIED THAT I was now in danger, a known informer, but curiosity overcame me. I decided to walk over to Olive's to see what had happened during Mike and Stefan's arrest. I couldn't get any closer than two hundred metres because the area was blocked off by police tape.

Buzzing about were forensics units, police vans, squad cars, sharply suited detectives, and uniformed police officers. There must've been around a dozen people. A few of my street friends stood transfixed, watching the commotion from a distance. They didn't notice me. The investigative team carried out box after box of evidence, and one had Tim's leather jacket in his hand. I imagined lines of determined ants hauling away leaves to their colony-headquarters. Their industry was perfect, inhuman, insidious.

I saw the shattered back window of the apartment, glass strewn all over Olive's porch and out onto the parking lot, where, only two days earlier, Stan had warned me to be careful. The blue-and-red strobe of the squad-car lights refracted off the shards, sending rays of broken colour in every direction, dancing across my eyes, carving the scene into the back of my cranium.

The police must've entered, gangbusters, that way.

Olive, Frank, and Tim were nowhere in sight. I searched for Olive's cats and saw the bald detective arrive in his SUV. He ducked under the yellow tape and entered the apartment through the destroyed glass doors. He, again, seemed to be calling the shots, pointing his finger and making younger cops jump. I looked around for the big black cop but he wasn't there.

I walked closer and caught the attention of one of the neighbourhood street kids who stood watching. "What's going on?" I asked, pretending like I knew nothing. A look of disgust shot across his face.

"Don't chat to me," he said. "You'll get it soon enough, you fucking rat." He spit on the ground, mounted his bike, and flipped me the bird as he rode away.

An old lady nearby said, "What a rude young man."

I had broken a cardinal rule. *The* cardinal rule—*omertà*, silence above all else. Old friends I'd dealt drugs or gone to raves with wanted nothing to do with me. I was seen as untrustworthy, vile, scum—the worst kind of person.

People lured me to parties or to dark corners of the park with the promise of smoking a joint, then jumped me and beat me up. One tried to knife me in an alley. Another beat my leg with a baseball bat after he'd invited me into his place for a drink; the muscle on my thigh was clobbered so badly it was purple and black halfway up my belly, and it was nearly impossible for me to walk. I was lucky, though, that he never got to my knees—his original target. I surely would've been crippled.

I bumped into a friend at the mall, who I used to sell sheets of acid with a few years before. "I'd have done the same thing," he said when I saw him in front of the Chinese food stand. I was in between meals and he offered me a bowl of stew his mother cooked for lunch. He had it in a container in his knapsack. I ate it, but it tasted funny—bitter, sour, off or something. When I was done he looked me right in the eye and said, "Eat shit and die, motherfucker." I was sick for a couple of weeks afterward. It was the worst retaliation of all—biological warfare, street style.

The people who did talk with me only did so to give me attitude or tell me I wasn't worth the skin I was born in.

All the maltreatment left me wondering if I'd done the right thing, if helping to deliver justice was worth it. I mean, maybe the cops wouldn't have found me with the shirt. Maybe Stefan and Mike would have gotten away with it. Maybe I should've just laid low until things cooled off. Maybe I should've just taken my chances.

When I explained that to Uncle Ron, he assured me that I'd done the right thing. "It takes a lot of balls to do what you did, Jess. Don't doubt it."

I was surprised.

Jerry and Leeroy, too, remained steadfast. Leeroy got back from Vancouver right before the murder.

"What the fuck, guy?" he said when he first saw me. "You just left me out there to die."

"I'm sorry. The logs floated by, there was light on the mountains, we were starving, and I had to go." He crossed his arms, like he wasn't convinced, but we still started hanging out. Things were different, though. We didn't share or trust the way we did before I'd abandoned him, he wouldn't share dope with me as freely, or booze—but he stuck by my side and defended me.

Jerry and Leeroy were spooked by the company I'd gotten myself involved with, though—killers! But they stood with me, my brother and best friend, as everything collapsed around me. They never once told anyone where I was, even though I was sure people offered them rewards for my whereabouts.

Around March a couple of new detectives showed up at Uncle Ron's apartment. They said they were doing follow-up on the investigation. Apparently, they'd been searching for the knife I'd drawn but had come up with nothing. It was a key piece of evidence.

"We even dredged the pond next to the complex where Mike and Stefan ran after they killed the cabbie," one detective said. "We had a team of divers there for a month looking for it, but it wasn't there."

The detectives then told us that post-mortem examinations indicated that Baljinder Singh Rai had sustained massive stab wounds to the face and neck with a sharp object, most likely a knife nine inches in length or longer. Just like I'd drawn. That Rai had evidently picked up two males who matched Stefan and Mike's description at the bus depot in downtown Brampton at ten p.m. on December 31. That he'd then driven them to Gateway Six, just behind the Pizza Hut, where he'd been attacked. They said Rai had held on just long enough to alert staff at the store, before he bled to death.

That turned my stomach. My heart hurt for his two children—I was raised without a father and knew that horrible pain well.

"But Mike and Stefan aren't saying a word," the detective said. "And without the knife, we just can't be sure." His last comment lingered, like a poisonous gas that scorched my lungs, robbing me of breath.

I'm fighting in the trenches on two fronts now. Against the criminals and cops, I thought, because he'd implied the thing I feared most, the reason why they were in the apartment taking Uncle Ron's and Jerry's statements. Why they'd begun canvassing people in my extended family, like Uncle Ralph, who was a Metro copper down at 52 Division. In Ralph's case, they'd asked him for my character profile, and if I was capable of taking another man's life. In Uncle Ron's case, they'd asked for exact times of my movements on December 31, and if I acted strange the next night when we watched *The Saint*. Jerry never did tell me what they asked him; he avoided all my questions.

It also began making sense that they'd held me for twenty-four hours after I'd reported the murder, and that I was denied a phone call the whole time I was in custody. The way they had collected my cigarette butts and coffee cups, one by one, during the initial questioning also pointed to the fact that they'd been collecting my DNA.

I realized I was still a suspect, and had been since the night of the murder. I was a suspect the police couldn't rule out because they'd failed to find the murder weapon, and Mike and Stefan wouldn't squeal on each other. Moreover, I was roughly the same size as Mike, and Leeroy, amazingly, was the exact same height and weight as Stefan. It was well documented, too, that I'd had the shirt the crime was committed in. I wasn't sure if they ever considered Leeroy a suspect, though. I wasn't even sure if it was all in my head, or if any of it was true. Maybe the pressure of everything was beginning to make me see things that weren't grounded in reality.

"Just show up in court and tell the judge what you know," the detective said before he left.

I knew that the expression on my face betrayed me—my mind was fracturing.

"They're the ones charged, Jesse," he said, as if to comfort me. "But a conviction is another matter altogether. We have to look at all possibilities."

I held on to that sliver of hope for justice for two months until it was time for the preliminary hearing. But I questioned myself every day until then. I hid out at Uncle Ron's, and drank and smoked crack until the paranoia forced me to hide under my brother's bed for hours at a time. I wouldn't even take the dog out for his bathroom breaks. My weight dropped and I was afraid to even put garbage in the apartment building's chute, thinking it was the perfect spot for my enemies to ambush me and make me disappear, just like Dad had.

At the end of May, I was called to give evidence for the Crown at the old courthouse on Clarence Street, right in the heart of my old neighbourhood. The courtroom was filled with many of Mike and Stefan's friends—some from around our hood, others I'd never seen before. No one I knew came—not Leeroy nor Jerry nor Uncle Ron. I couldn't blame them. I could swear the people who were there mouthed, "You're dead," to me from the back benches. I tried to ignore them and sat up near the front, a few rows back from the Crown lawyer, where I knew I'd be safe if anything went awry.

Mike and Stefan entered the courtroom and glared at me from the bench behind the bailiff. I stared at them to show I wasn't scared, even though I was shitting bricks. Stefan leered right back. I couldn't turn away and let him win.

When I took the stand, the Crown asked me to run through the details. He paused in between questions and let me think, getting me to note exactly how Stefan got the knife and how I'd helped him scam welfare. To me, the whole thing made sense—I'd been framed, Stefan and Mike were the framers, they were the murderers.

I kept my head up after the Crown finished with me; I sensed it was important to keep an air of confidence. I adjusted my shirt and tie and glanced over and saw that the judge had sketched out a few notes—a couple of words had red underlines.

"Defence," he said, his voice a slab of granite authority. "It's your turn."

The judge peered over his glasses at me, and I held my back straight. I thought it might make him respect me more, but his head just swivelled, detached, unimpressed. He pushed his glasses up with his finger and continued on. I thought he might have secretly given me the middle finger. But the Crown smiled at me as he took his seat.

The defence, however, was having none of it. He walked up to the bench. It was hard to tell if he was angry or happy or what—his face was expressionless. He reminded me of an old west gunslinger at high noon right before a showdown—Johnny Fucking Law. He drew first, interrogating me on where I'd been on December 31.

I was frank. "I can't produce a witness as to where I was that night—I can barely remember where I was or who was at that party, but I didn't kill anyone."

He asked the same question a hundred times over, just in different ways.

I fiddled with my thumbs and thought of my grandma and the time she caught me stealing when I was young.

Finally, I yelled, "And, yes, I am a criminal! Have been since childhood. And, yes, I do drugs. And these are the drugs I do." I proceeded to list over a hundred different kinds of liquids, pills, powders, substances, herbs, plants, moulds, and cacti—every drug that I'd ever done since boyhood. I finished with, "But that doesn't make me someone whose word isn't good!"

The Crown's face had gone ghost white. He was flabbergasted.

Hell, I was flabbergasted. I'd just sunk my own testimony with my honesty. It was totally on the fly. I was an addict, a fucked-up addict. I had to deal with it. End of story.

The defence leaned over to the Crown's desk and whispered loud enough for me to hear, "Solid witness you got there." He turned to Stefan and Mike and grinned. I didn't wait to see their reaction before I again peered over at the judge.

"That's it, Mr. Thistle," he said. "You are relieved." His voice sounded like an ice shelf sheering off into the ocean—kaboom.

My legs wobbled as I slid out of the witness stand and bobbed toward the back doors. The onlookers were confused at what had just happened. Even Stefan, Mike, the lawyers, and the judge had puzzled expressions on their faces. I'd simultaneously given the Crown what it needed to go forward with a trial, while leaving the defence with enough ammunition to call my testimony into question.

As I exited the courtroom, I was approached by an East Indian man around my age.

"Hi, Jesse," he said.

My adrenaline made it hard for me to focus.

"My name is Paul Singh. We were in the same Grade 10 class."

It was difficult to tell, but I did recognize him as the quiet newcomer I'd gone to high school with, a boy who was unsure of his English back then. Paul had no accent at all now.

"Yeah, I remember you," I said, still not fully aware of what I'd just done, or if I'd get attacked outside.

"Baljinder Rai was my uncle." His lip quivered. "I want to thank you for doing what you did—calling the police. I know it wasn't easy." His eyes teared up and he moved in for a hug. I opened my arms like a thistle in bloom, wrapping every leaf around him, thorns outward, keeping us both safe.

"Don't mention it," I said. "I did what I had to do."

He invited me to a celebration of his uncle's life, but I declined.

A few months later, the Crown cut a deal with Mike. There was still no knife. Whatever happened, Mike MacDonald pleaded guilty to manslaughter and got ten years. Stefan Miceli pleaded guilty to second-degree murder and was sentenced to life without chance of parole for thirteen years.

Me, I got a lifetime of people thinking I was a rat. That I could live with, because I knew what really happened—they tried to make me their patsy, and I dealt with it. What other choice did I have as a young Native homeless man? And I knew that the code of the streets was bullshit—everyone cracks, no exceptions.

I never found out if Frank had my back with the jersey, or even if it mattered. When I reconnected with him, I didn't have the heart to ask him about it. I didn't want to put him in the same position I was in.

A BOTTLE FULL OF PILLS

I STARTED SLEEPING ROUGH IN parks, under bushes, on benches in my old neighbourhood—my whole social web was destroyed by the murder case. I went to Olive's new apartment periodically, but she banned me from her couch after a while—something that'd never happened before. I understood—she didn't want me around because of the mayhem I'd been involved in, and she had to protect her family. It became clear, too, that Tim had a score to settle with me.

"Where's my bloody leather jacket?" he'd yell, his fists held aloft ready to strike me. "Ask your friends, the cops, where the fuck my jacket is!" I never did find out why the cops confiscated his jacket or if they returned it later.

I ventured over to Mississauga and began using the Salvation Army shelter there. It was way back in the industrial section of town, at least three hours away by bus from my usual stomping grounds. I stayed for a month but felt isolated so I went back to Brampton. But I still couldn't go back to the Brampton shelter—I'd blown welfare start-up money after the preliminary hearing.

One night, around midnight, drunk and high, I ventured to Leeroy's parents' house. His father and mother had welcomed him home after Vancouver and forgave him—it was like the return of the prodigal son. Sylvia had long since gotten married and started a family of her own, working as a special needs teacher. She'd really come full circle from the Sylvia I remembered in grade school.

I banged on the window. No Leeroy. I pounded on the door and hollered and heard his dog barking. Still no Leeroy. I'd watched him jimmy open his bedroom window in the basement before, so I crawled down into the window well and pushed the glass up and over to the left in spurts. It popped right open. I poked my head in and yelled his name. The dog rushed over, barking. I dropped down into the room, rubbed the dog's head, wandered to the kitchen to make myself a snack, and started watching some TV in his bedroom. The phone rang, which startled me.

Then it hit me. I'd broken into my best friend's house. I'd violated his space, our friendship, his family. It was much worse than me leaving him in Vancouver. I got up, locked the door behind me, and went into his garage and fell asleep on a pile of wood.

When I awoke, Leeroy was standing over me.

"You broke into my house?"

I leaned back against the wall, my leg slipping on a log.

"You crossed the fucking line this time!"

"I'm sorry! I didn't have anywhere to go. I didn't steal anything."

"Fuck, man," he said, but then the expression on his face changed. "You can stay here if you want."

His pity wounded me, made me feel inferior. I told him I was sorry again and scurried away. I slept behind the arena attached to the school where I'd gone to junior high, across the way from where we'd smoked our first cigarettes together.

I felt like Leeroy was avoiding me, like I'd lost my best friend. I figured people would say I was out to rob him blind. Maybe it was payback for Vancouver. Whatever the reasons, without my best friend in my corner, I had nothing.

I was distraught about everything—the case, being a social outcast, being homeless and hopeless. I went to a drugstore and stole a bottle of a hundred acetaminophen tablets and ate them all before I could think better of it. Then I went and sat by the river with my feet in the water, the rush cool against my skin.

My toes numbed as I wiggled them in my shoes. A roar filled my ears—like an approaching hurricane. I checked the treetops and the leaves were still—there was no breeze. Stretched thin and sapped of energy, my vision crowded black at the sides, then formed into deep tunnels. I stood up, but my legs had a hard time holding my weight. I wobbled along the pathway, grabbing branches as I fell down on my knees. I hoisted myself up again using the edge of a garbage bin and attempted to breathe deeply, but no amount of air could fill my lungs—they gurgled and filled with fluid. My heart beat faster than if I'd run a marathon at full sprint. I was dying. I panicked and walked the half-mile it took to get to the hospital.

I glanced in the glass before the emergency department doors slid open and saw myself—deep-set charcoal eyes, plastic-looking skin. I looked like a grey alien.

"I swallowed a bottle of Tylenol," I said to the nurse at the desk. "An hour ago." Without a word, she ran into the back and a team of orderlies came out and put me on a gurney. I gave them Olive's phone number and then my world went white.

My eyes cracked open. I was in a room, strapped onto a bed, with doctors and nurses buzzing around. I heard a beeping, and a sound like Darth Vader next to me. There was a mask strapped over my face, and I called out, "Grandma," but heard nothing. The neon lights above captivated me. The doctors kept running around. I coughed. Breathing was even more laboured now. My head felt thinner, the ringing louder, the wind roaring through me, carrying me away.

A doctor appeared, ripped off the mask, and jammed a tube down my throat. I watched as black fluid crept down the tube and filled my belly, then spilled out of my mouth, down my neck, and all over my blue gown. Then lights. More doctors rushing. And silence.

———

"Wake up," someone said.

Their breath smelled like onions. Whoever it was peeled my eyes open and a light blinded me. I tried to look away.

"Hello," another said. "Jesse. Mr. Thistle."

I tried to respond but the tube made it hard to speak. Then silence again.

When I finally came to I was in a room with a guard. I was told that was so I wouldn't run away or hurt myself. Apparently, I'd woken up earlier and ripped the tubes right out of my body, undid the straps, and took off. The hospital rang the local police precinct and put out an APB on me—I couldn't remember if the police had brought me back, or if I'd wandered back myself.

"Rest easy," the guard said. "The doctors will be by shortly."

He looked familiar, and told me we'd played together as kids way back in grade school. "We used to scrap, but that school was nuts back then."

I laughed. I remembered him stomping me for playground supremacy. He'd been in one of the rival gangs.

"You've had a rough go of it, eh?" he said.

I broke down.

When the doctor showed up, she informed me that I'd taken a lethal dose of slow-release acetaminophen. "It's one of the hardest overdoses to treat. It releases acetaminophen at a steady rate. We try to treat it with liquid charcoal—which absorbs toxic substances—but you may still have a number of pills lodged in your digestive tract and so are very much at risk. Any more time and your liver would have been destroyed. Did you hear a roaring wind?"

"Yes."

"That's how thin your blood was pumping over your eardrums."

I had to explain to a psychiatrist that I'd meant to end my life, but I now wanted to live.

"Why did you do it?" he asked.

"I destroyed a lifelong friendship, and I don't have anywhere to go. I just can't stop fucking up."

"More common than you know."

He filled in a form, told me I needed rest, and decided to hold me for at least another week. I'd already been under observation for seventy-two hours. I gave the attendants the phone numbers of everyone I knew— Leeroy, my grandparents, Olive, Jerry, and Josh. Only my brothers called to see if I was okay. No one came to see me except a friend of Olive's who'd let me crash on his couch from time to time. He gave me some money, so I could take the bus to Jerry's new place.

SMITTEN

WHEN MY STRENGTH WAS UP after the overdose, I got a job at a local grocery store near Jerry's as a produce clerk, stacking fruit, cutting lettuce, crushing boxes. Josh sent $1,000 to help get me on my feet. "I love you," he said on the phone. "We all do. Just don't kill yourself."

I kept chasing death, though. Each time I got my paycheque, I went out and spent it on comfort for my mind. I started banging needles of crack, melted down with vinegar, with working girls in the train yard at Dufferin and Queen, across from Toronto's Gladstone Hotel. They didn't judge me, and there was an honesty to what they did, like they had the courage to take things all the way. I had respect for that. *There is perfect order in perfect chaos*, I philosophized. We'd shoot up in the abandoned trailer one of the ladies lived in. I brought food from work sometimes, and we'd listen to Charlie Parker or the Velvet Underground or some other brilliant junkie band. They were my friends. My only friends.

One morning while I was stacking apples, my boss, an old Italian guy, glanced down and saw the bruising on my arms and my track marks. "You know, Jess, there's no shame in being sick," he said, but he was polite enough not to say anything outright.

I knew he couldn't complain about my work performance—I worked hard and got the job done, just like Grandpa had trained me to do.

Sometime later I saw a crisis support line number scrawled on the job chalkboard. I called, but the addictions worker told me, "You need three months or more before your employee insurance kicks in." I wasn't surprised. I'd tried accessing treatment before, many times, but the places all had long waiting lists, or needed insurance, or were outpatient only—there was always some kind of restriction. Detox worked, sure—but after that, I'd be left with nowhere to transition to and would relapse. I knew I needed quick isolation to get clean—total, immediate immersion for months and months.

My addictions had become unmanageable. I couldn't escape the horror of being involved with people who'd taken someone's life in such a gruesome way. And I had recurring nightmares of that jersey melting into my body, of being stabbed in the neck, of people lying in wait to ambush me around every corner.

With rent squirted up my veins, I ran away, leaving Jerry and my boss high and dry.

I fled to the Brampton shelter and, to my surprise, met the most beautiful girl. She was just sitting there, surrounded by a pile of plastic bags and suitcases. Her hair was blond and pulled back into a tight ponytail that lifted her eyebrows up, and she was well taken care of.

I went into the washroom to comb my hair and straighten my shirt, and then went over to her.

"I'm Jesse," I said, holding out a cigarette. "You smoke?"

She smiled and took it. Her name was Samantha. She placed her bags near the front office and asked the staff to watch them, then we went outside to the smoking pit.

Straight away I knew she was fearless and powerful, like a lone she-wolf who didn't need help fending for herself. She had no problem talking about how she'd ended up at the shelter—her parents had kicked her out because she was an independent thinker and she'd lost her job at the local gym.

"They're very Christian," she said. "Not me—I love to party."

For two and a half months we tripped around, getting high, staying on people's couches, then decided to combine our welfare start-ups and leave the shelter. We finally got a place and began picking trash to furnish it. She didn't mind, and even brought stuff home herself—an old couch, chairs, a microwave, and a TV.

Uncle Ron saw that we were trying and got me a job building counter-tops. I still took off on paydays trying to numb myself out, but now Samantha blasted stones right by my side—we were like two quarry workers chucking dynamite and smashing crack boulders together.

I ghosted work so often that the owner of the business, Randolph, changed paydays from Thursday to Friday just so I'd make it into work on Friday mornings. I worked my ass off, though, doing the jobs of four men—made sense, I was jacked on cocaine and moved faster than Ben Johnson at the Seoul Olympics.

Randolph ended up firing me, furious because I was so unreliable, but as soon as he axed me, he'd hire me right back—he knew no one could work like me. I was probably fired and rehired over twenty times.

Samantha and I soon lost our place and started moving constantly, gathering household belongings and then jettisoning them like spent rocket-fuel containers whenever we missed rent and entered homeless orbit—we must've moved about thirty times. Everything I pulled in at various temp jobs went to feed our addictions, to keep those nightmares at bay, and we always ended up at another shelter, in another city, or at Jerry's. He always had his door open, and Samantha and I were thankful. But I could tell he was reaching his limit.

In between cheques, food banks, and jobs was the hardest. We'd have no food, no alcohol, no fun, and no hope. I began stealing ground pork and ramen noodles at a market over in Chinatown. I did it at least a dozen times, stuffing my backpack and booking it out the front doors, until one day a security guard stopped me. I broke free and ran but was headed off. Security brought me to the backroom. I shouted and fought, but the security guard restrained me, pushing me to the ground and holding me tight with my arms behind my back. I was sure they'd call the cops, and I'd go to jail on a theft-under-$5,000 charge—the standard Canadian charge for shoplifting. I sat weeping, and when my energy was spent, the owner came in.

"Why you steal from here all the time?" she said with a thick Cantonese accent. "Go steal somewhere else, bad boy."

Bad boy? I thought, thinking that was kind of demeaning and strange. She was right, though. I always chose her store. It was big, and I believed its size concealed me. Obviously not.

"I know the other owners," she said. "They see you, too!" Her neck turned red as she flailed her arms.

"I'm sorry, miss. I—"

"I know you, crackhead."

Her voice made me feel ashamed.

"I see you steal ginseng and steel wool for your pipe." She wagged her finger, a look of disgust upon her face.

How did she know about that, or where I got my gear? I wondered, shocked. *Had she seen me steal it from the local convenience stores? Did she know all the local merchants?*

She pulled up my chin and forced eye contact. "Too skinny," she said, then slapped my cheek, but not with anger. It was like she was sorry for me. "Look at you. Too skinny." She took my backpack and opened it. "You have my pork and noodles." She shook her head.

I felt like an idiot.

She motioned to the security guard and the few employees who were there to leave the room. When we were alone she squatted next to me.

"I was hungry a long time ago, too, you know," she said. "Someone fed me, too."

She got up and went over to a skid and grabbed some noodles and yelled something. A man came through a plastic flap door with a big clear grocery bag of ground pork. He handed it to her, looked at me, then left. She stuffed both the noodles and meat into my bag and plopped it into my lap.

"Go now. And don't ever come back." She stood me up, and then shooed me out the back door before I could thank her.

I never stole from there again.

Everywhere else was fair game, though—thieving was the one thing I was good at that Samantha and I could count on. I grabbed her whatever she wanted—meat, alcohol, smokes, the odd article of clothing. I was smitten with her, and it was my selfish way of keeping her by my side.

Maybe I should've just let go and let her be.

THE KING OF SOMALIA

"**GOOD NIGHT, ABDI, YOU CRUSTY** old bastard," I said and rested my head on my pillow. Abdi was a Somali man of about sixty-five. He was my buddy and always slept in the bed next to me at the homeless shelter. Samantha was off on the women's side.

"Hey," I said a minute later. "I've been meaning to ask. You said you were the king of Somalia. Is that true?"

As expected, Abdi's face flushed and his eyes bulged. "Would I lie, peasant? Of course I am the king of Somalia. How dare you question my royal blood?"

Obviously I knew he wasn't Somali royalty. I liked joking with Abdi to get him going, and he'd do the same to me. It was our only form of entertainment in this hospitable yet horrible place.

Life hadn't been good to Abdi. He'd fled Somalia with his family when civil war broke out in the early '90s. Soon after he'd become an alcoholic and his wife had left him for another man. Abdi would reminisce about his homeland, telling me how he used to shepherd massive herds of cattle between Kenya and Somalia, and how he'd sit every night watching the orange-red African sunset. By the way his eyes lit up, I could see it was something he missed dearly. I tried to imagine how hard it must have been for him to be forced out of his homeland, to end up in a homeless shelter in a foreign country that seemingly didn't want him or his problems.

"Hey, Thistle," Abdi said as he leaned over. "You know how I know you're a real streeter like me?"

"Maybe it's the way I drink the last of the Olde English piss water?"

He cringed. "That's just disgusting—dirty Canadian drinking dirty American beer. No, young blood, it's in the way you sleep."

"How do you mean? And why are you watching me while I sleep?"

"I always watch out for you when you sleep, to make sure no one steals your stuff."

I thought about it, and he was right—I watched out for him, too. It was just what friends did in this place.

"Indian, you've had your shoes stolen so many times you sleep with them on. See?" He pulled up his blanket, exposing his grungy, mud-covered black boots, and smiled. "You see those young guys?" Abdi pointed at two men with their shoes placed under their cots. "They're little puppies, down on their luck momentarily. One day, if they're at it long enough, they'll learn like we did: never take your shoes off."

Having no shoes and being homeless was the worst. It could take a day or two to find a new pair that fit from the donation box—and that was if you were lucky. Other times you'd have to leave the shelter shoeless at seven a.m. to go and wait at the chaplain's office until eight a.m. to get a voucher to take to the Sally Ann up the street so they could outfit you with a new pair. Or you had to go without for a few days. Or steal a pair from Zellers and risk your freedom. When you were shoeless in the winter, it was almost unbearable.

I surveyed the shelter beds. Only about a third of the guys had their shoes on.

I'd never noticed, but every night I tied my shoes on with triple, even quadruple, knots, just to give myself a chance of keeping thieves from stealing them right off my feet. Even then, they got them sometimes.

"I guess I do sleep with my shoes on, eh, Abdi?" I said, and laughed.

LIFE AT GUNPOINT

FLIP'S 38 WAS PRESSED HARD into my forehead.

Flip was one of the more aggressive and secretive crack dealers who served the downtown core. He'd been doing it for decades and was a wild card, trigger-happy, too, and even the rival gangs let him chop uncontested. I didn't like going to him—no one did as far as I knew—but he always had good dope, at all hours, and was one of the only choppers who'd exchange goods for crack at a fair price.

I was hoping he'd buy the Gucci bag I'd just stolen from a car with my high school friend Marko, but, in desperation—no one else had dope— I'd disregarded the various rules Flip had put in place to protect himself from crackheads he didn't know.

His number one rule: no new customers.

His number two rule: no new customers, and so on.

I thought our longstanding relationship might supersede the formalities. Marko kept bugging me to sell the bag, and thought maybe our friendship was good enough to get him access to Flip.

"Who is this fool you brought here? I told you not to bring anyone to see me!" Spit and angry breath hissed through Flip's clenched teeth as the hammer cocked into firing position.

"That—that's m-my bu-boy . . . Come on, dog . . . I—I've known you for ye-years." We only wanted to score some dope, and Flip was flipping out.

Just then a cruiser rounded the corner. In an instant Flip rammed his pistol through his belt, pointed his finger at me, mouthed something, and fled down the street toward the Dairy Queen. He was gone before I could process what had happened.

"Man, I'm sorry, guy," Marko said. "I never thought your buddy would react like that. What is his problem?"

I looked at Marko. His astonished words told me that he didn't really understand how close I had come to death.

———

A week after, the pinkish purple imprint of the gun muzzle, the size and shape of a Life Savers, remained engraved between my eyes.

I never did another run with Marko again.

WE ALL FALL DOWN

THE HALLOWEEN PARTY AT JERRY'S friend's house ran late into the night. I was dressed up as William Wallace from *Braveheart*, half my face blue and with a diaper of fake fur and a plastic sword. Jerry was a Viking with huge horns and a plastic battle-axe, and Samantha was the Pict girl from *King Arthur*, with leather armour and a bow and arrow made from household items. The rest of the partygoers wore costumes ranging from ghosts to Spanish matadors, but a couple of people were just dressed in regular clothes.

One was a beautiful redhead in a tight black sweater. She was the girl from grade school who'd been nice to me on the hill.

"Hi," I said to her. "My name is Jesse. You're Lucie, right?" I stuck my hand out like I had years earlier.

"Yes." She reciprocated like she had years before.

"Do you remember me? I'm Jerry's brother—we were in middle school together." I motioned toward Jerry, who was chatting over near the kitchen.

"No." She grinned, shrugged, and then turned away to talk to a bald guy. Samantha came up with her bow drawn, half-drunk. I disarmed her, and we mingled into the heart of the party, asking people if they had any coke, but I kept looking back. I was enchanted by Lucie, and the fact that she wasn't interested attracted me even more.

After a couple of screwdrivers, I was hit with addiction cravings so bad I ran to the toilet—I needed to take a dump—then I ditched the party and Samantha and went out scouring for a twenty stone. I found plenty, spending our rent money and shoplifting things to generate more cash. Before I knew it, it was around four a.m. I drifted back to the party, but almost everyone had left. One of the last people trailing out told me to get home quick because Samantha was livid. I did my last toke and walked back to Jerry's, which was miles away.

When I got there, I picked the outside lock with my health card. I didn't have my own key—Jerry's rules, even though Samantha and I'd been staying with him for months at his new place in Toronto after we'd fled from Brampton. The inside door to the apartment was locked. It was steel, bolted shut, and impossible to bypass with any of my thieving skills. I banged on it.

"It's me. Open up!"

Nothing. I banged some more. Again nothing. I started kicking the door, the boom echoing through the hallway, and a neighbour stuck his head out his door and said, "Keep it down!"

I kicked the door again. I wondered if Samantha was being faithful to me. Why would she be? I was a terrible provider. I didn't treat her the best. *Maybe she and Jerry are inside having sex. Maybe she's exacting revenge on me for stealing our rent, for smoking it.* Or maybe it was just the copious amounts of crack that was making me paranoid.

I noticed the window down the hall. It was about three feet wide by four feet tall and opened onto the street. I went and stuck my head out of it. Our living room window was about ten feet over to the right. It was open, almost begging me to climb over. I decided to go for it. After all, I'd scaled up the sides of apartment buildings before, and this shimmy between windows was only thirty-five feet above the ground.

Piece of cake.

I charted out my climb. I'd swing from the ledge of the hallway window over to the brick notch between the two windows, where there was a good grip, then swing over to our window and plant my toe, and then pull myself up.

I lowered myself out, swung over, grabbed the notch, then swung over again and grabbed the window ledge.

Perfect so far.

I took a second to collect myself for the pull into the apartment. Scar, Jerry's dog, a pit bull–Rottweiler mix, stuck his head out and started licking my hands.

"Get. Get," I shooed. The fucker was blocking my entrance. He didn't budge. He must have thought I was playing a game or something. A drop of his saliva fell off his tongue and into my eye.

"SCAR, GET!" I blinked to clear my sight. My strength was fading, my fingers slipping. I yelled "get" one more time, desperately, and he finally listened.

I hoisted myself a quarter of the way up and planted my toe against the wall and pushed, but slipped. I was still holding on, but barely, my arms carrying my full weight. I examined the wall closely and noticed a cluster of black cables—rows of them, one over the other, stapled to the bricks. I hadn't seen them in the dark. I mustered my last bit of strength to pull myself up toward the window, planting my toe higher than before—but there was another cluster of cables. My toe slipped. My hands let go.

People who say your life flashes before you when you're about to die are full of shit. What does happen is your world slows down—seconds feel like hours, the sounds all around become clearer, colours and lights become so bright you can see everything—every bug and creepy-crawly thing in existence.

The milliseconds I was falling to my death I thought of a hundred different ways to fall so I wouldn't die. I could try to land square on my feet like I was doing a powerlift, but my face and skull would be ruined as I fell forward into the brick wall with thousands of pounds of force. I could try to do a commando combat roll off to the side but would hit the air conditioner and break my neck. Or I could try to catch the ledge of the windows below. I tried that, but this wasn't *Die Hard*, and I wasn't Bruce Willis.

My last option was to do a break-fall, something I'd learned in judo as a kid—land on my feet, tip backward onto my back, and then slap my arms out straight and let the force ride out my bone structure, out my shoulders, humerus, radius, and ulna, and blow out through the constellation of wrist bones, and finally the fine bones of my hands and digits. That was the only way to stop from smashing my head like a watermelon. Every other scenario ended with brain trauma.

It was my only chance.

When my feet hit the ground, I leaned back. A wave of pressure fired down my arms, followed by two loud cracks that sounded like shotguns. I rolled on the arc of my spine and saw my feet jut above me, and the back of my head lightly hit the sidewalk.

Tink.

The wind knocked completely out of me. I wasn't in pain but tried to scream. Nothing came out. I looked at my hands—they were folded in upon my forearms. I tried to wiggle my fingers. They didn't move. I held up both legs and saw my right heel was in the middle of my shin and my right foot pointed backward. The other foot and my skull were fine.

Scar was looking out the window. He howled.

I managed to pull in a lungful of air and yelled. "Help! Help! I've fallen."

No one came.

I yelled three more times—crickets. I shifted my strategy.

"Fire! There's a fire!"

From every direction people came, in seconds flat. I asked one guy to call my brother and tell him that I needed help.

Moments later, Jerry was downstairs.

"Jerry, I broke my leg and wrists. I need you to call an ambulance."

Jerry just scratched his head, disappeared, and then reappeared with an old set of crutches he had. "Here." He threw the crutches at me. "I don't need this shit. I have work in the morning." He turned and walked away.

In shock, I managed to get up using the crutches and hobbled up three flights of stairs into the apartment. I never wished more that Jerry's building had an elevator. I was still not in any pain, somehow. Samantha came out of our room.

"What's going on?" she said, half asleep, shielding her eyes from the light. She grumbled and swore, I heard the word "asshole," and then she went back to bed.

I grabbed the phone, my hands flopping about, and tapped 911 with the meat of my palm.

The paramedics were confounded that I'd survived. "This isn't Hollywood. Thirty-five feet spells death most times."

The pain was finally hitting, like molten nails driven into my leg, over and over again.

They laid me on the floor and told me not to move because I likely had internal bleeding. "You should have stayed where you fell. You probably have a broken back or neck."

One of them turned to Jerry, who stood watching from the bathroom, and asked, "How did he get up here?"

Jerry was silent.

"I used the crutches," I yelped.

They turned to me, mouths open. They jabbed something in my leg, strapped me to a plank-like stretcher, and carried me down to the ambulance, where they placed me on another softer stretcher.

On the way to the hospital, one guy kept cracking jokes to me even though I was so tired, I just wanted to go to sleep, and then said, "When you get out, you should leave those people. They aren't good."

I felt a slap on my face and saw tubes sticking in my arms and hands. The lights returned to normal, and I felt a sudden warm rush, a fuzzy feeling—I knew it was some kind of opioid. I felt safe.

A doctor appeared by my side as they ran with me down a hall.

"Whaddya call a guy who fell out a building and survived?" He cracked a smile.

"I dunno."

"You. You call him 'you.'"

I laughed, but my back and neck hurt. My foot and wrists pulsed with such sharp pain that the dull ache radiating from my forearms and shins was manageable. The doctor flashed a light in my eyes. I could feel someone cutting my clothes off, and then I was rolled onto my side, and a cold, wet sensation slammed into my asshole. It bloody hurt, sharp with immense pressure like a jagged chili fart scraping my lower intestine.

"You aren't even gonna buy me flowers?" I remarked, as high as Lou Reed in 1967.

The doctor laughed and said he'd take me to dinner when I recovered.

"I like steak."

"You're in good spirits. Just hang in there." He moved the object around inside my anus, then said something to the others around me. There were flashing lights, a giant white machine rotated up and down my body and over my head, and then blackness.

I drifted upon a cloud afterward. Doctors and nurses came in, filled me with fluids, told me I was "lucky" and to "cool it on the morphine drip," got me to sign forms, and then, before I knew it, I was rushed into surgery.

When I awoke in the recovery room, Samantha and Jerry were by my side, apologizing that they hadn't known how serious the fall was.

Samantha cried. I yelled at first, but then forgave them. They didn't know. I was the idiot who'd gone all strung-out-and-drunk Spiderman.

The doctors told me that my fall had shattered my right heel, destroyed my right upper ankle joint, broke my left wrist, and sprained my right wrist. I was told to keep my leg elevated.

The surgeons decided it was best to leave my wrists exposed so I'd be able to walk with crutches. They said they'd fixed my right heel and ankle with a ninety-degree incision on the outside of my right foot—it rode six inches along the back of my ankle and heel, and another six inches along the side of my foot. Two pins protruded out the back of my heel, holding my heel and ankle together.

They sent me home after three days—scabs hadn't even formed.

WESTERN DOOR

SCAR SAT BESIDE ME, NUDGING my arm every few minutes. He was my primary caregiver, along with Samantha. I lay in bed with my leg elevated, just like the doctor had told me to do. World War I documentaries rotated across the black-and-white TV, remnants of Remembrance Day programming. The horrendous 1916 battle at Verdun, with its massive craters and fractured trees, lacerated trenches and knotted barbed wire was the current feature.

This has got to be the worst battle in history per square foot, I thought as the narrator described the sheer number of deaths. It sounded worse than the Somme, and I wondered why we'd focused so much on the latter in grade school.

I gazed down at the tips of my toes. They were red, and the cast on my foot grew tighter and tighter. A strange itching had gnawed at my shin these past few days—I couldn't get to it, not even if I stuck a pencil down the cast. Almost like the itch was several layers below my skin, in the marrow of my leg. A throbbing dull pain radiated up into my buttocks, too, and even the Tylenol 4s I was prescribed couldn't stop it. When Samantha turned me over to clean me, she said that the back of my leg was turning a weird kind of grey, green almost, and was starting to emit an odd sweet smell.

All I could keep down was chicken broth, the nausea was so bad. I thought it was the medication. I'd stopped shitting five days before and was sure I was bunged up from it; I found no relief from the chamomile and senna tea the doctor said would loosen my bowels. Only weed and hash seemed to make me regular and helped with my appetite, but even that wasn't working anymore. The pile of cigarette butts in the ashtray beside me loomed ominously—I wasn't supposed to smoke, the doctor had warned—it'd impede blood flow and increased the chances of infection. But I just couldn't stop cold turkey—I needed something to occupy the time.

I took a handful of T4s before bed. I wanted to sleep all night for once. Scar and Samantha were beside me and I knew Jerry would check up on me every few hours. It felt good to have my older brother watching out for me, despite our growing animosity. I entered the dead zone about thirty minutes after.

My dreams came, as always.

Bombs exploded near my head as I moved down the trench to deliver a vital message, warning our men not to advance. A concussion knocked me into a puddle, and I dropped the letter as soldiers ran past to their deaths. I reached up toward their jackboots to stop them, but my fingers slid off their ankles. One young man looked down at me and startled me. He had dark features, a long braid, and bronze skin. He was an Indian, and looked like me, but different—older, wiser—and I knew somehow he was already dead. He turned and disappeared into an explosion as he went over the top.

The chatter of World War I artillery gave way to the slower, more powerful reports of a nineteenth-century Gatling gun. But the hulking gun sounded more menacing, more real, there were houses burning all around, and children and women were screaming and running into the bush for cover. They were all Native, like me. A handful of Indian men lay beside me in shallow pits dug into the ground, long rifles in hand. We'd pop up periodically and fire down a large prairie slope at redcoat soldiers near the banks of a large river. Our enemies stood in ordered columns and outnumbered us. The man beside me said something to me in a language I'd never heard before but understood, then reached over and took my last bullets. He cocked his rifle and returned our enemies' fire. He looked familiar, like the young man in the trench, and I could tell he was a half-breed like me. He, too, was dead; I somehow knew this.

I looked back out of the pit and suddenly saw myself on the bed at Jerry's apartment. My body was broken, my leg propped up on pillows, Samantha, Jerry, and Scar weren't there anymore. I floated higher above the battle and saw a white church get smaller and smaller on the horizon of the plains, and I knew I was part of this long-ago battle—it was real. I saw my grandparents' house in Brampton, and the house number—eight—appear above the church. The number turned sideways and formed into an infinity symbol on a blue flag. I heard voices on the wind; they told me it was my destiny to be raised under that symbol.

Just then, a great shaft of light from the west broke through the clouds. It was dusk, and the orange light of twilight was fading fast. The guns and cannons fell silent. I saw a vast field before me with mesas and buttes off in the distance, and from the brightest spot of the setting sun a vast herd of horses emerged and ran toward me. I watched their muscles ripple with power, their manes float on the wind as their heads bounded with each stride, and their hooves kicked up a cloud of dust so big it enveloped the whole earth.

A tug, soft at first, then stronger and stronger, pulled me along with the herd as they ran by me and then back again. I was galloping with them, but I was not yet a hooved creature like them. I stared back and saw my broken body on the bed get smaller and smaller, until I could hardly see it. A great sadness came over me. I knew they were taking me home, but that I hadn't yet done what I was destined to do. I tried pulling away, to return to myself, to my body, but the force of the herd was too powerful. I pleaded and cried, and still they pulled me with them.

Just as I was about to cross into the brightest spot of the setting sun, through that western door, I cried out one last time.

"I will do my work, I will change, I will finish it."

Without a sound, the herd pivoted and released me. I watched as they turned into the light, their hooves thundering, then fell behind the great façade of the western door.

As soon as they were gone, my eyes opened. I was with Samantha on the bed. Scar tilted his head, and Jerry burst into the room.

"What the hell is going on?" he asked, his voice shaking. "You were screaming, 'Help, help.'"

"I don't know what happened—I think I have a fever," I said as I looked down and saw my body was covered in sweat.

Samantha slept through it all.

CAST OF HORRORS

WHEN THE DOCTOR'S ASSISTANT CUT away the orange-and-black cast, she gasped. The smell was horrid: like Toronto during a summer garbage strike.

"Excuse me one moment, Mr. Thistle . . . I have to get the doctor," she said and rushed out.

My toes had turned a bluish grey-green and the back of my cast was leaking a swampy crimson, so I'd pushed my post-surgery checkup ahead and was lucky to get a spot. It had been many weeks since my fall. The surgery should have worked. But I couldn't listen to the doctors. It's not like I didn't try to follow their orders. I did. But I was an addict. More important, I didn't have anywhere to live.

I'd been at Jerry's, but after one of my friends stole a neighbour's vintage bicycle, he'd kicked me and Samantha out. He had to do what he had to do. If he'd kept us, he'd have been evicted, and we all would've been homeless. But I figure his place was probably where I caught the infection I likely had—it was full of cat shit and dog piss and hadn't been cleaned properly in years. It was a veritable cesspool.

Samantha and I moved into her parents' house. She got a good job. She was trying to fly straight, but I'd never really been welcome there, as we weren't married and for a bunch of other reasons, so I took off on my own. I thought she could do better without me cramping her style.

When the nurse came back in with the doctor, they both had masks on their faces. My stomach dropped. Their hands were full of instruments, including one that looked like wire cutters, lots of gauze, a kidney-shaped tray, and medical tape. When I finally got the courage to look down at my exposed leg I nearly fainted. There was a black puss-filled blister on the front of my ankle that resembled a giant, deformed pierogi. My foot and lower leg were swollen, green, red, and greyish yellow. When the doctor took the staples out of the incision, the edges of the skin peeled back, exposing fat, muscle, bone, and metallic hardware.

"Not good at all," the doctor said. "The surgery has been a complete failure. Your leg is infected and gangrene is setting in. I'll clean it, cut away the necrotic skin, and trim the bone, but you're at serious risk of losing your leg if you don't take care of yourself."

He gave me something to freeze the area and set to work. Even with the numbing, when his full weight bore down on my leg and I heard a sharp wet pop from the bone clipper, I bellowed, and tears began to stream down my face. As it went on, my field of vision narrowed to pinpoints, and my hearing dulled, with the voices around me becoming distant, then inaudible. I vomited, then passed out.

When I woke up my leg was again in a cast. I had on someone else's clothes and a numbness everywhere that smothered my arms and made my legs flop about.

The nurse came in and told me I was free to go but I had to speak to the doctor before I left. She had a prescription for antibiotics, and a suction-pump machine to attach to my leg to improve its circulation, as well as a schedule for an aftercare nurse who was to come and change my wound dressings twice a day. The doctor came in and asked me where I was staying. When I told him I was staying at the shelter, I could see his expression change. I knew it was a shithole of a place to recover in. I'd always been able to hold my own on the streets and in the shelter system, but I had to admit things weren't like before. And I knew I couldn't stay at the hospital.

When the doctor and nurse left me alone a moment, I grabbed the pump and scrip and hobbled out, getting in a cab. The driver kicked me out halfway to my destination when he found out I didn't have the fare.

The first night at the shelter, the pump disappeared. By the third and fourth nights, my prescription was stolen. A week into my stay, the infection was back. Not surprisingly, the nurse never came. When I had the pump and my meds, I could at least feel hopeful, I could at least dream of keeping my leg and walking on my own again. Now I had nothing. I wanted to forget everything. I gave up.

The Personal Needs Allowance (PNA) I got every day at the shelter bought me my morning wake-and-bake hit of crack. That killed the pain in my leg long enough for me to make my way to the nearby drugstore, where I could steal some mouthwash and razors—it was surprising how much crack you could get for a pack of triple razor blades and how stupefied a bottle of mouthwash could make you.

Other homeless people I knew tried to help me. Some gave me free tokes of crack when the pain was unbearable, others shared their liquor. Outreach people who knew me came by and gave me bus tickets, cigarettes, and clean pairs of socks. After they left, I broke down and cried. I couldn't even wear both socks.

After about a week, I realized that I couldn't feel my toes. They were cold and they had changed from greyish blue to waxy black—I hadn't noticed because I'd been too busy feeling sorry for myself. My toenails started to fall away at the slightest tug and the skin sloughed off when I scraped it with my finger.

It was happening: my foot was dying just like the doctor said would happen.

I rushed myself to the hospital again.

The doctor was furious.

"Do you know how sick you've made yourself?" he yelled. The nurse rammed a thermometer in my ear.

I knew I was sick. My upper leg and torso felt like they were on fire and my head had been spinning for over a week.

The doctor told me he didn't even have to cut the cast off, he could smell the damage I'd done to myself. "Mr. Thistle, based on your condition during your past visit and your condition today, I regret to inform you that we might have to amputate your leg. The infection is severe, and if it spreads to your brain or heart it will kill you."

His words thundered into my brain. "Like fuck you are!" The words came from somewhere deep within me. They were a knee-jerk reaction to an impossible proposition. They left the room to attend to someone else, and I frantically stumbled off the bed, mounted my crutches, and see-sawed down the hospital corridor, tossing myself out the back door. Before I knew it I was in the dorm room at the shelter. Not wasting any time, I packed what clothes I owned into a plastic bag, collected my PNA, and fled.

I got to the subway and jumped on a train. The ride to the northern part of the city felt like an eternity. I clutched my Pyrex stem the whole way. It was loaded with crack I'd bought before I left the shelter with the hoard of bus tickets I'd got from the outreach workers and my $3.75 PNA. I had about a fifty-piece. I promised myself I wouldn't smoke it until I got to Brampton. I needed to get as far away from the hospital and the threat of my leg being amputated as I could. Where I grew up seemed a safe and logical choice.

Getting on the 77 bus was easy. It was something I used to do all the time. I'd just tell the driver I was homeless and needed to get to a shelter and they'd let me on every time. Now I had a cast—how could anyone say no? I slumped back in a seat, and we were soon cruising along the highway. When the bus started coasting through some of my old stomping grounds, a thought entered my head. We pulled into Bramalea City Centre, the air suspension hissing as the driver lowered the bus for me to get off. I hurried to catch the 1A bus to Four Corners, downtown Brampton.

I had a plan.

TURNING POINT

WHY THE FUCK AM I *wandering in the desert like a wounded animal?* I asked myself as the 1A entered the terminal.

"Last stop!" the driver called out. The bus pulled to a halt, and I stepped off onto the platform and closer to relief. I lit my stem. The sizzle of the stone gave way to a milky stream of smoke that coated the back of my throat. A fire engine howled in my ear, and my heart raced. I found myself striding to a nearby convenience store. I knew what I had to do. It didn't matter that I'd never done anything like it before, or even wanted to. This was beyond wanting. This was need.

Leftover crumbs that resembled bone shards peppered the centre of my palm. With the tips of my fingers I packed them into my pipe and lit it. My leg still hurt, but when I took this last blast, the pain completely subsided. I was ready. I gritted my teeth, opened the door, and walked in.

It's too late to turn back now. There's nowhere left to go.

I swallowed hard and grabbed the first thing in sight—a submarine sandwich wrapped in foil and a small jug of kitty litter. I brought both to the counter and waited until the clerk rang open the register, then made my move.

"Give me all your money or I'll kill you!" I yelled as I pointed my sub sandwich at the clerk. Lettuce and mayo flew everywhere.

The guy looked at me with a half-smirk. "Are you serious, pal?"

A long, awkward silence ensued, or at least it felt that way.

"Of course I'm serious! Give me the cash and hurry the fuck up!"

I could hear my voice rising to a falsetto pitch, but I meant it.

"Look, cowboy, I only have $90—store policy. You can take it; we're insured, so I really don't care. I just want to get home to my family. Understand?"

I understood. He stepped aside. My hand jittered and rifled through the till, firing change and bills all over the place. My other hand squeezed my sandwich through my fist like beef through a meat grinder. Out of the corner of my eye I could see the clerk picking up the phone. I scrambled and tried to bolt out the front door, but missed the handle and slammed headfirst into the glass.

"Ah!" I yelled, clutching my head and dropping even more cash. A goose egg instantly formed. I almost passed out, but kept running.

"You won't get far with that cast on your leg," the clerk hollered as I rounded the corner. "The cops are on their way right now, they'll get you soon enough!"

That was supposed to be the plan: get arrested and go to jail, so I'd get taken care of, so my foot could be fixed, and so my life would be saved. I was desperate. I didn't know what else to do anymore. I felt as though I had nowhere else to go, nowhere else to turn. But as soon as I was out of his sight, I jumped into the store's dumpster and covered myself in trash. I sat there as frozen as a statue for a good four hours until the sounds of the police cruisers, helicopter, and dogs were gone. I was lucky, I guess. The juicy garbage smell must've masked my scent, and the police never even thought to look in the dumpster.

I emerged as smelly as a New York City rat and counted my take: $37.20.

I thought, *This has got to be the worst moment of my life.*

INDESTRUCTIBLE PINK DRESS

I IMAGINED COPS EVERYWHERE—BEHIND TREES, under cars, behind doors, inside toilets, under the fridge, in my coffee. The sheer terror—the constant looking over my shoulder—was maddening. Drugs didn't help, and I couldn't bear the paranoia.

I couldn't go back to Samantha and the little apartment she'd rented for us. I'd cleaned out her bank account, $400, while she was at work one day and blew it all on coke and booze, afraid of withdrawal after my Tylenol 4 prescription ran out and couldn't get it renewed because I'd gone through them too quickly. I wandered around feeling sorry for myself for about a week while my health deteriorated when I should've worried instead about the damage I'd caused Samantha, about how she'd eat and get to work for the next month. We'd gone through a lot of adventures together, living precariously in emergency services, in shitty rooms all over the city, on people's couches, and under constant threat of violence for a long time.

It was the end of our four-year relationship.

I drifted in and out of shelters giving false names and slept on benches and in parks until one night a dive bar let me use the phone and I called the cops and told them I was the guy who'd committed the convenience store robbery in Brampton a few weeks earlier. I knew I'd be safer in jail than wandering around with no place to go. Society, I figured, cares more about criminals than they do about the homeless.

They came and picked me up.

The details of my arrest are sketchy at best. I remember the squad car ride to the station, how the officers were laughing at how bad I smelled, and the relief of knowing I was headed to jail, where I could rest and clean up and get some medical aid.

I also remember the brief statement I made against myself. "I did it," I said. "Now lock me up and throw away the key."

I just wanted a place to hide from the world. More than that, I wanted a place to crawl into and die in, like some wounded dog under a porch somewhere.

They charged me with robbery and shipped me off to the Maplehurst Correctional Complex in Milton to await my first court hearing.

Upon arrival, I was processed, strip-searched, and clothed in an orange jumpsuit, then thrown in the general population bullpen with the other prisoners. I broke a jailhouse rule the instant I was caged—I whistled. Four young guys jumped me from behind and stomped on my head until I was almost unconscious. I'm not sure why they stopped—there wasn't a guard in sight. Maybe they just ran out of energy.

When a guard finally came to take us off to our individual pods, I told him I was suicidal, and that I'd tried to swallow a plastic spoon near the toilet.

"What happened to your face?" he asked with a smirk, spinning his keys on his finger.

"I fell over when I was taking a shit," I replied, my head throbbing. The guys in the bullpen laughed and confirmed my story when he asked for verification.

They pulled me out of gen pop and stuck me in the protective custody holding cells, then processed me out to solitary confinement a few hours later.

I came to realize solitary confinement, or "the hole," usually isn't that bad a place to go while doing a short stretch of time. Sometimes prisoners earned their way there by beating someone senseless or because they wouldn't squeal on their comrades—both commendable things inside. Sometimes those prisoners even got to wear their orange overalls down to the hole, and you could almost see the laurel wreaths on them as the guards paraded them past everyone.

Not me.

I went into solitary confinement because I'd been banged out of general population and then squawked on myself because I was suicidal. From that point on, I was marked as a bitch during my stay at the Milton Hilton, and I was always paranoid someone might find out I'd chirped on Mike and Stefan. To underscore my humiliation and horror, I was outfitted in an indestructible pink dress with no arms or legs—the standard garb given to prisoners on suicide watch. It was made from space-age padded polyester, about eight layers thick, with diamond diagonal stitching and a collar wide enough to jam a pumpkin through, and it felt tougher than a bulletproof Kevlar vest. It was tear-proof, so you couldn't rip it apart and make a braid to hang yourself with. Which I tried to do.

It resembled a loose miniskirt crossed with a tight poncho, and all the guys whistled when the guards walked me down to isolation.

"Shake them fries, baby!" one inmate called.

"She's mine," called another, rattling the Plexiglas on his cell door.

The rest just blew me kisses and made hearts with their hands.

I wasn't ready for this shit.

Inside the hole, there were no blankets, no pillows, no contact, no respect. There was just me, my little pink dress, a blue jail-issue Bible, concrete, my thoughts, and time.

Graffiti was scrawled all over the cinder block walls, lavish script done in the finest dried feces, blood, and pencil someone must've smuggled in in their ass, addressed to God or Satan or other deities I wasn't familiar with. And, of course, there were pictures of giant penises and vaginas everywhere, decorated with old claw marks, broken fingernails, smears of snot, and magnificent pictures of the sun and trees for background effect.

The first few days were excruciating. I entered withdrawal on day two with no medical support—no Librium or Valium or anything. I was getting antibiotics for my foot, because I'd told them about it, but I was too whacked out to mention my addiction. *Just my luck*, I thought as the furies of Hades engulfed and drowned my brown ass in the river Styx.

Breathing was laboured and almost impossible. Vomit and diarrhea fired out of me every forty-five minutes or so. I never got to the toilet in time. My cell looked like it'd been peppered with a strange kind of mud, corn, and peanut shotgun.

My bones sang shrill notes of agonizing pain that vibrated right down to the marrow, shattering and pulverizing my frame into piles of bloody talcum powder. Vivid colonies of maggots burrowed through my flesh and brain and hatched out of my skin into plump flies the size of raisins that clouded the neon light the guards never turned off.

As I lay there convulsing and wishing I would die, the soft voice of my kokum whispered gently in my ear, but her road-allowance song couldn't drive away the insects and demons. She was gone as soon as she came.

I shook.

I vibrated.

I quaked.

The horizon of the cell shifted up and down more violently, I imagined, than the crust of the earth during an earthquake.

If the physical symptoms of alcohol delirium tremens just about killed me, the ever-increasing psychosis of withdrawal from crack broke me into shards of shame and pity and guilt that burned under my forehead like napalm watered with gasoline and lit by a blowtorch. The sharp edges of my memories stabbed into my consciousness, shredding my mind into fragile ribbons of dark introspection. Faces from the past—my grand-mother; Mrs. R., the French teacher; Leeroy; Karen; Ivan, the kid I robbed; Samantha—all came in like razor-edged knives to disembowel me on the altar of long-ago transgressions.

I'm sorry, I'm sorry, I'm sorry, I pleaded, my eyes riveted shut, my tears run dry, my hands held aloft, trying to shield myself from a lifetime of mistakes. Dimensions folded in upon one another with a force that crum-pled me in upon myself. I tried in vain to stop the implosion, to gather my intestines from the frozen cell floor, but the walls kept squeezing in and my guts just wouldn't fit back into the empty cavity that was my existence.

I writhed and squirmed, twisted and thrashed, and somewhere in my flailing, the side of my face chanced upon the only thing in the cell—the Bible.

Creator sends me a fucking message now! I sneered, pissed off by the timing.

I snatched it up and hurled it against the wall. It bounced back and landed near my throbbing leg. It lay open to Psalm 32, but the words in the passage ran like black ants in all directions. I kicked it away. It landed near the base of my concrete bed, pages splayed open once again, waiting.

I never read the damned thing.

SOLITARY CONFINEMENT

i dreamt i tread
upon cobblestones
of that ancient city,
Jerusalem.

where once
David betrayed Uriah,
his crown
replaced
by broken bones and sores,
withered in iniquity.

there,
upon marble floors,
he cried out.
met by all he was:
a coyote
languishing in the land of jackals.

selah

SHARING THE LOVE

I FINALLY SOBERED UP, AND within days the infection in my foot began to subside. I couldn't yet defend myself, so they put me in the protective-custody wing, where I could mend.

Lauriston, my cellmate, was a man of seventy from Bermuda. He said he was in for probation violation, but I was skeptical. People in on breach never get more than thirty days, and here he apparently was with two years plus a day. Had he committed some heinous crime? Or had he done just what he said he'd done? Was he just what he said he was? You could never trust other inmates.

I also wondered how he had set up the sugar trade that had made him wealthy in packaged sugars. Each inmate only got one sugar packet on his breakfast tray, one for lunch for our tea, and one for dinner, again for tea, but Lauriston had a pillowcase full of sugar packets, and he consumed at least five of them at each meal. They were a real commodity in jail and could buy food and help make mash liquor from orange peels, water, and bread; along with tobacco and dope, mash was a top jail product.

At mealtimes, the sugars would just pour into our cell.

"Here, Lauriston," said Bucky, the quartermaster—the inmate who gives out and controls the food, the most powerful and respected position on the range, a collection of cells that form a holding area where inmates do the majority of their time.

Lauriston reached both hands through the food port and Bucky dropped a sock full of sugar packages into them.

"Thanks, young blood. I have something for you. Hold up." Lauriston reached down onto his dinner tray and handed Bucky his potatoes.

Bucky dapped his fist on Lauriston's and thanked him for the carbs—much-needed fuel, as Bucky worked out compulsively three hours a day.

"I got you, wisdom. Always."

Bucky smiled and continued distributing the rest of the trays to the other cells down the line.

"You see that, Indian," Lauriston said to me. "Give to the next man and the next man prosper with you."

"It's a nice theory," I snapped, "but how do you know they won't just take your stuff?"

"What are you thinking, fool? Wake up. We are people, too, you know. We give and trust just like all those people on the outside, like all those good people. Know this: all brethren who give to his brethren prosper by his brother, and all those selfish *bloodclaat* that don't, get nothing but fire."

Lauriston was quite angry. It looked like he was going to start swinging. He kissed his teeth and muttered something, then became deadly serious.

"You see me? I'm an old man, I got no family, no drugs, no tobacco, no candy bars—I got nothing. But still my canteen's rammed with goodies and my belly full. These convicts can take anything from me, but I know to give, even in this place. And I trust these guys and they know it. Some of them never been trusted in their whole lives. You know what that's worth in Babylon?"

"I'm sorry, Lauriston. I just . . ." I scurried to the back wall to get ready to defend myself.

"Calm your ass, I'd never hit a cripple. Listen to me—I'm trying to help you. Try it. Give away your food and don't ask for nothing. That means a lot in here. Trust those guys to be good people. But never give it to a *bombaclot* who tries to take it; if that happens, then you beat his ass—life and death."

I agreed to heed his advice and went to bed, all the while thinking about his pile of sugar.

The next morning when Bucky came around, I took my breakfast tray, grabbed my cereal package and bag of milk, and handed it to Bucky.

"Here, take it," I said.

Bucky just glanced at me, put them on his tray, and continued on.

Nothing came back. I waited for an hour, looking over at him while he played cards with the other quartermaster, Priest. He didn't so much as peer up at me.

What a prick, I thought. At lockout, I walked over to the shower, took off my overalls, and was about to get into the stall when Bucky came up to me with Priest and grabbed me.

"What the fuck, you crazy, star?" he said. "You gonna wash your dirty ass in my shower? You never wash your dirty self, star."

Bucky was right, I never showered. I was as afraid of getting an infection in my foot as much as I was afraid of getting raped. Those fears kept me perpetually dirty and stinky. But today I had to shower, my terrible body odour was making it difficult for me and Lauriston to eat in our cell, and I'd forced myself into the stall. I could feel my face turning white at the thought of being beaten, even raped, by Bucky and Priest. I closed my eyes and wished it would end quickly.

"You can't go in there, bomba. Open your eyes. Open them and look at me!" Bucky yelled.

But my eyes remained glued shut, my body stiff as a board.

Bucky shouted again, only louder this time. "Open your *bloodclaat* eyes, star. You can't go in there. Not with your foot wound open like that. Here," Bucky said.

I felt something squishy press against my chest. I opened my eyes a crack, careful to protect them from a fist or finger gouge. Bucky was handing me his black jail sandals.

"You need to wear these to keep your feet off the ground. The bacteria is on the ground; if you step on it, it will get in your wound and you'll lose your foot."

As Bucky said that, Priest grabbed my shoulder and added, "Turn them over. Look. I carved the Star of David on the bottom to protect you against the filth of the place. One, bless."

There it was, the Star of David, engraved on the heel, right where my injured foot would rest.

When I returned to my cell, Lauriston was there, waiting. I told him what had happened.

He just grinned and said, "I told you so."

BIBLES BEHIND BARS

SOON I HAD ALL THE food I could eat, all the sugar I wanted, and all the juice crystals I desired. Moreover, I had all the respect one could hope for inside. The food helped to heal my foot, and in time, when Priest and then Bucky were moved to a supermax prison, I was chosen to take one of the jobs as quartermaster because the guys on the range knew I was fair and that I'd share.

As Lauriston said, "All people who give to those around them prosper by them, and all those selfish *bloodclaats* that don't, get nothing but fire."

I just wish I hadn't had to go to jail to figure that out—that and so much else.

Before Priest was shipped off, he offered me some advice.

"Indian, listen. I've exhausted my appeals. It's over for me."

The look on his face was of utter defeat and worry. It was an expression I hadn't seen on his face since I'd met him sometime earlier.

"It'll be alright, bro," I said. "Just keep to yourself, read, work out, draw . . ."

"I'll try. But shit's crazy down there. At least I'll get conjugal visits after a while . . ." Priest cracked a half smile and his eyes glazed over.

"Anyways, Thistle, listen. You have two official duties in this job: First, you have to make inmates read the rules when they first enter the range and make them shower—people need to be clean. If they don't listen, you have to bang 'em out. You're the first line of defence against disease and nastiness, the guys depend on you. Second, you have to distribute the food fairly, which I know you'll do 'cause Lauriston taught you well."

It was true, Lauriston had taught me the value of sharing and how it maintained order. "Is that it?" I asked, knowing that the quartermaster job was much more complex.

"Of course not. You have to keep the dope and tobacco flowing and you have to pass lighters to other inmates and other ranges. You do that through the cleaners who mop the halls. They come at 8:30 sharp every morning. You pass the lighter to them, they pass it to other inmates, and then they pass it back. It's simple. Here."

Priest handed me the purple lighter I'd seen used many times on our range. I grabbed it and rammed it in my jumpsuit pocket.

"When the screws come to shake down the range," Priest stressed, "it's your job to hoop the lighter. You've got to stick it up your ass, and fast. Don't give me that face, I've had to do it for two years straight! Do you know how many times I've been intimate with that thing?"

The laugh I let out relaxed Priest for the first time in our conversation. I felt happy he could ease up, if only for a second.

"Use soap if you can, slip the lighter up. If not, you're taking the dry hammer—it don't matter, just get it up there. I know it sucks, but the lighter is power. People can't smoke or do dope without it, and they will try to steal it from you. To prevent that, you have to buy protection with food; give it to guys who you want to fight for you—the big guys you work out with. They don't give a shit about you, but they do care where their calories come from, you can bet on that."

"Got it," I said, picturing myself having to repeatedly hoop the lighter during cell raids. "Anything else?"

"Yeah, when new fish come in, you have to take 'em to the toilet and watch 'em take a dump. Remember when I did that with you? There was a reason for that."

The memory of when I first entered the range shot across my mind. Priest met me at the sally port, made me read the rules, told me to shower, then took me to the toilet and watched me. He had his hand over the flusher the whole time. Once I was done, he pushed me aside and took a rolled-up newspaper and stirred the water, breaking up my waste. Then he told me to shower again.

"That's how the drugs come in. Some guys come in with suitcases up their asses and ruin the trade by driving down prices. You can't let that happen. If someone drops a suitcase in the bowl while you're quarter-master, you have to reach in and grab it, bang the guy out, then give the product to Bucky—it's his market. And don't worry about Bucky—he's got an army in here and will sort out any problems if it involves product. Got it? If you follow those rules, you'll be fine."

I assured Priest I understood, but I could see he wanted to tell me something else. I waited patiently until he looked comfortable, then asked, "Is there anything more?"

"Yes," he said intently. "I've seen a lot of guys hurt really bad in here. Some go to the hospital, some die. You see this book right here?" Priest pointed to his blue jail-issue Bible. "This has a lot of power in it and it can tell you things about people."

I tried to piece together what a Bible and people getting killed in jail had in common, while at the same time hoping Priest wasn't going to get all religious on me.

"Lots of people end up here," Priest said. "Some come to jail on re-mand, some on misdemeanours, some on transfer, some on breach, and some on really serious charges. Many of the fake cats brag about the crimes they've done; they do this to make themselves out to be badder than they really are, to intimidate others. They say they're bank robbers or jewel thieves or murderers but really they got caught with a dime bag of weed in their mother's station wagon at a traffic stop. Whatever they say, remember: braggers get daggers."

Priest paused and looked down at the guys pumping water bag weights at the end of the range; dudes getting their swole on. "But there are others inside who are real criminals, and there's a way to spot them."

"How?" I knew what he was about to say was valuable.

"At night, when you're giving out tea for Jug Up before bed, look at people's bedsides. Look beside the beds of those young punks who brag, then look at the bedside of the quiet guys. You'll see something different."

"What?" the question jumped from my lips before I had a chance to stop it.

"Those in for real crimes, the serious ones, they always have a Bible, Koran, Torah, or some other holy book by their bedsides. Night after night they stay up trying to make it right with God. Don't fuck with guys like that, they'll straight up kill you. The fake criminals, on the other hand, sleep like babies and never keep Bibles by their beds cause they don't need forgiveness cause they ain't done nothing wrong. The real hard nuts can't sleep and can't stop themselves from seeking God. They need forgiveness because they can't accept who or what they've become and what they've done, or accept the life they've made for themselves. It's a hard pill to swallow—to know you're a monster who's done monstrous things. They've got no other comfort than God . . . Somewhere along the line it went bad for them."

I kept a Bible beside my bed, and I asked, "What went bad, Priest?"

"All us criminals start out as normal people just like anyone else, but then things happen in life that tear us apart, that make us into something capable of hurting other people. That's all any of the darkness really is—just love gone bad. We're just broken-hearted people hurt by life."

There were tears in the corners of Priest's eyes. I could see for the first time the good man this muscle-bound criminal must have been once, the man he must have wished he could still be. I felt a deep sorrow knowing that he had no chances left.

The sally-port buzzer blared and the guards came to collect Priest. He composed himself, gathered his pillowcase of belongings, dapped my fist, and said goodbye.

I never saw Priest again. Someone told me that he'd been in for a homicide in a drug deal gone wrong. But I never did find out the details, because that was something he never talked about—except, I assume, in private, between himself and God, at night, with a Bible resting beside his bed.

AUDREY

"I GOT A CAR," SHE said. "We could work together." The gorgeous vanilla scent of her perfume filled my nose, and her deadly smile left me defenceless. I nodded like a moron.

I'd seen her around from time to time at some of the trap houses in the neighbourhood since getting out of jail. She had straight golden-blond hair and grey eyes plastered with mascara. She was a knockout and didn't look like one of us street people. Her cheeks were full, her body well-formed, and she had expensive clothes. She intimidated me at first. Then she introduced herself.

"Hello," she said. "My name's Audrey."

My heart jumped at her East Coast accent.

"What's your name?"

I was too enamoured to form a coherent response.

She twirled her hair on her index finger and giggled.

I was in love.

I learned that she lived around the corner in her own apartment. She was impressed that I fended for myself, begging and stealing, and did it without drug dealing.

"I don't believe in dope dealing," she said. "It's poisoning our kind. Broken-hearted people with nowhere to be in the world."

I related to that. I wondered how she kept her car on the road with such a serious crack addiction, but I never asked. It was none of my business.

One of the working girls who frequented many of the same dope spots wasn't a fan. "She takes away all the business," she said when I'd asked her who Audrey was. "I wish she'd leave some for us."

One day, when I brought in about two hundred dollars of stolen meat I'd pinched from the grocery store, Audrey was sitting in the back room of the trap house, watching the goings-on. I got my standard one-third the retail price for the haul and exchanged it for crack.

"A girl can do a lot with a guy like you, Jesse," Audrey said as she eyed me up and down, then looked at my rock.

We went back to her place that night. I thought we were going to have sex, but we just smoked until the dope ran out, and talked until our jaws hurt, about where she was from and how she wanted out of the life we were both caught up in. I didn't make any moves toward her. I figured she got that all the time—pigs invading her body.

She made up some blankets for me on the couch and said, "Anytime you need a place to crash you're welcome to stay." She covered me up, then went to sleep alone in her bedroom. I dreamt of her the whole night.

The next day we did our first run together.

We hit about twelve grocery stores. I went in with my gym bag, filled it with steaks, shrimp, baby formula, razors, and makeup, until it damn near broke from the weight. She waited outside, her van revving. A couple of times security guards chased me out, but I just hopped in the van and she floored it to our next destination.

The excitement in Audrey's face, the way we cheered and held hands as we sped away, like we'd accomplished something, turned me on. It made my foot feel better, made me feel better about myself, made me feel better about everything. We made a great team. When we cashed out in the evening, we had more dope than we could smoke. I fried up a few steaks, and we had dinner at her place like real people.

Soon, our scams became more complex. The easiest was the water bottle hustle. I'd go into a grocery store and grab two huge water bottles—the ones worth ten bucks when they're returned empty—and carry them out. If I wasn't followed, I'd dump out the water, go back in, and return them. I got twenty dollars for five minutes' work, simple as pie.

If store security did come after me, I'd drop the bottles in the parking lot then rush away. Security had the choice of either chasing me down or staying with the merchandise—they couldn't do both. If they did leave the bottles for someone else to steal, that someone was Audrey. She'd drive behind the action, pick the bottles up, then speed ahead and grab me before I was busted. That was the best scenario, because we'd just return them somewhere else down the road. Again, an easy twenty.

If security stayed with the bottles, Audrey would just drive ahead and pick me up, and we'd try it again somewhere else. In all three scenarios, I always got away safe. It was brilliant. We did it all day.

We hit liquor stores, too. We used what we called our blitzkrieg manoeuvre there, our most daring, but also our most lucrative. We could make upward of $200 or $300 a pop. I'd rush in and grab the first big bottles in sight—maybe five at a time—then I'd make for the front doors and dive headfirst into the van. She'd hit the gas, back door wide open, my legs dangling halfway out. I must've looked like a baseball player stealing second base. Audrey was one hell of a driver, fast and fearless, rubber wheels screeching through red lights and stop signs like she was Steve McQueen on meth. Often, we'd look back at the pack of angry floor walkers standing and screaming, shaking their fists at the van, and we'd yell at the top of our lungs, cheering our victories.

When the liquor stores caught on, we shifted to beer stores. Given the weight and size of beer cases, the runs didn't make as much money, but we still made hundreds of dollars over the course of the day. All of it went to crack.

We got thinner. There was a swagger about us, a strange kind of confidence, like we were rock stars or something. We *were* ghetto rock stars, just not the kind with guitars, and we partied like there was no tomorrow. No matter how much money we got, though, it was never enough. And the excitement was fleeting. Now, looking back on it, we were high, wild, and borderline out of our minds. I can't believe we did what we did. I regret it all.

In a matter of weeks it all fell apart. I was sitting at the end of Audrey's couch drinking a bottle of booze we'd just stolen, waiting for our nightly steaks to grill up. There was a giant pile of crack between us—our day's keep.

"I know you want me," Audrey slurred, drunk off her face. She cozied up to me and put her hand on my lap, sliding it toward my crotch. It felt weird. We'd never been intimate before, even though I'd wanted her since we met.

I sat frozen. She didn't look so hot anymore. It wasn't like she'd changed so much as to not be physically attractive—she was still a bombshell. It's just that I didn't like it when she talked and acted this way, nor did I like what we'd become. I thought we could make a real go of life together, get jobs, clean up, stay out of trouble. I wanted us to be something better and I didn't want to ruin it. It was silly to think this way, because it was clear that we were addict thieves, partners in crime—good at it, too—and that we adored each other and got along great. I just had too many feelings to take advantage of her.

I loaded up the pipe and gave it to her to distract her. She knocked it out of my hand and leaned in for a kiss. I reciprocated. My soul exploded, but it felt wrong. I pulled back.

"I can't," I said. "I think I love you." I reached for her hand. I wanted to explain myself, about how I wanted to wait.

"Don't," she said, sounding hostile. She hoisted herself to the edge of the couch and almost face-planted on the table. Her knee knocked over our little crack mountain and a portion of it tumbled onto the carpet.

I sat speechless. I knew I'd crossed a line.

"Take your half and get out," she said, not looking at me. "I'm done with you." She walked over to the front door and held it open. "Out."

I didn't argue as I collected my belongings and left.

We didn't even say goodbye.

DYNAMITE

THE WICK ON THE STICK of dynamite stuck out of my parka about five inches. I tucked it into my breast pocket as I headed to the dope house.

My crack dealer's name was Green, a gang member from Rexdale, Ontario, and his homies all had colours for names. I assumed they got the idea from *Reservoir Dogs*. Green told his mates that I was dangerous and willing to do anything. He was right. I had no fear of death after Samantha and I broke up and what happened with Audrey and Flip. Everyone was impressed that I'd robbed the convenience store, and that I'd eluded the cops with a cast on my leg. They started calling me "Hot Boy." I hated the moniker, but it gave me a kind of respect, homeless or not.

Piles of snow shimmered in the dusk as I hurried past the mechanic shop. The red stick felt heavy against my chest, like an iron bar. The Oxy-Contin I'd taken three hours earlier was wearing off. My foot was hurting like it'd been crucified with a six-inch railway tie—the staph infection had come back. Cold crept into my ankle and seized the wires holding my foot together. I couldn't run without the aid of pills, and pain could halt my mission.

It doesn't matter, I resolved. *I'm going to get a giant rock from those dealer scum whether I'm high or not.* My jaw muscles flexed and snapped the tooth I'd got fixed in jail. I spit the fragment on the sidewalk and it bounced off into a snowbank. A vision of Vancouver and the car came to me. I wanted revenge for the person they'd turned me into.

I whipped out my crack stem, loaded it with my last twenty-dollar rock, and lit it. I needed that extra push forward. Yellow flames licked the glass and the rock melted, releasing a stream of thick smoke. It sizzled like Rice Krispies covered in milk. A gush of spit poured out of my mouth and thwacked onto the ice below; it froze into a beautiful spiderweb of crystals, making tiny squeaking noises as it formed. In an instant my hearing had sharpened to superhuman levels.

I spun around 360 degrees scanning for the legion of hidden cops I knew tracked my every movement. I saw nothing, but sensed they were close. Once, I'd found a tracking device in my baseball cap—in the button on top. People told me it was just there to hold the hat together, but I didn't believe them. I ripped it off and chucked it into the Etobicoke River to evade capture. These tracking cops, I'd figured out, also sent coded messages to each other using car license-plate numbers. Nine meant they were close; two or five meant they had a lock on my whereabouts and were moving in.

I saw a car with a license plate with a two and a five, and it even slowed down as it passed. I searched around for cover. I contemplated diving into the bush but decided against it. My ears were ringing from the intense crack high, and I almost slipped on the ice and dropped my payload of explosives.

The blast of rock also brought out those Ewok-looking shadow creatures who shot death rays at me with their galactic sorcery. Their chatter drove me nuts; they sounded exactly like they did in *Star Wars*: "*Mechipy chuwa, ah!*" Fuckin' terrifying. They were stealthy creatures, melting in and out of the shadows. They reminded me of those demon shadows in *Ghost* that dragged that Puerto Rican—Willie Lopez—to hell for killing Patrick Swayze after he got hit by that car. I didn't want to end up like him. I lit my pipe again, hoping to rid myself of my paranoia, but an Ewok groaned from the darkness over near the curb.

They're coming for me!

I ran as fast as I could into the middle of the street where the light was strongest. My heart pounded until it hurt. I slapped my face to snap out of it. I slapped it again to remind myself that none of it was real. My arm knocked loose the dynamite and it tumbled down around my waist inside my jacket. I placed it back in my pocket and continued on.

When I got to the dope house, one of Green's men was guarding the door.

"Hot Boy!" he hollered as I approached. He held out his fist and I dapped it. He kept his eyes on my every move. The brown-black hilt of his Glock was exposed in his waistband, his shirt purposefully pulled up, warning people not to fuck around. It didn't faze me.

"Green around?" I smirked back, trying to play it cool. I felt a thunderbolt radiate up my leg. The Oxy had worn off.

"Inside, in the basement." He stood up and reached toward me.

I jumped back. "What the fuck?!" I said, pushing his hands away from my torso. He was going to pat me down. "You know me, dog."

His face hardened, and he put a hand near his pistol. "New policy."

"What do you think? I got a stick of dynamite on me?! Chill." I laughed and nudged his shoulder.

He laughed back. "Wouldn't be surprised." He eyed me one last time, then motioned toward the door with his head. "G'wan in."

My bluff had worked. I dapped his hand and passed.

The house smelled of crack and meth. The walls were caked with a clear layer of resin, enough to get high on if I scraped it off and smoked it. Half the light bulbs were missing or shattered on the floor; the whole place was lit by candles. A dim light radiated from the bowels of the basement. I steadied myself and made my descent.

A few crackheads were in the corner hitting their pipes near the foot of the stairs, and a few tweakers were over near the bathroom smoking broken light bulbs. The door at the back was closed. That was a good sign—it meant the ladies were turning tricks with Johns because there was dope around; no one used that room but them. Green emerged from a door in the hall. He had a sock in his hand—his trademark dope carry-all. It bulged with a load of luscious rocks.

"Crackula, my man," he said to me. "What can I do for you?"

I stood there a second. I felt the explosive press hard against my ribs. Green must have sensed something was up and backed away. I reached into my coat, yanked out the dynamite, and thrust it above my head.

"GIVE ME ALL YOUR FUCKING DOPE OR I'LL LIGHT IT!" I screamed and waved the red cylinder around, my lighter held near the wick, ready to ignite it.

Green's eyes opened wide and all the heads in the room spun around, a look of terror on them. Everyone jostled for shelter, tossing their gear. Green backed up against the wall, almost dropping his plump sock. The gunman at the front door appeared at the top of the stairs and stood there motionless, seemingly stunned. Another emerged from the door where Green had been earlier, gun in hand. He, too, was shitting himself.

"I'LL LIGHT IT—I SWEAR!" I yelled again. I flicked my lighter. A bead of sweat trickled down my forehead, and I wiped it away on the sleeve of my dynamite arm.

Green cracked a smile.

That wasn't the reaction I'd hoped for.

He grabbed the explosive out of my hand. "A fucking road flare?" He laughed and tugged at the wick and it fell onto the floor. He sniffed at the red stick like he was examining a fine cigar. "Doesn't smell like sulphur to me."

Silence fell over the room like a blanket, until I heard the safeties on the guns click. Green stared at me. I was trapped.

I'd picked the flare up near the gravel pit by my old public school. It looked like a stick of dynamite, so I stuck a piece of string in it to make a wick, and hatched a scheme to come to the dope house and threaten maximum carnage to get a rock. I'd gotten the idea from an old story Uncle Ron had told me about when he went into a biker clubhouse with a live grenade to scare the shit out of everyone. It had worked for him, but my plan failed miserably. I waited for Green's men to open fire.

To my surprise, Green giggled. "That's why I like you," he said. "Because you're fucking crazy like me."

He reached into his sock and pulled out a twenty rock. "Here." He placed it in my hand and waved his men off. "Great joke. You had me for a second."

PUSH-UPS

I WAS IN JAIL IN 2007 for assaulting a couple of police officers.

I'd done a huge toke of crack after breaking into a car and was having bad hallucinations and thought the Ewok creatures were coming for me. I ran into the middle of the street hollering that I needed help and was dying and losing my mind.

From a side road, a van flew at me then slammed on its brakes and five huge bearded men jumped out and began chasing me. They looked like bikers. I hobbled as fast as I could, headlong into traffic, cars veering out of the way, horns honking, but the bikers were all larger and faster than I was. They tackled me, but I fought back with all my might until I saw a police cruiser pull up. I knew I'd be safe—the bikers couldn't murder or kidnap me—but they still choked me from behind, and I almost lost consciousness, my arms punching forward until I heard a loud crack and gurgle in my throat.

I was dumped in the back of a paddy wagon, scratching the steel sides and growling, like an injured mountain lion in shackles, and brought to Maplehurst, where I was charged with assault with intent to resist arrest times two, possession of a scheduled substance, break and enter, and theft.

The guys on the range were impressed that I'd fought off so many undercover police—the bikers, as it turned out—and had gone fist-to-cuffs with three uniformed police officers, and in the process re-broke my wrist and fractured my jaw. Truth was, I was just terrified and high and had gone mad, there was no toughness involved.

One.

My arms wobbled as I pushed up. Hands: shoulder-width apart. Feet: together. Body: straight. The latest song from Rihanna blasted across the protective-custody range in the jail in Milton, Ontario. A dank scent of male swamp entered me as I sucked in air for energy.

Two.

The pressure increased in my head as my sternum touched the floor, and my wrist throbbed, but then my arms straightened again. I peered down at myself and saw a rack of bones and a stomach that sucked back toward my spine. My skin was grey and lifeless.

Three.

I gritted my teeth and felt a burn in my triceps as I dipped down and up another time. There was a tightness in my core I hadn't felt for years. These were the first set of push-ups I'd attempted to do since I'd been arrested again.

Four.

I tried with all my might to keep straight but as my nose touched the floor first, my bum shot up in the air. I glanced over at my cellmate, who was drinking his orange crystal drink out of an empty shampoo bottle. A stain of blood near his foot had seeped into the pores of the cement.

Five.

Faintness overtook me. I kept going. My blue jail underwear dangled low, finding the ground before I touched down and hoisted myself up again. The echo of the cell wasn't as bad as the hole, but it still made focusing difficult.

Six.

Halfway down my muscles failed. My arms locked and wouldn't push up anymore. I gave it one more go—they wouldn't budge.

I tucked my legs underneath my bum and pulled myself upright using the side of the steel table. I swayed as my knees buckled and I found myself clinging to the bars of the cell. Last thing I remember was my hands letting go, then the hollow sound of my skull smashing into the pavement.

When I awoke I was in another wing of the jail with an attendant hovering above me.

"You shouldn't be exercising, Mr. Thistle," he said. "Your blood pressure is too low, you're still too emaciated."

"But how am I supposed to defend myself?" I asked. I tried to raise my arms but couldn't. I swallowed and heard a click in my throat.

"I wouldn't worry about that right now." He pulled back the cover revealing my foot. "The disease in here is way more serious than the other inmates."

I wasn't sure if he was talking about my infection or the detention centre.

INCEPTION

I SAW A GUY ON our range at the sally port talking with an older man in a red-and-grey uniform. The geezer wasn't stiff like the guards. He had a peaceful presence about him, but still a hardness about his body language, like he'd been one of us, like he'd done time in the past.

"Who is that?" I asked my cellmate.

"That's the chaplain."

I watched as the inmate gave the chaplain an envelope and took a pile of papers to the back table where he always sat.

When I walked over and asked him what he was doing, he said, "I'm getting my high school. You do that through the chaplain. It's a great way to pass the time."

I observed him for about a week. He was quiet—the mark of a true gent, like Priest said. He never bragged or talked bad or gambled chocolate bars or traded dope—the guy just did his time real classy like. I admired that. I thought maybe I could make a better life for myself in those books, too, like he was trying to do. Or maybe it was silly.

"I'd like to try that out," I said to him one day after I'd finished working out with the water bags. "School. Give it another go."

He lifted his head from his notes.

"But I can't read too good. I dropped out a long time ago. And years of drugs and hard living—well, it's kind of done my head in."

"Nah. It's easy—don't believe those lies." He turned around a piece of paper. "This is my reading assignment. Try reading the first line."

My eyes had trouble focusing, I stumbled and stuttered, and I messed up pronouncing a few words, but I eventually got through it.

"See. Walk in the park. I can help you out if you want."

A week later, I received my first assignment from the chaplain in English. I got help with my reading from other inmates when I needed it and handed in my work the following week. A month later, I got an 85 percent on the final.

Something within me shifted.

Philosophy and world religions classes followed. I got 83 percent in philosophy. World religions was way harder—I didn't finish because I didn't understand all the big words. The local school board, however, recognized my efforts and gave me six maturity credits. Three months into my sentence and I was only two credits short of graduating high school—it was a miracle.

Unbeknownst to me, most of the guys on the range were suspicious. Rumours spread that I was flying kites to the screws, squawking, because cell raids always happened right after I'd handed in my homework or sent a letter to Grandma. After I submitted one of my last assignments, I was confronted in the washroom by a group of inmates.

"Why would you chirp on your brothers?" they asked and slammed me up against the shower wall.

"I'm just trying to finish my schooling," I said, afraid but determined.

They roughed me up some, clocked me in the eye a few times, but eventually stopped, satisfied, I assume, by the fact that I didn't break.

THE MESSENGER

I HAD A VISITOR. I was so excited. No one ever visited me or sent me letters—ever. Grandma didn't even respond. That didn't bother me anymore.

The guard handcuffed me and took me to the visitor's area. I was surprised to see Jerry on the other side of the Plexiglas. Somehow he'd found my hiding spot—again—like he always did. No matter where I ran—to a shelter, jail, or to some far-off random street corner across the country—the fucker kept tabs on me and would track me down. Trying to hide from him was like a souped-up version of that TV show *Mantracker*, except Jerry didn't have a horse or cowboy hat, and I wasn't running and leaping through the bush. This, however, was the first time he'd actually come to see me in jail.

"So, here you are," he said, "hiding like a frightened rat. When is this going to stop?"

"Fuck you," I said. "I'll go back to my cell! You watch!"

"Go then, go back to your hole and die alone, you sad, sad man!"

I wanted to kick the Plexiglas and have it shatter in his pudgy face, blinding him for life.

"I see through your macho bullshit," he said. "Always have. One day I'm going to stop searching, then you'll be fucked."

I fidgeted with my coveralls.

"You put up all these walls to keep people out. Literally—look around.

I just don't have the energy to break them down anymore. No one does. I'm the last—no one else gives a shit anymore. I had to dig really deep to come see you here today. I hate seeing you penned in like some animal, but I forced myself to do it because I have a message."

I looked up at him.

"Grandma is sick. She doesn't have many years left. You living like this is hurting her, and it makes me want to beat you up—seriously. She's been waiting all these years for you to stop living this way. If she dies and you're like this, you'll never recover. I hope you realize that."

I slammed my fists on the counter in front of me and closed my eyes. I didn't know what to do. When I opened them I saw Jerry's hand pressed hard against the Plexiglas. I didn't dare lift my hand to his, but looked up at him.

"See, I knew you were still in there. That's the little brother I remember."

As soon as he said that, the buzzer of the timer went off—our visit was over. As the guard snapped the handcuffs back onto my semi-healed wrists, I turned and saw Jerry's hand still on the glass, his eyes locked onto mine.

A couple weeks later I was released with time served. I felt hopeless—I'd come so close to finishing high school, only to be released right before I could see it through, to be released right back into the life that I knew was slowly killing me. I was in bondage to the dealers, a twenty-four-hour money-generating machine, and the thought of lurching forward, and the pain that shot up my leg with every step in the desert out there, terrified me.

STEAK KNIFE

I WAS STEALING BIKES FROM people's backyards. My dealers took them, thirty dollars a pop, without question. I desperately needed the money to get high. I'd been up for a week solid since being released from jail, and my addictions were worse than ever.

The street I was on in Brampton is gang territory. Crack in Brampton travelled through there before being distributed throughout Peel County. I shouldn't have been jacking bikes there, I knew better. But I was desperate, and my mind wasn't working well. Jail time had softened my begging and thieving skills, too. People just didn't believe my lies anymore. "You're a healthy young man," they'd say. "You should be working."

I spotted a BMX bike, with gold pegs and chrome handle bars, and hauled it over a fence. Before it hit the ground, a group of angry young men confronted me from behind.

"Hot Boy!" one of them hollered. "You know this block's off limits!"

They stripped me of the bike and shoved me into a parking lot. There were five of them. Bandanas flying.

"Now we gotta make an example of you," the smallest one said as he circled behind me to cut off my exit.

A guy in front of me pulled out a steak knife and lunged at me. The knife hit me right in the mouth. I tumbled onto the ground, smashing the back of my head on the concrete. Blood poured down into my throat and I choked, but I swung forward, wildly, punching up at the sky, the instinct to defend myself kicking in.

"Look at him," one guy said. He kicked my ribs repeatedly, pushing me sideways. I felt nothing but heard the dull thuds echo through my body. I saw the knife handle sticking out of my face and covered my head.

I heard laughing, followed by the close whine of sirens and wheels grinding on concrete, and raised my head, saw my attackers running off in all directions like cockroaches as a cop car mounted the curb. I yanked the knife out of my face and tossed it in a bush. A stream of blood gushed onto my shirt—it looked like a massacre. My hands fumbled over my head. The left side of my face was numb. There was a hole above my upper lip. I stuck my finger into it and it slid over my front teeth.

Right down to the bone.

A policewoman ran over. "Who did it?" she asked.

I stayed quiet, fearful that people in the complex nearby were listening.

She helped me to my feet, then put me in her squad car and drove to the hospital.

I was shipped to 21 Division after and charged with theft. Didn't matter. The arrest probably saved my life.

After being attacked by a gang, I was taken to the hospital to get stitches; then the police processed me and shipped me back into custody. The scar is still visible today if you look hard enough.

RANDOM DUDE

"NAME. BIRTHDATE. SOCIAL SECURITY," THE shelter worker rhymed off, thrusting a clipboard at me under the Plexiglas. She looked like she was having a rough day, her hair all frizzed out.

I grabbed the clipboard. "I don't have any ID," I said. "I just got out of jail, and I'm going by bus to Ottawa to rehab tomorrow. The chaplain bought me a ticket." I pushed my Greyhound stub against the glass.

The rehabilitation centre I was going to was Harvest House, a last-chance Christian rehab that took the worst of the worst cases that no other place would touch—I know, I tried calling them all from jail. Given my record, it was my only option. Olive had given me the phone number one day when I called her collect from jail trying to set up a release plan.

"I'm going to be brutally honest with you, Jesse," she said, as I scribbled down the digits. "I've known you forever, and you can't make it another season the way you are. You don't look right anymore. Please call."

Olive was always so optimistic, so hopeful—she believed God could rescue people even in the most wretched of cases—so to hear her talk this way really caught my attention. I phoned Harvest House the instant I got off the phone with her and discovered that they had GED schooling as well as treatment—I could finish what I'd started and graduate high school. Plus, they'd take me right away—no other program would do that. That gave me such hope. When I told the chaplain, he bought me the one-way ticket and gave me a pair of jeans and a shirt, right before the jail gates opened to freedom.

"These don't fit," I said.

"Trust me," he told me when he dropped me off at the shelter. "You'll put on weight."

The electro-haired lady behind the Plexiglas ignored me and my bus ticket, slid a pen through the opening, and started talking with her colleagues.

I filled in the form and passed the clipboard back.

"Jesse Thistle," she said, and I nodded. She buzzed me in and told me to wait near the front to get my toiletries and to finish the intake process.

The shelter was empty, or at least it appeared that way. A few people were playing cards near the doors to the washrooms. A couple were on the phones by the office. I hadn't been to this shelter in months, but had been a regular for years, starting way back in 2001 when they moved it from the old fire hall. I sat down beside an old man with grey hair. His clothes and shoes told me he'd just gotten out of jail or lost his home—they were too nice to be lived-in street gear.

"Did she say you were Thistle?" he asked and motioned with his thumb to the office.

"Yeah." I studied his body language and wondered if I should bolt—thought maybe he could be a friend of Mike and Stefan's.

"Was your dad Sonny by chance? I only ever knew one family of Thistles."

"Cyril Thistle Jr. is my dad."

The man's face changed from hard convict to friendly dog. I noticed a few prison tattoos under his sleeve as he stuck his hand out.

"Name's Rodney. I was a good friend of your pop's."

I took his hand. "I've never met anyone who's known my dad other than my own family. I'm just on my way to Harvest House in Ottawa. I leave tomorrow."

"Been there. Treatment. Not Harvest House."

The tips of his fingers were burnt and swollen. Telltale signs that he suffered from the same addiction I did. Only lighters or crack stems burn like that; that, or maybe he was a mechanic.

Not likely, I deduced. *Working mechanics don't usually stay in homeless shelters.*

"Your dad was a great man. One of the best in Weston back in the day. Too bad what happened."

I nodded. I had no words and just wanted to hear him riff—thought maybe he'd reveal some details I hadn't heard before—but he fell silent.

I finally said, "I wish I knew him." I glanced over to the intake worker, then back, not sure of what was on my new friend's mind. "I grew up at my grandparents'. Last I saw him was when I was three. I've been keeping an eye out for him."

"Keeping an eye out?"

"You know, in case he pops up somewhere. I heard he's homeless. I've been searching all over for years."

He shook his head and sat up. "No one told you? He's gone, son. They got him in '82."

The lady in the booth called my name, but I didn't move.

"Who got him?"

"You better go get signed in," he said. "If you don't, they'll discharge you for wasting their time."

"Who got him?" I asked again before getting up and walking toward the office, glancing back at him the whole way.

He didn't answer.

The worker closed the door behind me, and I sat there the entire time thinking of what he'd said.

When I emerged, he was gone.

THE PROCESS

I DIDN'T GET IT RIGHT the first time in rehab. No one ever does.

I arrived at Harvest House in November 2007 and stayed for three months straight. I didn't really work the twelve steps of Alcoholics Anonymous when I got there, nor did I dig deep in personal development classes to the root of my addictions, like everyone else. I believed I was better than everyone, than the program. I kind of coasted after the initial detox and withdrawal, white-knuckled it, as they say in AA speak. I stayed dry with no cigarettes, sure, but never really achieved sobriety, even though I thought I did. I just repeated the first drugless day for ninety days.

Eventually dreams of liquor and drugs drove me out into a pitch-black February night with my roommate Max, another guy who was lackluster about the program. I was in no shape to face Old Man Winter in Ottawa; I didn't own a jacket or even a sweater. I didn't care. All that mattered was that I was free and that I was going to be high and drunk and that I didn't have to listen to the counsellors yell at me in group therapy while I avoided revealing any of my resentments about Dad or Josh or Grandpa or Jerry, or read the King James Bible, begging God for a forgiveness I knew I didn't deserve.

"Fuck it all! Tonight is mine," I proclaimed. I knew I'd most likely get arrested, so I was going on a tear until my cash ran out and the police caught up with me. "I'm going out in a blaze of glory!"

Max grinned a demonic grin and let out a hellish AC/DC scream, complete with heavy-metal devil horns thrust into the air.

We made it to the fence, and under the cover of darkness, we scrambled over it. My pants tore open as I leapt to freedom, leaving my balls blowing in the freezing wind.

The freedom that first day felt incredible. Like I'd been some cooped-up dog who'd discovered the gate left open.

Frickin' party time!

We arrived at a homeless shelter an hour after we jumped the fence and immediately scored some dope and divided it between us. After the first blast of rock, Max saw an old working girl he'd dated before his stint in rehab. He waved to me, and they disappeared.

I ran to the liquor store, swiped a sixty ouncer of Crown Royal, and slammed it down without even tasting it. Then I went in to steal another to buy a huge chunk of crack. Store security didn't notice me for once with my full cheeks and laundered clothes. My put-togetherness was like a cloak of invisibility.

I went ballistic. I know now that the compulsion to get high had eroded any moral judgment that I had. I was totally out of control. I was doing things like ripping open pay phones, and shoplifting in what felt like every store in the whole Ottawa area—razors, bras, makeup, baby formula, shrimp, whatever the cab drivers in front of Rideau Centre wanted me to steal, I got it for them. They were like my bank account—a twenty-four-hour drive-through cash bar that never closed. I must've been up for fourteen straight days before I finally fell asleep in the parking garage in the market. By then, I knew I was starting to look like some creature, slinking about. And I'd begun to be reduced to begging, worse than I ever was in Brampton, like my addictions had been at the bottom of the Harvest House driveway doing push-ups, getting stronger than before, waiting for me to fuck up.

THE MEANING IS GONE

I RETREATED INTO DARKNESS.

I walked along the boulevard in Ottawa, and the colours of the storefronts drained down across the sidewalks, faded under the blackened snowbanks, and seeped into the storm grates. Grey on grey, followed by more grey. The city hummed its droning hum, a cacophony of horns and car tires rotating across slick pavement, splashing through puddles. People hustled past me as I limped forward. My bowels loosened and let go, sending a stream of waste down my legs.

I'd held it in the best I could, stopping several times to ask store employees if I could use their washroom, but they'd said, "Sorry, for paying customers only," before ushering me back out into the cold. I shuffled into an alley and attempted to clean myself with a discarded chip bag. After, I asked a restaurant for napkins, and they refused and grimaced. It was impossible to hide my shame.

I steadied myself against a bus stop, pulled out a bottle of Listerine, and took a swig, hoping that the antiseptic would cleanse my spiritual wounds. Mouthwash was the best I could do. Most of the liquor stores had caught me stealing and wouldn't let me in. I heard the LCBO even had pictures of me in their backrooms. When the noxious fluid hit my belly, it torched my intestines but worked its dark magic. I faded into a groggy, chemical drunk, the kind that obliterated existence into fragments, just like I liked.

My digestive system was in tatters. The past few weeks I'd been puking blood mixed with bile, a sour, putrid liquid that burned when it came up. It made eating near impossible, save for a dry slice of toast or some weak chicken broth. The lack of regular meals caused my throat to close up. It hurt in the most ungodly way when I tried to force anything down it. The shelter staff worried. They'd come over and ask me why I wasn't eating. I never answered. It was none of their business and they could fuck off as far as I was concerned. They didn't even know my real name.

A passerby paused and said, "I don't have any money." I hadn't asked. He looked me up and down then glanced at my bottle of Listerine.

"Fuck your money," I said. "Cocksucker." I belched caustic air in his direction then took another swig. It burned as though I'd eaten a forest fire. My stomach contracted, and bile shot onto my shoes and the sidewalk. The rose colour of it used to frighten me, but I didn't care anymore. I wiped my hand across my mouth and started toward the Giant Tiger, where I hoped to steal a new pair of pants. My legs were like wooden stilts underneath my baggy, soiled jeans, knobby knees knocking. It took all the strength I had just to keep steady, my vision wavering. I gave up on my mission after a few laboured steps.

The smell of bread from the bakery on the corner made me think of my grandma and our Christmases in Brampton. There was an ember of that time still alight within me. I inhaled deeply, hoping to set it ablaze. Nothing. The memory passed.

My stomach gurgled, and I searched the ground for lost change and cigarette butts. I found nothing but garbage, more dirty looks, and a bench out in front of a bar. My foot was numb, and I decided to take a rest—I wouldn't be able to fish change from the Centennial Flame fountain on Parliament Hill, either. I'd gotten so used to the pain from my ankle that I routinely forgot about the gaping sore. It'd been over two years since the operation. The hole was the size of a dime, but the flesh around the edge of it was white and shrivelled, like skin submerged in water for too long, and it expelled a green-grey ooze that crusted yellow when it dried. It reeked like the dead. My foot, too, used to frighten me, but now I was indifferent.

A song came on the loudspeaker of the bar. I turned my head to listen, wondering if I recognized it. I didn't. I didn't recognize much anymore—not music, or movies, or anything. Signs blurred into smears of jumbled incomprehension. Faces, too. I was a wild animal, a stray wolf with matted fur covered in filth, one not even a dogcatcher would want to mess with. The world screamed past me. I lived amongst the Ewok shadows; I groaned misery and shifted as they did. I longed to be part of something again, to be known and accepted, to hear my name. No one ever said my name anymore. I never told anyone who I was for fear of being found out. For what? I didn't know. I'd forgotten years ago.

I slumped forward on the bench and held my head in my hands, trying to remember how my name sounded. I spelled it aloud to myself.

"J. E. S. S. E. Jesse."

I smiled, but molten bile bubbled up into my throat, followed by the rude smell of feces, bringing me back to the street. Olive was right, my body was giving out. It wasn't strong enough to endure any more punishment.

SALVATION AND THE SOUP KITCHEN LADY

"HEY YOU!" A VOICE CALLED up to me. "Get down from there."

It was some woman. I paid her no heed on my ascent to the summit of the half-completed building on Rideau Street.

"I said get down, or I'll call the cops."

My bony hand grasped the edge of a roughly finished ledge. My muscles may have atrophied somewhat from addiction and soup-kitchen slop, but I was still as spry as Gollum of Middle-earth looking for his Precious.

"What do you care?" I shot back. "Beat it."

"Why do all these do-gooders keep fucking with me?" I muttered to myself. "Why can't they just mind their own goddamned business?" I hoisted myself up another floor.

"I work over at the Shepherds of Good Hope shelter. I've seen you on the breadlines." The pitch of her voice raised the higher I went.

"So what?" I replied without looking down.

Her efforts were useless. I'd worked out my plan in jail. After I got released, I was going to climb to the top of a construction tower, close my eyes, spread my wings, and float away, crack and alcohol coursing through my brain for courage. I'd had enough. If shuffling around on the streets like a homeless rat on cocaine was bad, a recent stint in jail in the nation's capital was worse. It wasn't like in Maplehurst with Bucky and

Priest—here I got no respect. No one would take my calls—not family, not friends. Rapists and murderers got their calls taken, but not me. And letters—forget about it. I'd wait every day at the front of the range for word from the outside world, and every day I was disappointed.

I shouted down to the woman on the ground. "Listen, lady, I'm just going to go to sleep up here cause it's safer than on ground lev—"

"It's still winter weather and cold as hell. You'll freeze up there."

A gust bit through my H&M hoodie, and I felt weak all of a sudden. "Listen, can you please just leave me be? I just want to be left alone."

"I don't believe you."

I quickened my pace. I didn't want to lose my nerve, so I reached for the next floor. My hand slipped on some ice, and I fell onto my back on the floor below. Writhing, I almost rolled off the edge.

"You almost got what you came for!" she shouted.

Gasping for air, my heart racing, I curled up and covered my ears, trying to hide from both her incessant voice and what had just happened.

"Hey, you know what? I think I do know you. You told me about your grandmother and your brother. You said your name was Jesse or something."

The sound of my own name dropped into my consciousness like a sledgehammer. The tears creeping along the bridge of my nose froze as I thought of my grandma and Jerry—memories that shattered and warmed me at the same time. The woman below was right, I did know her.

I could hear her yelling again.

"You said you missed them and wanted to make them proud. I remember."

I rolled over and peeked over the ledge. Sure enough, it was her, black hair hanging behind her shoulders as she looked up at me.

"Come on now, enough of this nonsense," she said with a big smile. "Get down, and let's get you some soup and socks."

I picked myself up and began my long descent.

When I got to the bottom, she greeted me with a brisk hug. "That was close."

"It sure was," I replied.

RECONCILIATION

2008–2017

FIGHTING THE DARKNESS

once, in a not-too-distant life
i was a different person.

it was a dark time
loveless,
cold,
violent.

a time when I no longer cared about the world,
a world that had taken so much
and left me with nothing.

wîhtikow (monster)

i lived by the criminal's creed:
live for today,
forget the past,
damn the future.

i took what i wanted,
stole what i needed,
and robbed when i could.

dwelling in shadows,

amongst the murderers and thieves,

the highwaymen,

and outlaws.

that is how i can fight the darkness now.

because i once was the darkness,

an apparition,

driven by worst part of the human soul.

a beast lost in resentments.

once, in a not-too-distant life.

DAWN OF THE BRONZE AGE

"WE FOLLOWED A TRAIL OF money from the scene of the crime," the constable told his fellow officers. "Right to where he was smoking crack in front of the Shepherds of Good Hope. Can you believe that?"

It was shamefully true. For my very last crime the cops had literally caught me red-handed. I put up little resistance when they chucked me in the back of the squad car. I'd had enough.

I faced break-and-enter charges and was processed at the Elgin Street police station in a nice part of town I rarely ventured into, except when arrested. Then I was shipped to the Ottawa-Carleton Detention Centre (OCDC).

So there I was, once again, heckling the screws and counting the days and cinder blocks.

Those cinder blocks seemed to follow me wherever I went—the ones found in jails, mental institutions, probation offices, hospitals, detox centres, detention centres, shelters, Sally Anns, welfare offices, court holding cells, police station bullpens. I hated the monotony of doing time, but if I was sick of anything, it was seeing those institutional sixteen-by-eights. I once counted around 180 of them in my cell at the Don Jail in Toronto; around 190 at Maplehurst in Milton, Ontario; and around 160 at OCDC. But the Harvest House rehab centre had over 360 blocks per dorm room; that made it like the Ritz-Carlton to me.

I called Harvest House, dreaming of their abundance of blocks, hoping to get someone to vouch for me in court and bail me out.

The intake worker picked up the phone. "Have you had enough of the life, of the Stone Age, Thistle?"

Employees at Harvest House could be so smug.

"Get me outta here!" I begged. "I'm sick of it all and I'm especially sick of this jail food—reminds me of crappy retirement scraps they feed old people."

"What, you don't like steamed dog food?" He laughed.

Eleven days later, someone from Harvest House came and bailed me out, and I was released directly back into rehab where I could do my dead time before sentencing.

The judge who granted my surety said that if I made the year in rehab, it could serve as my jail time. "But if you skip out, Mr. Thistle, we will

Rehab. I was arrested before I could sell the gold chain to get cash for dope. I can't remember where I got the chain from, but I gave it to my roommate after he achieved three months' sobriety.

find you and send you down to the darkest prison we have because the justice system has had quite enough of your nonsense." The sound of his hand pounding down scared the shit out of me.

A few hours later, I was back at Harvest House shaking and vomiting and praying for mercy. But it was a chance at redemption, and I was grateful for it.

RUNNING ON GLASS

THE LACES ON MY BLUE ASICS were discoloured and frayed, evidence of previous ownership, but they were brand spanking new to me and I loved them for what they were—a second chance.

The shoes had been donated to Harvest House by the local Running Room—all the guys got them when they came to rehab. Some guys mocked them, but they were the ones who relapsed and ended up back in the can within weeks. Those who appreciated them lasted a little longer but still seemed to go back eventually—usually within two or three months.

Harvest House director Gary Wand was a recovering addict like us who had turned to running to get sober some fifteen years earlier when he washed up on the front lawn of Harvest House from Montreal. Everyone at the centre said that he'd been worse off than all of us, and his entry photo, taken the day he arrived at Harvest House, seemed to confirm that. He looked like a real bag of shit in it.

Wand now ran the running program at Harvest House, and had arranged the shoe donations. The concept of running as therapy was brilliant, actually. "The dopamine from running affects the same part of the brain as coke," he said. "Running quells cravings." Lots of guys were in the program, and those who did the ten- or twenty-kilometre runs instead of just running away to smoke cigarettes seemed to fight relapse better.

I wanted what they had. I thought if I ran I might have a chance to stay clean and honour my surety. I had to go all the way this time around, give it my best.

"If Wando can do it, I can do it," I said to myself as I hobbled onto the driveway for the daily five-kilometre jog. The reality of my foot, however, quickly snuffed out my newfound courage, replacing it with doubt and apprehension. It was withered and meatless, bones popping out where flesh should be, and the pins and screws holding my heel together dug into my ankle joint whenever I took a step. I'd never run on it without vast amounts of drugs or alcohol to numb the pain.

"Gary, I'm scared," I said, as the pack gathered. "I don't know if my foot will hold . . ." The grind of pebbles under shoes drowned me out, as everyone began running. I waddled to catch up. I must have looked like a penguin shuffling against the wind on a sheet of ice.

Gary looked back and smiled. "Just go slow. Trust me," he said and turned to join the others.

"Go slow?" I shot back. "Are you fucking kidding me?" No response. "Fuck you!" I yelled. It was no use, everyone had already gone.

I looked down. My damaged foot was longer than the other one, due to the surgery, and the leg it was attached to was atrophied and resembled a sad dollar-store broomstick, the hollow kind that bends if you sweep too hard.

Will it bend and break if I run? I contemplated. *Better that than my foot falling apart.*

I laughed out loud at the image of both gruesome scenarios, even though I felt like crying. Then Grandpa popped into my head. "Get going," I heard him bark in his thick Cape Breton accent. "Get going and stop feeling sorry fer yerself." It had been a long time since I'd thought of the old man, but there he was, kicking my ass again, as always.

I got pissed off and let go and ran. I didn't think about it, I just put one foot in front of the other and went. I tilted and slipped on stones, my leg and foot buckled and shook and wobbled—but they held. I had no push or spring to my gait, burning pain shot up from my ankle to my brain, and the bottom of my foot felt like I was running on broken glass—but it was bearable.

Is this how it feels for babies to walk? I wondered. As soon as that thought ran through my mind, my leg gave out and I tumbled down into a cloud of dust and pebbles.

The dirt in my mouth tasted glorious.

"Holy Christ, I did it!" I exclaimed.

AT LAST

MY HAND SHOOK AS I dialled the number Nicole, the CEO of Harvest House, had given me.

I sat listening to the phone ring. When it clicked, I panicked and hung up. I sat staring at the dial pad. It seemed to get bigger the longer I gazed at it. I dialled again, and again I hung up when I heard an answering click.

I just don't have it in me yet. What do I say to her?

Earlier that day, Nicole had come to my bedside in the dorm room and asked me into her office. She was solemn as I took a seat. I thought I was in trouble for violating a rule—what, I wasn't sure.

"I got an email today," she said. She typed something into her computer. I thought for sure the police were bringing a new charge against me, for something I'd done, from somewhere, some time ago. The long arm of the law was something I always dreaded but had to accept now, in my second attempt at sobriety.

"There's no other way to say this," Nicole said. Her eyes were welling up, but she was smiling.

So not the cops. I was puzzled.

"I'll just let you read it," she said. She turned her screen toward me, and I saw the email.

Hello,

I've been trying to contact my son Jesse Thistle for quite a while and he is never where I'm told he is. I heard he was in Harvest House and I'm sure God had a hand in it. It's a long story, but I haven't talked to Jesse for a long time and I don't know what problems he has anymore. I hope he's not suffering too much. Our family was torn apart a long time ago and I wasn't able to be around Jesse too much, but he always seemed to calm down around me.

Anyway, if he is there, tell him I'm happy he's getting help if he needs it. I love him very much and please just let me know if he is there. If he needs anything, socks, underwear, whatever, let me know and I'll try to send it.

Thank you.
Blanche Morrissette

It was my mom. I couldn't believe it. I held my head low, but my emotions rolled out and down my cheeks onto my lap.

I dialled my mom's number one more time and tried to steady my nerves. Ring—it was picked up straightaway this time.

A shaky, small voice answered, "Hello." It sounded like an old lady, not the mom I remembered from the snowy mountains.

"Mom . . ." was all I could muster before losing my breath. I tried to say more but couldn't.

"Jesse? Is that you?"

I'm not sure if I answered her, but we both began crying. Not sobs, more like sweet sucks of air, the silence between us saying more than any words. Finally, she told me that she'd been searching for me for ten years, since just after she saw me in Vancouver at Josh's wedding. In shelters, in the jail system, at places I'd just lived for a spell, in mental health facilities, in detoxes all over Ontario, and at Jerry's.

"You were like a phantom," she said. "I almost caught up to you a couple times, but always just missed you. I'm sorry life has been this way for you. I'm sorry I wasn't there."

I'd forgiven her before the words even left her lips.

The rest of our conversation melted into a drizzle of emotions that fogged my heart in the nicest way. Like a silent summer rain that lightly quenches the prairie after a long drought, or the cloud of droplets that kicks up at the bottom of a waterfall, delicately misting your face. Refreshing and warm, like I'd rediscovered some fragment of home, some lost piece of myself.

It filled me up.

A PLAIN PIECE OF PAPER

A PROFESSOR FROM THE UNIVERSITY of Ottawa who specialized in human relationships was overseeing classes her grad students were giving us Harvest House goons on communication skills, including basic etiquette.

Many of the guys in class mocked the lessons.

"What kind of idiot needs to relearn how to wash their ass," said one.

Another said, "Only total ratchets and baseheads need this."

Maybe I'd been at "the life" longer than they had—over a decade—and had forgotten more than them, but I was determined. And maybe hearing my mom's voice again made me feel like I could do this, made me feel like I could try, gave me that small bit of courage I needed to open my heart once more. I sat in those classes every week. I was embarrassed to admit to the professor, Dr. Jenepher Lennox Terrion, that I needed help with everything—brushing my teeth, combing my hair, dressing myself, washing my clothes. I was really rough around the edges.

Over two months, I relearned everything—I practiced in my dorm room. I looked at myself in the mirror and timed myself while brushing my teeth. I trained myself to look people in the eye and not interrupt them. I shaved with such precision I could run a credit card up my face and not hear it flick.

Perfect.

I spent months working on my reading and writing. When I got to Harvest House, I'd pore over the stack of encyclopedias I got from the rec room every night before bed, forcing the words to make sense. Just like my cellmates did years before, my Harvest House roommates teased me, calling me "Einstein" and "Mr. Spock," and some said it was ridiculous, a crackhead trying to get an education.

"You think people will hire you?" someone said in the slop hall one night. "You're a criminal, junkie piece of shit. You're no better than the rest of us." The table laughed. I wanted to respond, to tell him I had dreams now, but I just took it and kept the bigger picture in mind, kept pressing forward. I took my GED and passed with flying colours. When I received my final report card, I thought of my buddy in jail who'd got me interested in school—I hoped he'd gotten free and found a new life, away from the cinder blocks.

When it was time to graduate the etiquette modules, Dr. Lennox Terrion handed out our certificates as we walked up single file to collect them. She was beaming, and so was I. Some of the guys trashed the certificates as soon as they left the room. But I kept mine. When I got back to the rehab centre, I placed it within a large book to keep the edges from folding or crumpling. It meant the world to me. Every now and again, I'd open the book and just stare at it.

It lit me up to see my name, "Jesse Thistle," alongside "University of Ottawa." I'd done something significant. I'd actually achieved something in my life. I didn't have a driver's license, ID, a proper high school education, a health card, nothing—but here was this completion certificate that had "university" with my name under it!

A PUSH

"HEY, THISTLE . . . GET OUT OF bed, you have a phone call!"

It was 9:30 p.m. and I was already passed out, exhausted from my daily responsibilities at Harvest House. I barely heard Rob's voice when he yelled for me a second time.

"Dude, get up! It sounds important. It's your grandma in Toronto!"

Rob was always the type to be joking or laughing. He was never serious, but he sounded like he was this time. I jumped out of bed and ran to the phone.

"Jesse," whispered Grandma. "I need you."

I hadn't seen her in over four years.

"Where are you, Grandma?"

"Room 525 at William Osler hospital. Come see me."

"But what about Grandpa? I can't come if he's there."

"Just come. It's my time. He'll come around someday, you watch," she said. "He really does love you, you know."

I had betrayed Grandpa and all the good he had taught me and I knew he resented me for it, but I also knew she was right.

"I love you, Grandma. As soon as I get my day pass I'll be there." I hung up. By the end of the next day, I was on a moving truck on my way to Toronto. Randal, my AA sponsor, was my driver. Harvest House let me out on furlough on the condition that he never leave my side.

Grandma's arms were frail and covered with deep purple-black bruises. I tried not to stare, but she caught me looking and pulled the covers over them.

"Don't worry, Jesse," she said. "That'll clear up soon enough."

But I knew the bruises were a sign of the leukemia that was threatening her life and almost broke down.

"You know," she said, "I love science fiction novels. I've already finished the ones everybody brought me and need some more. Could you send me one or two from rehab?"

"Sure," I mustered, immediately thinking of *Doctor Who*. I knew she was trying to distract me. "Anything you want."

She looked at me. She rarely showed her front teeth all the way—one of them was black—but she did now, her face beaming, her smile so warm it could defrost Siberia in January. "Why don't you keep going with the school, baby boy, and give it your all? You were always smart, just a little angry."

I could see the hope ignite in her milky-grey eyes. "Of course I'll keep going," I said.

"Good." She perked up, her grin widening even more. "And university? You don't wanna half-ass it; you've gotta take it all the way."

"Yes, Grandma. Just get better." It wasn't quite a promise, more like words I blurted out to try to comfort her. Anything to make her feel better, to make me feel better, here in this hospital room.

"Good. And don't you worry about me, I'll be fine." She drew me in for a hug from my chair near her bed. "Remember, I'm always with you."

I wrapped my arms around her and could feel how feeble she was, but she squeezed me with all her might. Then all of a sudden she let go and pushed me away. I remembered my first day of kindergarten, right before I met Leeroy. I cried the whole way and didn't want to go in. I was so afraid to let go of Grandma and go to the teacher until Grandma knelt down, looked me right in the eye, and said, "Go on, Jesse, it's okay. Grandma will be here at the end of the day. I promise." She smelled like old cigarettes and perfume as she pushed me toward the teacher.

It was that same push she was giving me now. A push that said, "Go on, make your way in the world. Make me proud."

Two weeks later, she was gone.

THE CLEANEST BACHELOR IN THE WORLD

ON THE DAY MY GRANDMOTHER died, Harvest House took pity on me, I assume, and graduated me. There was no ceremony, no fanfare, no anything. Nicole just came into the dorm room, informed me that I'd completed the first phase of treatment, and told me to pack my things. I was upgraded to a room in reintegration housing, aftercare dwellings adjacent to Harvest House that guys moved into after they'd completed the immersion part of treatment and were transitioning back into the real world.

On my way over, around the boundary fence I'd hopped with Max a year earlier, a gust of wind hit me. It carried a faint smell of burnt hickory and cedar, like a campfire. I wanted to believe it was my grandmother's spirit telling me to keep going. I said a prayer and felt her presence leave this earth, galloping away to the west.

When I got to reintegration, one of the first things I did was start a Facebook account. I didn't even know what Facebook was, but the guys there told me about it and helped me get it set up. Minutes after I signed up, I started getting messages from people I knew from years before—Derick, Brian, Karen, and other neighbourhood friends. They were glad I was still alive—they'd all been searching for me for years, just like Mom.

I heard Leeroy had cleaned up and joined the army and was shipped off to Afghanistan five years before. I was glad he'd straightened out and said a prayer for my old friend. I also heard Stan had gotten a good job and was doing well, and that he often asked if I was okay. He was solid—always was.

I also got a message from Lucie. She was the girl on the hill in middle school who'd been nice to me in front of the popular girls, and she was the red-haired girl at the party the night I'd fallen off Jerry's building and wrecked my foot.

Her message was consoling. She'd heard of my grandmother's passing from Jerry and wanted to make sure I was okay and wouldn't fly off the handle and use again. I thought that it was kind of her to think of me when I needed it most. Her gesture reminded me of Karen—that unconditional kindness, a kindness I hadn't felt for decades.

———

Intimidated isn't the right word to express how Lucie made me feel as we got to talking—it was more like a mixture of shock and fright, total excitement and extreme pride. I was super pleased with myself for catching the attention of such a respectable woman: she was in university as a mature student, she had her own place, she knew what she wanted out of life, she was more or less sober, she was independent, she didn't need a man to support her or take care of her, and she was beautiful—like some kind of red-headed fire goddess. Me, I was just a recovering addict trying to do right by the world.

Connecting with her, though, I felt like the luckiest guy in the world.

I hadn't talked to a woman so powerful, so bright, and so intelligent in years. I didn't own anything because I'd been on the streets for so long. All I had were words and a desire to impress her.

I wrote her poetry. I'd had corrective surgery on my wrist to fix the break that had never healed properly since the fall from the building, the fight with police, and the thousands of push-ups I did in jail, so I had to do it with one hand. It often took me hours to type one page. I bled for each one. This was one of the first ones I sent:

once in a lifetime

two people meet.

not knowing what the universe has designed for them,

they form a bond so strong

that it holds the very fabric of time at a standstill.

this is true love,

it is infinite,

i will always love in this moment forever with you.

now is ours.

Lucie loved the poem. A week after she got it she sent me Michael J. Fox's *Always Looking Up* and *The Alchemist* by Paulo Coelho—books with messages of hope and making the best of our gardens, our lives, even with our shortcomings, that I devoured. I knew it was her way of helping me, of saying it was okay that I was a little broken.

We started to Skype like crazy after that. Before every call, I showered, combed my hair, put on my best hat, my crispest pressed shirt and pants, and my brand-new leather jacket, even clean underwear.

Life on the streets had been horribly dirty. Many times I'd wished I could have had a shower but simply couldn't—I often went for weeks without one. So when I got sober, I collected an abundance of soaps, shampoos, skin creams, face scrubs, toothpastes—I must have had, no exaggeration, about two hundred of each. So many that I filled an entire bookshelf with them and kept them on display in my room at Harvest House behind my computer seat, perfectly lined up.

When Lucie called, I'd sit in front of my wall of soap and shampoo, so she could see that I was clean, so she could see that I was respectable just like her.

I really wanted to impress her.

THE OTHER HALF OF THE SOLUTION

MY PROBATION OFFICER, MR. F., came to Harvest House for our last weekly visit. When he sat down, the sun was shining behind him and carried summer warmth onto my face.

"You've done your time, Jesse," he said. "How does it feel?"

"Not sure," I said nonchalantly. The immensity of release was not yet upon me, but I wasn't afraid of freedom for once.

The manila folder he put on the desk that housed my case file was thin, not the usual thick ones I'd had back in Brampton. That alone felt like a major accomplishment. He rifled through it, stamped the last page, and then got me to sign a confirmation of release from the Justice of the Peace.

I was a free man.

"What are your plans when you leave here?"

"That girl in Toronto I told you about, Lucie?" I said. "I'm going to see her."

Mr. F. studied my face for a moment.

"You know, when you first came, I thought you were a long shot," he said. "Wasn't sure if you'd honour your surety bond, thought you'd take off and relapse like the rest of them." He motioned to the long line of clients crowding the hall. "But something was different about you . . ." He tapped the end of his pen against his teeth then went over my activity report.

"You did every chore in the joint—cleaning washrooms, toilets, and showers; kitchen duty; waxing the floors; sold calendars. You mentored the young guys, helped others with reading, academic bridging, ran marathons in the program. You did everything over twelve months without a single violation. That's not normal."

I thought back to my first day at Harvest House the first time around. I was skin and bones, just off the Greyhound bus from Brampton, and as rusty as an iron rivet on the hull of the sunken *Titanic*. I had a real hate for the world, but also a glimmer of hope after hearing news of my dad. It was like that dude in the shelter freed me to move on, made it okay to let go and stop chasing my father's ghost—something that didn't really sink in until I started talking openly in group therapy during my second attempt at rehab. That, and I was desperate—I didn't want to die, which almost happened after I relapsed with Max.

"I guess I just chose to live. And that meant trying my best at everything."

"Come on now." He shook his head like I'd given him the wrong answer. "That's only half the solution."

I didn't know what he meant. I'd put in the work this time. I'd set micro goals and chose to follow through on each one of them, just like Brian and Mr. T. told me was possible years before. I chose to stay sober, pushed myself in therapy, until the minutes turned to days, the days to weeks, and the weeks to months. I'd literally set one- or two-minute goals—*If I can just make it to the next minute*, I thought, *then I might have a chance to live; I might have a chance to be something more than just a struggling crackhead.* I chose, repeatedly, in everything I did until I reached my first three months of sobriety and I thought I'd achieved the impossible—to me it had seemed impossible. My name looked so triumphant on the achievements board: *J. Thistle—90 days.* And now that I'd reached the year and had worked the AA steps properly, I felt I could just keep on choosing a better future forever and ever.

"There's no doubt it took lots of dogged hard work. But don't forget the team of great people behind you, the rehab itself, and the addicts who've struggled and won victories with you these last twelve months—they held you up and gave you the chance to choose better for yourself. They deserve credit, too."

I sat back and thought about what Mr. F. was saying. There was truth in his words, an external factor Brian and Mr. T.'s empowerment philosophy had missed. The support of family and love—Harvest House gave me both; they gave me the opportunity to choose.

"And you, Mr. F. You played a part, too. You got me to write the letter to the convenience store guy I robbed—that helped me move forward in so many ways."

He smiled and slid another paper my way.

"You still have eighteen more months of probation in Toronto. Here's where you report."

I read the form and saw that my new probation office was just down the street from where I fell off the building, on an old corner where I used to use. My gut stirred with crack cravings, but it wasn't enough to send me to the toilet—that was real, tangible progress.

"I hope this Lucie girl will hold you up like everyone here did," Mr. F. said, "and that you remember to keep making the right choices."

I nodded. "I'm sure she will and so will I."

BRAVERY

I WAS MORE AFRAID THAN I'd been in my whole life.

I walked to the oncology ward thinking of what I was going to say, my hands sweaty and heart trembling uncontrollably. I squeezed Lucie's hand like a vise grip.

She smiled. "Have courage, Jesse. Just tell him how you feel."

Afternoon light cascaded through the hall window, shining on her beautiful red hair. It calmed me.

"It's time," she said. "Put pride away."

I nodded. I'd been in Toronto at Lucie's for just two days, but I already knew she was the one. We sat awake both nights discussing my grandfather and how people fight and waste the best years of their lives trying to be right, but that "right" doesn't exist when precious time is spent in such useless ways. She listened to me talk about the void I had within, how I'd tried to fill it with drugs over the years, and how I knew I'd broken my grandfather's heart by hurting myself long after we'd fought in the van over me wanting to buy a car.

"Don't you see?" she said. "You two donkeys just loved each other so much that this fight broke out—and neither of you is willing to admit it's gone on long enough."

She was right. We Thistle men never learned how to express ourselves. We were raised to be tough and unemotional, with the thickness of our calluses and fists the only way we were ever allowed to show how we felt—lessons that went way back to Grandpa's horrible boyhood in Cape Breton—lessons my dad, no doubt, struggled with, too.

The last time I saw my grandfather was at my grandmother's funeral. I'd been granted furlough with my AA sponsor Randal again, a week after she passed, but he left me alone when I walked into the funeral home and up to my grandmother's casket. My grandfather sat with his sisters and my aunts and uncles beside him. He wept softly, as if he was trying to hide his grief, even then. I bent in and kissed my grandmother's face. She had a peaceful smile, almost like Buddha.

When I'd turned to face my grandfather and offer my condolences, he'd wiped his cheeks and barked, "It's too late, asshole. She's gone."

I never felt so sorry for him in all my life—I knew he didn't mean it. I'd used anger myself to hide from emotions I couldn't handle.

I returned to Harvest House. I occasionally worked in the shop making duck decoys or building furniture to sell to support the program, and every time I lifted a drill or held a saw, I thought of the old guy and wished, for just one day, we could work side by side again like we did when I was a boy. That I could hear him say "attaboy" one more time. I missed him so much. I ached to wipe away his tears, to tell him how I really felt.

When we entered his room in the hospital, he was alone with my aunt Sherry, who I hadn't seen in nearly five years. She was holding his hand, tears streaming down her face. She whispered to him, and he looked up at me. I had no words, and neither did he. Soon we were both crying, too.

Finally I said, "I'm sorry, Grandpa."

"I know, Jesse. It's okay." He held his arms out, and we hugged.

I knew he'd heard from the family, Aunt Sherry primarily, of all the things I was doing to better myself, and I knew he knew me better than anyone. I was sure he could look right into my heart and see I really was trying my hardest.

"I'm proud of you," he said and gave me a karate chop on my forearm, like he used to do on my knee when I was a kid, then held my hand. His hands were shaking. He told me that he understood what it was like to be an orphan. "That's why I was always hard on you. To make you strong. Like my granddaddy did with me. That was the only way to protect you. Just keep flying straight or I'll kick your ass." He gave me his trademark Popeye wink.

That was the nearest he'd come to saying he loved me in nearly two decades.

He passed away a month and a half later, six months to the day of my grandmother's passing.

FOLLOW YOUR DREAMS

LUCIE AND I SAT ON the couch in our apartment. My leg rested on the coffee table and shook from pain after a long day of work with Uncle Ron. Fourteen- to sixteen-hour days working again for Randolph installing kitchen countertops had become the norm, and Lucie was always there to help me recover at night—rubbing Swedish bitters on my wound, which had opened back up from the heavy work, binding my leg in special bandages to keep the swelling down, drawing on my shoulders to distract me.

"Ah, watch it," I yelped as she shifted on the couch. "You bumped my foot." I wasn't nice about it, something that was happening as of late—me being snappy and grouchy after work.

"I'm sorry," Lucie said, kissing her hand and placing it on my foot. "I didn't mean to."

I huffed and crossed my arms, making more out of it than I should've. Lucie turned to face me.

"I've kept quiet this last year," she said. "But I'm not going to anymore." She sounded dead serious—she clearly wasn't having it this time. "When I picked you up from Harvest House you had a garbage bag full of donated clothes, a wall of soap, a toothbrush, and tons of shampoo." She paused, her expression even more focused. "But you also had a dream. Remember we'd talk about university, and remember the promise you made to your grandmother?"

I nodded. I knew to drop the act and listen. When we first started talking when I was in rehab, we spent hours on the phone, getting to know one another as I worked nights watching over the new guys. Lucie was at York University, her first year back in school after over ten years of drifting about, and her resolve to give it another go inspired me. We'd talk about her assignments, how she was sacrificing going out with friends to do homework, getting things done on time, with good marks. We were talking about moving in together, too, and how I could do the same once I moved to Toronto. We schemed about how we'd study together, support each other, look over each other's work. We were a lot like each other—late bloomers.

"Remember when I helped you get into academic bridging at the University of Toronto last fall?"

"Yes."

"Well, since you dropped out of bridging to work with your uncle, you haven't been happy. I've watched you day after day come home miserable and limping." She crossed her arms. "I can't watch you break your body anymore—you're not supposed to be a construction worker."

"I'm trying my best!" I said, slamming my hand down. I thought she was insulting the labour that put food on our table and helped pay our rent. I thought she was saying it wasn't good enough.

"You can have a tantrum all you want. I need to be with someone who's living their truth. Because I love you, because I love us, and I know what you're capable of." There was a long pause. "It hurts me so much to watch you keep neglecting your dream."

She reminded me of my grandmother, that power and uncompromising attitude, when she knew she was right. I remembered when we argued over the placement of the TV when I first moved in. I tried to force it onto the stand and hollered when she told me not to because it wouldn't fit. Then I ran out of the house sure that I was right, like I'd learned to do in anger management when I got too worked up.

She didn't chase after me. She waited until I returned an hour later to explain why the TV had to go where it did. She was calm and kind, but firm.

"I understand why you throw fits," she said. "I would, too, after years of having no control over anything." She then said she'd always be there to help me figure out my emotions, even if it was an ugly process.

God, I loved her so much. But I tried to be mad now as she challenged me to face the truth—I'd given up and broken my word to myself, to my grandmother, and to her.

Finally, she said, "You chased the money—I get it, we have to survive—but money will not make you or me happy. Following your heart will."

I thought about it. There was something about the way we'd talked those nights, like we were planting dream seeds in fertile soil, our hopes and desires spigots of water, nurturing a future we both wanted and saw in each other. She gave me the courage to hope and dream, because I saw that in her, and she believed it was possible for both of us. It was contagious.

She was right.

And she trusted and loved me back when I was just a newly recovered criminal, back when it felt like no one else would. I promised myself I'd honour and protect that no matter what. Trying my best in school was part of that.

⸻

"Just fill in the line that asks for your major." Lucie's red hair brushed across my arm as she walked me through the York University application process. "What do you want to do?"

I scratched the top of my head. "I like history," I said. "I watch lots of World War I documentaries." I peered down at my callused hands and couldn't picture them writing academic papers. I still doubted my decision—I'd quit installing countertops a few weeks before.

"Good—historian is a great profession." Lucie moved the mouse and clicked a box on the computer and scrolled onto the next screen. She smiled. "Almost done. Now just add in all your personal information here and we're good to go."

She walked away and put the kettle on for tea.

"But—" I said. The application was just halfway finished and it looked like Chinese to me.

"No. You have to do this one on your own."

She wasn't trying to be mean, I knew that.

"I've taught you how to fill in enough forms, my job is done."

I couldn't argue. Since living with her, Lucie had helped me fill in health card forms and taught me how to drive and how to fill in all the car driver insurance forms. She taught me how to email and use the computer halfway decent. She taught me how to make doctor's appointments and fill in the forms at the medical offices. She taught me how to access my debt information and then chart out a plan to pay it all back. She taught me how to open a bank account and how to access credit, and she also taught me how to write properly—she edited most things I wrote and taught me grammar and sentence structure, adding to what I'd already learned in my GED.

Lucie basically taught me how to access society again.

"Okay." I sighed and worked my way through the rest of the application and the Ontario Student Assistance Program forms. She came over occasionally when I got too frustrated, but she was resolute—she made me do it all.

When I pressed return and the forms were submitted, she hugged me.

"You did that." She smiled. "I didn't want to take that away from you."

I felt like I'd climbed a mountain.

THE FINES ARE FINE

WHEN I WAS HOMELESS AND in trouble with the law, I collected fines like boys collect hockey cards. The police slapped fines on me; the courts, too, used to slap fines on me for every missed court appearance; and judges slapped fines on me every time I got convicted. Each fine ranged from $50 to $200. Eventually, my collection added up to over three grand.

The fines had long been a black stain that I believed I could never wash off. They were just there, reminding me I was a criminal who owed a pound of flesh to the state—a pound of flesh I didn't have, would never have. I'd often thought in the past about changing my life, but thinking about those fines would make me give up before I even started. When I got sober, I put the fines aside; mainly because I was struggling just to live. But when I graduated rehab and started working, I began saving with Lucie's guidance, and one day, before I started university, I realized I had over $3,000.

I finally had enough to pay my fines.

I drove to Brampton with Lucie, and we walked into the courthouse together. I licked my thumb, peeled off each fifty-dollar bill, and slapped them down one by one until I'd counted out the full $3,071 in fines.

The teller was gobsmacked and grinned back at me—he knew what paying those fines represented: a break with the past.

FINDING THE COURAGE TO STAND

MY FIRST CLASS AT YORK University was at 8:30 a.m. on September 8, 2011. It was in Canadian History.

"Just remember to breathe," Lucie said to me as I threw my book bag over my shoulder and walked out the door. She waved to me with a tea towel, and I remembered Grandma doing the same when I got my first job at the grocery store. I smiled, but was trembling inside.

I was the first one to arrive, and I found a seat in the front row. I placed my brand-new binders, pens, and paper on my desk in neat rows and readied myself for the lecture. I watched as people trickled in, filling the hall. They were half my age. Everyone—around four hundred people—had laptops, smart phones, or recording devices—only two others that I could see had pen and paper like me.

No one sat beside me, and I fidgeted and tried smiling at some of the kids, but they were more interested in people their age.

Maybe I've made a huge mistake coming here, I worried. *Maybe it was foolish of me to try this.* Me, an ex-con, mid-thirties, barely two years sober, amongst all these glowing young people who had years of education on me, and who still had that bright spot within them that hadn't yet been crushed by the world. I got scared and gathered my things, ready to run away.

Then a memory came to me of when I was in jail and saw the chaplain and started working with him, and then of Professor Lennox Terrion and how I'd relearned everything in rehab.

I wasn't sure why I thought of that when I looked at all the young people with their computers and innocence, but I did. Maybe it was because I was frightened, like when my cellmates tuned me up after I handed in my homework, or maybe it was because I was reaching really deep not to run away, trying to remind myself that I didn't break then, and that I wouldn't break now.

Whatever the reason, I came to the realization that I'd earned my way here and that I had the right to chase my dreams. That even I deserved a second chance.

I thought, *I belong in university, just like everyone else.*

INDIAN TURNED MÉTIS

I STARTED TAKING INDIGENOUS HISTORY classes to figure out who I was and why I saw so many other Natives in all the homeless and justice institutions and out on the streets over the years. I thought I might be able to get some answers in my classes or readings and understand why I had made some poor life choices and keep from relapsing. It was a long shot—but I had to try.

For one of my first assignments, one of my professors, Dr. Victoria Freeman, asked us to look at our family history within the context of Canadian colonization.

Since my grandma in Brampton hardly ever talked about her Native background, I called my mom to ask her questions.

"We're Michif rebel fighters," she said. "Canadians call us Métis."

I recognized that word "Michif" from when we'd all been talking in Aunt Cecile's kitchen after Josh's wedding.

"Your great-grandmother Marianne Ledoux, Mushoom Jeremie's mother, is related to Louis Riel," Mom said. "But talk to your aunt Yvonne, she's the family historian."

When I called Aunt Yvonne the next day and asked her about our involvement with Riel, she could hardly contain herself.

"I've been waiting a very long time for you to get interested in who you are," she said. "A lifetime actually." She asked me to hold on while she turned on her computer to access her genealogy files. "I'm addicted to Ancestry.ca, so if I get a little strung out on the call, just send over the blue bus to take me away." She cackled, and her laughter stirred up a memory of her in our place in Moose Jaw after we ran away from Dad in 1979. She was taking care of us when Mom went off to work and tucking us in. I'd never remembered that before.

"Let's see," she said, and it sounded like she was slurping a drink of some kind. "Ah! Here. The Morrissette family tree. I'll email the link, so you can explore it yourself. If I explain it, you may need to go back to rehab." She cackled again, but I could tell she was serious. "The picture I sent is Chief Mistawasis—a Cree chief. He's your three-times-great-grandfather."

I remembered Derick's brother Moses asking me what I was when I was growing up.

So we are Cree . . .

I checked my email. There, upon my screen, appeared a big black-and-white picture of an old man sitting with other old Indian men. The caption read, "Cree chiefs Ahtahkakoop and Mistawasis." I examined the medals around their necks, and then minimized the image and clicked the link. A huge family tree appeared—hundreds of ancestors with pictures, names, dates, and places of birth beside each box that represented each ancestor. Many had feathered bonnets on, like plains Indians from the movies, others looked like old cowboys, others were just dressed in regular clothes.

"You're Cree and road-allowance Michif, Jesse. You come from a long line of chiefs, political leaders, and resistance fighters." Auntie's voice glowed like fire and lit my curiosity.

I went through the photos faster and faster, trying to drink in the rushing river of information. Those of the Cree chiefs fascinated me most. They were strong and epic in appearance, in their beaded buckskins, feathered headdresses to the ground, and spears in hand, many on horseback and surrounded by warriors. But they looked staged.

Then I saw pictures of my kokum Nancy and mushoom Jeremie and their little shack near the train tracks and felt a lump in my throat—I hadn't seen an image of them in nearly four decades. Below those was a battlefield picture with the heading "Batoche," and underneath it was that blue flag with the infinity symbol I'd seen when I'd had the fever after my operation.

"What is this battle—Batoche? And what's this flag, Auntie?" I asked. Visions of the western door and the horses and the fear I'd felt welled in my chest again, but I fought against it now with my auntie on the line.

"That's where our family fought for our land during the resistance— when Canada attacked us. And that's our flag—the Métis flag."

The reports of Gatling guns thundered in my soul. The face of the Indian I'd been with in the rifle pit in my dream came to me. I searched the family tree and couldn't find him, but I remembered that Iron Maiden song Leeroy and Derick sang near the dumpster.

Could this be part of the same conflict . . . ?

I searched the pictures and saw the same columns of redcoat soldiers near the large river, charging up the same slope of hill, toward that same white church. I couldn't believe what I was seeing. It was real.

I stayed on the phone for a half-hour with Aunt Yvonne and she explained how our people had fought and been pushed off our lands around Batoche, Saskatchewan, after 1885 and were made to squat on public Crown lands on the sides of roads and railways, known as road allowances—land nobody owned or wanted. The Métis weren't taken care of with a treaty like First Nations peoples with reserves, but cast off to wander, unprotected and dispossessed—we were the forgotten people.

The waist-high grass along the old highway in northern Saskatchewan rustled as warm wind blew from the south. I took my camera out and snapped a photo of the now-deteriorating railway line running from Debden up to Big River. Its steel bed snaked up over the crest of the hill then disappeared into the shrubs and thistles; I couldn't trace where Kokum took me berry picking, but knew it was somewhere here. Standing beside me were my mom, Aunt Yvonne, and Dr. Carolyn Podruchny, a York University professor and expert in Métis history.

I'd met Carolyn after Dr. Freeman marked my family history paper.

"This is one of the best papers I've read all year," she said. "I think you need to meet a friend of mine."

Two weeks later, I was at Carolyn's office in York University's History Department, a binder of Aunt Yvonne's and my own genealogy research in hand. Yvonne was right: genealogy was addictive, but in the best possible way.

I learned quickly Carolyn hadn't read my paper, but she wanted to know my family's history. After some explaining, she said she knew exactly who my mother's people were—Arcand, Morrissette, Montour— some of the major Métis resistance fighter clans, bison hunters, and road-allowance families in the northern parkland belt in Saskatchewan.

She agreed to take me on as a student.

"You'll do an independent reading course," she said, adding that she'd hire me as a research assistant on her Social Sciences and Humanities Research Council project, "Tracing Métis History Through Archives," which involved fieldwork at various Métis historical sites in Saskatchewan.

I was thrilled. It meant I would see my mother and our people in our homelands, where I hadn't been since I was three.

Carolyn flew me home in June.

It felt so good to hug my mom after so many years. I don't think I mustered any words in the airport, I let my tears do the talking. We growled like wolves the same way Josh and she did years ago in my grandparents' doorway. Carolyn clapped her hands in excitement.

For two weeks, Carolyn and I, along with my mom and Aunt Yvonne, drove all over the province to interview about a dozen Cree and Métis Elders, visiting historical sites relevant to the 1885 resistance, including Batoche. Many of the Elders told us they'd never shared their history with outsiders before. Given their traumatic history and treatment by the Canadian government, it was understandable.

The road allowance where my kokum and mushoom lived was the last stop on our research trip and my quest back to my identity. The land stretched about an acre back from the old road, right over to the train tracks. I recognized the ash and poplar trees off in the distance, bending and moaning as they arched over the now-derelict property. Mom wandered ahead of us to the old smoker, a small shack where my grandparents used to smoke moose, bear, and deer meat. There was nothing but a few rotten pieces of wood where it once stood.

Aunt Yvonne hiked toward two depressions in the grass and pointed to the ruts. "You can still see where the cars and carts used to drive up, doctor."

I took this photo of my mom (*right*) and Aunt Yvonne (*left*) in the Park Valley schoolhouse, about three kilometres from the Morrissette cabin, on the day we visited the road allowance. Mom said she was so happy I was home that she'd dance—and she kept her word.

Carolyn batted at the mosquitoes buzzing around her head as she struggled through the overgrown grass. I limped alongside her, like usual, but energy radiated up my legs—I was stepping on ground I hadn't tread in thirty-seven years—and it was like the road allowance remembered me, the prairie roses all across the property appeared to be smiling at me, welcoming me home, waving their heads this way and that.

Aunt Yvonne motioned her hand over another depression some thirty by sixty feet with small shrubs and trees growing within it—fauna not as tall as the surrounding forest.

"This is where they lived, *ma mère* and *mon père*." She looked at me and her black eyes seemed to hug right around my whole body. Carolyn turned to face me. She, too, had eyes as big as moose tracks in the snow.

I stepped within the depression of the building and fell to my knees.

The smell of lard and my kokum cooking bannock washed over me. I heard kokum singing to the hornets and mosquitoes, lulling them away, as we picked berries. The sweet sound of the Morrissette reels my mushoom played throbbed in my ears, the flicker of moonbeams on his vest danced across my eyes. The faint scent of smoke from my kokum's hearth wafted across the air. I saw my mushoom whittling a toy sword.

I remembered them.

I remembered my mother's people.

I remembered who I was.

IN THE CUSTOM OF THE COUNTRY

LUCIE AND I DIDN'T HAVE a big wedding. We didn't have the money nor did we want the headache. We just went to Toronto City Hall with a handful of our closest family members and friends.

Jerry was there. He was my best man, and he was wearing his finest black shirt, with his hair slicked back.

We didn't talk much, but when he adjusted my tie, he said, "It's been a long road, Jess—time for a new pact, though, eh? She's a wonderful woman," and his voice cracked. Uncle Ron and his daughter were my witnesses. They shed some tears, but he kept a straighter face than she did, the way we Thistle men were trained to do by Grandpa.

Lucie's best friend came, too, along with her boyfriend, a professor at Humber College. He was in charge of the music and was supposed to play "Sweet Disposition" by the Temper Trap after the Justice of the Peace announced we could kiss, but he missed the cue and didn't hit play until a few minutes after everything ended. There were cheers and laughter behind us as we embraced.

Liba, my mother-in-law, sat weeping in the front row. Her smile was so big it filled the whole of Canada.

After the ceremony, we gathered in front of the Jack Layton memorial in Nathan Phillips Square, and everyone drank and clinked together glasses of semi-expensive champagne—I had my bottle of 7Up, ever the teetotaller. My clinks made more of a blopping sound.

———

We went camping in Killarney Provincial Park for our honeymoon. We brought Luna, a golden Labrador retriever Lucie was dog-sitting for a friend, and got a campsite way at the back of the park. When we arrived near dusk, we saw we had neighbours: a little girl and her father. They were roasting marshmallows and singing. We waved to them, unpacked, got a campfire going, and settled by it, smiling and happy and hopeful of what the future held.

The next morning, we awoke early, walked down to the lakeside, grasped hands, and promised one another that we'd love and support each other and be friends until our last breaths.

Lucie and I were married on August 25, 2012, at Toronto City Hall.

TARA NOELLE BATES

The city hall ceremony had been just a legal formality; the real wedding happened while the two of us were alone in the woods, by the lakeshore, in the misty sunrise. We submerged our hands in the water and the bond was sealed.

In that moment of love, continents joined and the gaping maw within me closed, silent and forever.

Creator and Luna were our only witnesses.

The water ceremony was the way I imagine my ancestors would have married. It was the best wedding we could have asked for.

AMENDS

Today I walked back to where we used to live
Same old fence surrounds,
Same old paint on the windowpanes
This, the place where it all happened.

Guilt pushes me here; I can't live these excuses anymore.
You've long since passed, I know this.

But here I am regardless,
Reaching through time,
Staring at our door
Apologizing for breaking your hearts.

A silent amend you'll never hear.

SIXTEEN LETTERS

WHEN MY AUNT SHERRY DIVIDED my grandparents' estate she discovered an old shoebox, tucked away in the closet, up top, in the hardest to reach spot, with the rest of my grandmother's most precious belongings. Inside it was a stack of old letters from the Ontario Correctional Institute (OCI) in Brampton, where Dad served his last sentence before being released on day parole in December 1982. After that, he vanished forever after getting into a car outside Aunt Sherry's place.

"He just got in and we never saw him again, Jesse," Aunt Sherry said. "I really miss my big brother, too." She cried like she always did.

I was shocked when Aunt Sherry gave the letters to me along with a tiny black prison Bible that OCI sent my grandmother. I didn't know they existed.

"These should go to you," she said. "You're the most like him, lived a life closest to his."

My father's name was scrawled inside the front of the Bible, once in printing, which was scratched out, and then in flourishing cursive script underneath.

I knew what that meant the instant I saw it. The curve of the letters, the gentle pressure on the rounded S and roll of the Ns and T: he was trying to perfect what he'd learned in school and discarded years earlier, he was trying to better himself in his cage.

I'd done the exact same thing in a letter I'd sent to my grandmother when I was practicing my writing in jail years earlier.

I pored over his letters, memorizing every one word for word, and I saw the same effort. He wanted to be a better man, to change and love, and be home for his family, but couldn't for some reason.

My favourite letter was the one addressed directly to me where he talks about Yorkie, my absolute best friend growing up.

"Don't be afraid of the dog—he's a good boy," he assured me.

I was just four years old when he wrote it, and apparently afraid of Yorkie then. In another letter he wrote, "Grandma tells me you have all the women."

I guessed she must have told him about the time I ripped up the catalogue and had the pictures of models strewn beside me under the covers,

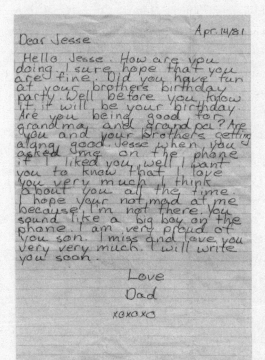

One of the letters Dad wrote to me from a corrections facility in 1981. I would have been four years old when he sent it. I didn't see it until I was in my late thirties.

and how Yorkie busted me by romping about on the bed. I had a hard time keeping it together reading that one.

Those sixteen letters and the black prison Bible are all I have of my dad—that, and the world of resentments I had to sort through on the streets, then in rehab. But it's more than I ever had, and I was grateful for the journey back to him, even if the old shoebox, some thirty-four years later, was as close as we'd ever get to being father and son.

57 YEARS OF LOVE

ON OCTOBER 14, 2015, I graduated from York University.

As I stood waiting to collect my degree, I smiled at Lucie and her mother, who were sitting in the audience, then patted my left breast pocket, which held my grandmother's picture. I swear the picture glowed over my heart as my name was called, I walked across the convocation stage, shook the chancellor's hand, and accepted my degree.

I'm sure my grandmother was there with me, cheering me on, proud that I had found my way, and that I'd kept the promise I'd made to her.

Grandma never did get to see me sober, or out of trouble with the law. Nor did she ever meet my wonderful wife, Lucie.

Lucie now wears my grandmother's engagement ring, a surprise gift from Aunt Sherry after I told her over dinner one night at her house that I wanted to marry Lucie but mentioned that I couldn't afford a ring on a student budget.

"You can have the most precious ring of all," Aunt Sherry said to me. She got up, went past Uncle John, got her jewel case, and pulled out a dusty box. The two of them were just beaming.

"It's your grandmother's wedding ring—fifty-seven years of love on there—she'd want Lucie to have it, I'm sure."

I like to think Aunt Sherry was right, and that Grandma sent Lucie to take care of me—she's the only woman strong enough to watch over Grandma's wayward, rebellious grandson.

WHEN WALKING IS A PRAYER

MY RIGHT FOOT STILL HURTS over a decade after "the accident." I guess it always will.

Every morning when I place my foot on the ground, a shock of electricity shoots up my leg into my brain like a bolt of lightning striking a rusty country weather vane. That first step is always the most torturous, and the jolt of pain it produces hijacks my cerebral cortex as I try to gain my balance. I hobble toward the bathroom with my hands braced on the apartment walls, my cat, Poppy, slithering between my legs. Sometimes, when I can't face the pain, I simply hop on my left leg, leaving my right leg dangling behind me.

Bone grinding on wire: that is my morning cup of coffee, that is what wakes me up every day, and that is what reminds me that the fall from my brother's apartment window was real—and that I'm lucky to be alive.

The pain also keeps me sober. It reminds me what it was like years ago when addiction and homelessness almost did me in. For that, and those harsh reminders, I am thankful.

The psychological pain, however, is sometimes almost too much to bear.

I have nightmares in which my leg is amputated just below the knee and I'm begging for change on Rideau Street and no one hears me. I dream that a colony of maggots is eating the gangrenous flesh around the incision and my toes are nothing but exposed bone. I dream that I'm scraping the skin off my dying foot like I would scrape soft candle wax off a glass table.

When these nightmares visit me, I feel like I'm drowning in some uncharted region of the icy North Atlantic. I feel helpless and utterly alone—just like I did when I was homeless. Just as I'm about to give up and lose consciousness, I come fully awake, gasping for breath, sweat soaked, and frightened. I am frantic. I cast aside the blankets to catch a glimpse of my foot to see if it's healthy, to see if it's still attached to my shin and knee, to see if all my toes are still there.

Without fail, my foot is always there, waiting for me; toes wiggling and fleshy, assuring me that we've made it, and that the leviathan can never drown us as long as we're together.

Lucie always knows when I've had one of my nightmares. Her method of comfort is always the same: she smiles and tells me it's okay, then she shifts across to my side of the bed, pulls me close, and squeezes me until I fall asleep. When I am lost at sea and drowning, her arms rescue me.

She's also there in the morning when I step down on my foot to receive my morning jolt; however, she's not so understanding then—she almost always shoos me out of the room so she can catch those precious last five minutes of sleep. But when the pain in my foot is too much to bear after a hard day of work, Lucie is there to offer me an arm.

I often wonder how I came to run with my foot the way it is (the doctors told me I'd likely never walk on my own again without medical aid). The truth is, I don't know, but what I do know is that my mangled foot and the pain it brings changed everything. It almost destroyed me, but somehow I survived; it forced me to do something unthinkable to save my life, it forced me to challenge and push myself when I was utterly defeated; it taught me to trust my body, myself, and my wife; and it forces me every day to remember what happened when I gave up and blamed the world for my problems and expected something for nothing.

In these ways, the pain in my foot has been a blessing, and I value each and every step I take. Every step is a gift, every one is sacred, and each, in its own little way, is a prayer for me.

EPILOGUE

I'M HERE IN OTTAWA PRESENTING at a conference on homelessness organized by the Federal Homeless Partnership Strategy, which oversees millions of dollars for emergency homeless services across the country.

My panel is on enumerating homeless people in census surveys called point-in-time counts. I'm also presenting a talk on a preliminary draft of the Definition of Indigenous Homelessness in Canada—I've been working on it at the Canadian Observatory on Homelessness, where I sit as the Resident Scholar on Indigenous Homelessness. But Jesse Donaldson, my boss and co-worker, is my co-presenter, and, truthfully, she carries our presentation—I fumble my words and have trouble reading, just like always.

People have started listening to me lately, though. Apparently, I've become an expert on homelessness and Métis history, and I won the top two doctoral scholarships in the country a month before—the Pierre Elliott Trudeau Foundation Doctoral Scholarship and the Vanier Canada Graduate Scholarship—and I also won the Governor General's Silver Medal for graduating with one of the highest grade point averages in the country—the first student, Indigenous or not, in York University's sixty-year history to do so.

The attention is a bit overwhelming—I just do my work like Grandpa taught me, listen to Lucie's advice, and remember the things Olive told me about being a good human. But people at conferences such as this listen now, instead of batting my hand away. I belong somewhere, finally—in academia, of all places.

People say and know my name now, they remember me when I introduce myself. I'm not just a blur to them. I'm no longer a blur to myself.

***

After the conference, I'm supposed to go out to dinner with some colleagues, but I pass up on the free meal. Instead, I decide to go for a walk, down Bank Street, along Rideau, past Parliament Hill and the Peace Tower. I gaze over at the Centennial Flame, where I used to scoop piles of change, its flame of justice forever flickering over crests of our country's provinces and territories. I look for my RCMP friend, but he's not there.

Downtown Ottawa has changed quite a bit since I was here last. There's massive construction, but the Zesty Market on Dalhousie and

Taken the day I gave a lecture at McMaster University in Hamilton, Ontario.

LUCIE THISTLE

Rideau is still there, as ghetto as ever. So are the multitudes of shawarma joints that stay open late to feed the hordes of drunk people that spill out onto the block after two a.m. when the bars close. The windows on the one I burgled have long since been repaired.

As I walk up Dalhousie toward the Novotel hotel across from the Mission shelter, I find myself taking off my numerous silver rings and placing them in my pocket. I do the same with my shiny aviator watch and the bracelet Lucie got me for Christmas a few years back. I'm afraid my jewellery might betray me to the local homeless people and make me a prime target for robbery—I would've robbed me back in the day. I also try to hide the rectangular impression of my iPhone in my pocket, but the blasted thing is just too damned big to conceal.

If they rob me, I think, *I'm suing Apple for making such a humongous and unconcealable phone.*

The homeless men who glare at me from out of the Mission's front entrance on Waller Street, however, don't make much of me—they aren't like I was. They aren't interested in me or my huge iPhone. They simply stand and survey the city landscape, glancing at me like I'm some awkward shrub rudely growing out of the sidewalk.

I stand there, the human shrub, trying to find the courage to uproot myself and walk over to see if I know anybody. But my legs won't take me. I just stare in the direction of the Mission and rustle around, wishing I could say hello, but can't.

This place isn't my home anymore, I think. *Maybe it never was.*

After a moment or two I head toward the beer store next to the walkway that leads to the nearby Salvation Army.

As usual, the dealers are in the alley slinging dope to the homeless clientele of the ByWard Market. One is thick and muscular, too thick and muscular to be a long-time regular—just out of jail perhaps, or maybe just a few months shy of drug-induced emaciation. On either side he's flanked by two beautiful but pockmarked working girls.

As I emerge from the alley, the dealer's eyes dart upon me and he jams his hand in his underwear, hiding his dope in the crack of his ass. As he does this, I see him mouth "cop" to his associates. They in turn whistle to other street sentinels. A chorus of whistles echoes into the distance and the dealers and their drugs vaporize into thin air.

They think I'm a cop? I laugh to myself. *I guess I am a burly boy just like those donut-eating mofos.*

It's true. The flesh on my bones in these parts means I'm either that or a lost pedestrian. But even softened by years of luxury and stability, I can still read the street like an open book. I can still see plain as day where the zombies live, where the vampires shift in dark corners, where they sell bones and batwings to the undead, the broken-hearted, and the lost.

As before, I long to go up to the homeless people in front of the Sally Ann, but my legs won't take me. I just stand and watch them from afar smoking their crack and cigarettes, and drinking the beers I assume they must have stolen only moments earlier from the liquor store. It's all so familiar. A man in a wheelchair rolls past me and breaks my trance, reminding me that I have no business watching the homeless consume themselves in this hopeless realm. I gather myself and walk toward the McDonald's. There I spot a guy I knew, but he walks right past me to ask the crowd of people behind me for change.

"Hey," I ask him when he's finished. "Do you remember me?"

"No . . ."

I can tell he's trying to place me. "I stayed at the Mission many years ago—"

He interrupts before I can finish. "Yeah, I remember someone like you. But he was really skinny, and you're fat!"

"That I am," I say and laugh at his honesty. "Life has been good to me these last few years. I'm sober, have a home, a wife, a cat. And you?"

"Oh, you know, same old. I stay on the second floor of the Sheps now. My mind doesn't work so well anymore—they feed me, keep me sorted with clean clothes and bug juice."

I know he means psychotropic medication. I can tell the physical damage the drugs have done to him over the years from the way he can no longer keep himself from fidgeting. His shoes are held together with duct tape and his pants stained with the grime of his thousand-year wanderings in the Ottawa desert. His bloodshot eyes shift about aimlessly, but they still carry the intelligence I remember.

"You used to be my friend, Omar," I say as I shake his hand. "You used to watch my back, give me tokes when I got sick, and we used to joke around and drink beers. Remember?"

"No. Sorry." His eyes break from mine. "I don't remember that. I just remember your face. Nothing comes easy anymore. Sorry, friend."

"No worries. Rest easy, old buddy."

Before he leaves I ask him to take care of himself. He promises he will, but that he needs some change to make it through the night. I give him what I can, then we part ways.

As I sit in my hotel room later, I don't regret missing my dinner meeting with my colleagues. I explored homelessness in a way that would escape them. They could only talk and write about it; I took a walk a stone's throw from my hotel room where I'd lived it.

And I'd said goodbye.

MY SOUL IS STILL HOMELESS

sometimes
in between slumber and consciousness
i sleepwalk.

my mind not yet aware
i shuffle out the front door
the crisp open air and night sky still call me.

at night
in between slumber and consciousness
i sleepwalk.

my soul not yet aware
that my wanderings are over
and I have a home.

MISSING PERSON

HAVE YOU SEEN THIS MAN? Investigators from 22 Division Criminal Investigation Bureau in the Region of Peel, Ontario, are trying to find a missing man, Cyril Thistle, and need your help.

Cyril Thistle, who was born April 3, 1954, disappeared in 1981 in the Region of Peel when he was twenty-six years old. He was last seen by members of his family, and his children have been searching for him for years but have not had any success.

The police note that, "At this time all investigative leads have been exhausted and assistance is being requested from the public."

If you have any information on the whereabouts of Cyril Thistle, please call investigators at the 22 Division Criminal Investigation Bureau at **(905) 453–2121, ext. 2233**. You can also leave information anonymously by calling Peel Crime Stoppers at **1-800-222-TIPS (8477)**, or by visiting **peelcrimestoppers.ca**.

ACKNOWLEDGMENTS

I begin by thanking my wife, Lucie. As always, you are my world, my everything—words fail me when I think how grateful I am to you. Liba, my mother-in-law, you're the best mom-in-law I could ask for, the great teacher of truth in my life. Thank you for letting me make sandwiches out of the *bramborák*. The Suriano family, you likewise love and have given Lucie and me a home; I feel like your son in many ways. Carolyn, you're my great mentor and changed my world in every good way imaginable—I'm infinitely grateful to you. To Thistle and Morrissette family members who shared stories in the crafting of this book—Mom, Dave, Sherry, Jerry, Josh, and Ralph—marcee. Randy and everyone at CASS, you made the academy my home—cheers. Auntie Maria, you walked me through such beautiful fields of reconnection and are a major factor in all I do. Aunties Nancy and Janet, thank you for the "auntie plan" with Tessa. Tessa, I know I was scared, but you got me to start speaking for the first time in my life, and without you my stories just wouldn't have been told. Nancy, you've always been there, along with Pat, back when the world literally had collapsed on me. The Hockley Crew, Bud Boys, and girls down east, you forged my soul and I think of you often. My Harvest House family and Jenepher, marcee for saving me when I was just an angry wolf. Randolph and Russian Andre—thanks for employing me over the years; sorry you had to fire me fifty times. Stephen and Allyson and the COH—

thank you for believing in me. My last two probation officers—Marta especially—I'm grateful for your light. Jesse Winter, your story changed everything and caught the attention of Adria and Nita at Simon & Schuster—thank you all for seeing value in me. And lastly, I want to thank Laurie, my Jedi master editor who taught me good writing, was patient and kind, and helped me cobble together my life into this memoir—your words and teachings also live upon these pages. Thank you.

A NOTE FROM THE AUTHOR

My memories are memories from my point of view. I have tried my best to remember and relay my life in a meaningful way. But because of my youth and, later, my addictions, I see what happened to me like fragments of light, flickers of a flame, shadows on a wall. And trauma distorts perspectives. I think my mind blocks out a lot, bends time, folds that trauma in on itself so that I can function today.

Much of what I recall is accurate, but my years clouded by drugs and alcohol have left me, at times, an unreliable narrator, so I employed court, probation, and school records in an attempt to help reconstruct the past; and many people who knew me during those turbulent times have helped me fill in the gaps—family and friends, police officers who dealt with me, social workers at rehab centres, shelter workers, probation officers.

Some of the names in the book are real; others aren't.

ABOUT THE AUTHOR

JESSE THISTLE is Métis-Cree, from Prince Albert, Saskatchewan, and an assistant professor in Humanities at York University in Toronto. *From the Ashes* was the top-selling Canadian book in 2020, the winner of the Kobo Emerging Writer Prize for Nonfiction, Indigenous Voices Award, and High Plains Book Award, and also a finalist for Canada Reads. Jesse won a Governor General's Academic Medal in 2016, and is a Pierre Elliott Trudeau Foundation Scholar and a Vanier Scholar. A frequent keynote speaker, he lives in Hamilton, Ontario, with his wife, Lucie, and is at work on multiple projects, including his next book. Visit him at **jessethistle.com**.